Transforming

Psychology

Department of Psychology

Jain University

Bangalore

2018

ISBN: 978-1985783072

Distributed by Mishil & Js

This book is dedicated to

all those who admire psychology and

apply psychology to transform the society

Preface

Jain University, accredited 'A' grade by NAAC, is an intellectual destination that draws inspired students from more than 25 countries to one of the world's greatest cities - Bangalore. Certified ISO 9001:2008 for quality management, Jain University has been consistently ranked as one of the top private universities in India. It promotes innovation and entrepreneurship by bringing people, ideas, and resources together at one platform through interdisciplinary collaboration and interaction. From academic discoveries to athletic records, from artistic creations to scientific breakthroughs, students are inspiring, impacting Jain University success in many ways.

Department of Psychology, Jain University imparts quality education in order to help students actualize their potential and develop skills that have local and global significance. It promotes the culture of pioneering, innovative, inter-disciplinary research among students at all levels of higher education. The department comprises of faculty members who are accomplished researchers and practitioners in the field. The faculty has published extensively in the form of books, articles, reviews, perspectives and research papers in reputed journals. Some of the faculty members have also been on the editorial boards of journals and are members of professional bodies. Most of them are actively involved in guiding Ph. D as well as M Phil students.

In addition to Ph.D and M.Phil., the department offers programs of M.Sc. and Post graduate diplomas. A wide spectrum of courses are offered in order to equip the students to pursue specialization in areas of their interest and the focus is on bridging the gap between academia and real world by laying emphasis on experiential learning and hands on training through internships and research projects. Course curriculum has both academic as well as societal relevance as it incorporates contemporary debates as well as demands of the changing world and the PG Diploma in Sport Psychology and PG Diploma in Psychological Counselling are two such courses which showcase innovation, insight and a progressive vision of the department in the field of Psychology.

Change is the only constant, although may not be so evident in this transforming world. Those who are most aware of this are psychologists because they are in the best position to understand the strengths of human potential vis-a-vis their surroundings and they address the challenges and effects of change. Being human is more about becoming, facing the challenges and transforming themselves keeping abreast of the changes. This book *Transforming Psychology* highlights the challenges, problems and solutions in the various fields of human endeavour and the role psychologists can play. The book contains 38 research articles ranging from stress management to corporate climate. This book will provide a vision intended to inspire others to help build an understanding of how best to facilitate individual, community, organizational and societal flourishing.

Editors

Prof. S.T. Janetius

Dr. Smitha Baboo

Dr. C. Gnanaprakash

Dr. MadhuriniVallikad

Dr. Guneet Inder Jit Kaur

Dr. J. Lakshmi

Dr. Pooja Varma

Ms. G. Shambhavi

Contents

Chapter One

Work Engagement, Cognitive Distortion and Mindfulness[1]

Introduction: The desirable condition for any organization to run efficiently and profitably is that, the workers should be in the best of their mental and physical health. The contribution of each and every worker serves to create a comprehensive whole which is why the proficiency of each individual matters. A positively oriented, dedicated and motivated individual shows maximum work engagement (Schaufeli, Salanova, Gonzalez-Roma & Bakker, 2002). In a field like the Information Technology (IT) sector, which is highly competitive and demands huge workload from the employees in a short amount of time, a proper and dynamic mental disposition is crucial to work engagement. The field has irregular working hours (like night work and shift work) which leads to less time for personal needs and decreased involvement in family matters, and also has been found to be a strong determinant of health issues like cardiovascular morbidity, as well as other psychological and physiological distresses. (Härmä, 2006). A phenomenon that is seen increasingly these days is that of Burnout (Maudgalya, Wallace, Daraiseh & Salem, 2006). It has been observed that job stressors such as role overload is a predictor for burnout (Jung, 2013).

Cognitive distortion is a pattern of negative thoughts or emotions which may cause individuals to have altered perception of reality, and can lead to psychopathological

[1] **Swathy Sathyapal, K.R Anjusha, Pooja Jayan**, Student, Little Flower Institute of Social Sciences and Health (LISSAH), Calicut
Prajeesh Palanthara, Asst. Professor, Little Flower Institute of Social Sciences and Health (LISSAH), Calicut

states like depression and anxiety (Coyne & Gotlib, 1983). They will often be occupied with their internal thoughts and worries and are unable to be in the present moment. They are unable to regulate their emotional state, as people who are cognitively distorted will find it difficult to practice mindfulness. People with mindfulness are able to generate emotional stability (Brown & Ryan, 2003) and manage their emotional crises. It is also linked with increased focus. (Ortner, Kilner & Zelazo, 2007).

Mindfulness is a quality that promotes adaptive human functioning, maintaining clear and open awareness which leads to internal balance and peace of mind (Hollis-Walker, Colosimo, 2011). Mindfulness practice has been shown to reduce high stress levels (Wolever et al., 2012), which themselves have been shown to be associated with compromised sleep and increased health risks, which is a major adversity for IT employees. Researchers have found that mindfulness meditation practice both improved energy levels and enhanced the immune systems of employees in high-stress jobs and it also has been linked with decreased anxiety (Davidson et al., 2003); as well as depressive symptoms (Farb et al., 2010).

Mindfulness may improve a person's performance in many areas, including social engagement, task performance and resiliency (Glomb, Duffy, Bono & Yang, 2012) to dedication, enjoyment, and memory (Levy, Wobbrock, Kaszniak & Ostergren, 2012), which is an important quality for an effective worker. Previous researches have indicated that mindfulness plays an important role in determining the attitude of employees towards their work (Hyland, Lee & Mills, 2015). Mindfulness causes high engagement in work. However, individuals with cognitive distortion have less work engagement because they will have reinforced negative thoughts. This results in consistent pessimistic attitude which in turn leads to behavioural resistance. It damages the individuals' association with other employees, management and organization. Cognitive distortion also leads to decreased engagement in work and organizational commitment and increases the level of intention to quit, leading to negative effectivity for an organization (Ullah, Jaan & Qamar, 2012; Bovey, & Hede, 2001).

Objectives

- To find the correlation between mindfulness and work engagement among IT employees.
- To find the correlation between Cognitive distortion and mindfulness among IT employees.

- To find the correlation between Cognitive distortion and work engagement among IT employees.

- To compare work engagement, mindfulness and cognitive distortion between males and females.

- To compare work engagement, mindfulness and cognitive distortion between people in nuclear families and joint families

Methodology: This is a quantitative study. The sample for this study consists of 65 IT employees, between the ages of 20 and 50, working in different companies. Random sample method is used here. Random sampling can also mean taking a number of independent observations from the same probability distribution without involving any real population. Measures used: The Freiburg Mindfulness Inventory, The Cognitive distortion scale, Utrecht Work Engagement Scale (UWES). The SPSS was used to analyse the quantitative data collected. Descriptive statistics were conducted for demographic variables like age category, gender and family type. Karl Pearson product-moment correlation analysis was used to assess the relationship. Independent sample t-test was also used.

Results: Pearson's Product Moment Coefficient of Correlation was used to check the relationship between mindfulness and cognitive distortion on work engagement among IT employees. For this purpose, Statistical Package of Social Sciences (SPSS) was used. In the present study, the alpha level was set at 0.01.

Table 1 Inter Correlation Coefficients among the Study Variables

Sl. No	Variables	Cognitive distortion	Mindfulness	Work engagement
1.	Cognitive distortion	---	-.415**	-.168
2.	Mindfulness		---	.600**
3	Work engagement			---

N=65   ** Significant at .01 level

Table 1 shows the correlation between cognitive distortion, mindfulness and work engagement among the IT employees. There is significant negative correlation between cognitive distortion and mindfulness, as the correlation coefficient was found to be -.415 (p<0.01). There is a significant positive correlation between mindfulness and work engagement (coefficient of correlation = .600, p<0.01). Correlation coefficient between cognitive distortion and work engagement is -.168. This suggests a mild and insignificant negative correlation. The results suggest that employees who score high on mindfulness have high work engagement, and also that mindfulness is considerably lower in people with cognitive distortions.

Table 2 Gender wise comparison on Cognitive distortion, Mindfulness and Work engagement

Sl no	Variables	Groups	N	Mean	SD	SE	T value
1	Cognitive distortion	Male	34	81.85	32.23	5.53	.306
		Female	31	74.58	23.42	4.21	
2	Mindfulness	Male	34	38.59	7.94	1.36	.881
		Female	31	38.25	9.69	1.74	
3	Work engagement	Male	34	72.03	16.97	2.91	.446
		Female	31	68.42	20.95	3.76	

Table 2 shows the comparison between male and female employees on Cognitive distortion, Mindfulness and Work engagement, done by independent sample t-test. 34 males and 31 females responded. The mean score for the group of female employees for Cognitive distortion, Mindfulness and Work engagement is 74.58, 38.25 and 68.42 respectively. The mean score for the group of male employees for Cognitive distortion, Mindfulness and Work engagement is 81.85, 38.59 and 72.03 respectively. The 't' value for the difference in Cognitive distortion, Mindfulness and Work engagement between these two (Female & Male employees) is .306, .881 and .446 respectively. The analysis shows no significant difference between the two.

Table 3 Comparison between Cognitive distortion, Mindfulness and Work engagement on the basis of family types

Sl no	Variables	Groups	N	Mean	SD	SE	T value
1	Cognitive distortion	Joint	22	74.27	22.51	4.80	.408
		Nuclear	43	80.49	31.01	4.73	
2	Mindfulness	Joint	22	38.73	8.58	1.82	.847
		Nuclear	43	38.28	8.93	1.36	
3	Work engagement	Joint	22	72.59	19.96	4.26	.491
		Nuclear	43	69.14	18.48	2.82	

Table 3 shows the comparison between people in nuclear families and joint families on Cognitive distortion, Mindfulness and Work engagement, done by independent sample t-test. 22 respondents were from joint families whereas 43 were from nuclear families. The mean score for the group from joint families for Cognitive distortion, Mindfulness and Work engagement is 74.27, 38.73 and 72.59 respectively. The mean score for the group from nuclear families for Cognitive distortion, Mindfulness and Work engagement is 80.49, 38.28 and 69.14 respectively. The 't' value for the difference in Cognitive distortion, Mindfulness and Work engagement between these two (joint and nuclear) is .408, .847 and .491 respectively. The analysis shows no significant difference between the two.

The results of Pearson's Product Moment Coefficient of Correlation showed that there is significant negative correlation between cognitive distortion and mindfulness, as the correlation coefficient was found to be -.415 ($p<0.01$), which means that the respondents with high cognitive distortion had significantly decreased mindfulness. Distorted cognition may lead to intrusive and irrational thoughts, increased self-blame and self-criticism, and a preoccupation with negative thoughts, which impairs their ability to keep an open mind to the present context.

There is a significant positive correlation between mindfulness and work engagement with correlation value of .600 ($p<0.01$), suggesting that individuals who practiced mindfulness seemed to have high engagement in their work. Similar findings were stated in a article conducted by Hyland, Lee & Mills (2015) for examining the role of mindfulness at work. Our study supports their findings. The practice of mindfulness may cause the individual to be completely immersed in their present work, and could lead to increased work engagement. Positive emotions increase the flexibility, creativity, integration, efficiency of thought and the flow of synergy between the co-workers of an organisation.

Correlation coefficient between cognitive distortion and work engagement is -.168. This suggests a mild negative correlation. The study by Ullah, Jaan & Qamar (2012) suggests that cognitive distortions lead to high behavioural resistance which ultimately leads to reduced work engagement, and causes increased intention to quit the job. Our study supports this finding.

Independent sample t-test for Gender wise comparison on Cognitive distortion, Mindfulness and Work engagement showed that there was no significant difference between men and women for the three variables. The 't' value for the difference in Cognitive distortion, Mindfulness and Work engagement between female & male employees is .306, .881 and .446 respectively. This 't' value is less than minimum needed value for significance. In other words, there is no significant difference between males and females for the three variables. A study by MacKillop, & Anderson (2007) suggested that there is no significant difference between men and women for the variable of mindfulness. Our study supports this finding.

The comparison between people in nuclear families and joint families on Cognitive distortion, Mindfulness and Work engagement, done by independent sample t-test showed that the 't' value for the difference in Cognitive distortion, Mindfulness and Work engagement between these two (joint and nuclear) is .408, .847 and .491 respectively. The analysis shows no significant difference between the two.

Conclusion: In conclusion, this study yields useful insights for further exploring the role of mindfulness and cognitive distortions on work engagement. Based on these findings we may hypothesize that increasing mindfulness will: 1) increase work engagement and well-being, and 2) help to cope with cognitive distortion.

Chapter Two

Health Issues Among Tribal Students[2]

Introduction: Physical health of an individual cannot be separated from his / her mental health. Each one affects other in complex ways. Health psychologists are increasingly exploring how physical health and mental health works together for the wellbeing of a person's psychological and physical standards. Symptoms of poor mental health can be disruptive to a person's daily life and limit potential and place stress on relationships. Accessibility to better physical and psychological health is not found to be evenly distributed to people in our country. The issue is of utmost importance when it comes to the plight of minority groups, such as tribal students in India. Scheduled tribes refer to a group of historically disadvantaged people who are descendents of the tribal communities. They do not believe in caste system but dwell in deep inside forest far away from the chief part of the society (Srivastava, Srivastava, & Ramasamy, 2013). It has been indicated that India has a long way to go to improve its health status (Mahajan 1996, World Development Report 1993). Periodic Food Consumption Surveys reveal the poor nutritional status of the Indian population. This problem is further aggravated by communicable diseases establishing the vicious cycle of malnutrition and infections (Bhaskaram, 1996, Reddy et al. 1993). The issue is increasingly complex in the case of Scheduled Tribes in the state of Kerala.

---

[2] **Kesiyamol Mathew, K.,** Student, Union Christian College, Aluva
R. Malini, Ph.D. Asst. Professor, Union Christian College, Aluva

As per the Indian Constitution, special consideration has to be given to certain ethnic minority groups such as Scheduled Tribes (ST's) who constitute around 8 per cent of the total population of the country. Most of them inhabit the interior and inaccessible parts of the country and their personal, physical and psychological concerns are rarely addressed. Though the state of Kerala stands first in literacy rate, there is an increased gap between tribal and non-tribal population with regard to their economic, educational, and social status. The tribal communities are isolated from the main stream and are in need of special programmes for their development. They are also the most exploited and neglected group and more prone to malnutrition and diseases. Therefore the education system has got a major role to play in imparting health related knowledge and fostering health-promoting behaviours.

Objectives: The present study was intended to explore the physical and psychological wellbeing of students belonging to the tribal community of the state of Kerala. The study tries to understand their health and hygiene practices as well as the extent of psychological well being they experience in comparison to non-tribal students. In addition, effort was also taken to gain understanding regarding the hygienic practices of girl students in the case of both the groups.

Methodology: The participants in the present study included 50 students (23 females and 27 males) from a State Government funded school within the forest area of Idukki District (in Kerala) named Mamalakandam. The students belonged to the age range of 12 to 19 years. Another group of 60 students were also identified from a state Government funded school where student involvement in NCC, NSS and Student Police force were ensured. 60 students who were actively involved in Student Police Cadets (SPC) but hailing from low socio-economic background were selected as a comparison group. Both the schools, viz., from the tribal and non-tribal areas were run by the Government and the medium of instruction was the native language, Malayalam

In order to obtain information regarding the health practices of students, a schedule was prepared by the investigator. The areas covered under the schedule included six areas.

   a)   Personal hygiene (oral and dental hygiene, taking bath, washing clothes etc.)
   b)   Public hygiene (waste disposal, spitting/urinating/defecating on public spaces etc.)
   c)   Physical environment (clean wells, toilet facilities etc.)
   d)   Personal health/fitness (proper nutritious diet, exercise and vaccination)
   e)   Home psychological environment (safe and protective environment)
   f)   Personal self efficacy (ability to tackle stress etc.)

A total of 45 items were prepared in the local language (Malayalam) in the Yes/No format which was to be completed by both boys and girls. Apart from this, a separate schedule (12 items) was prepared to understand the health and hygiene practices of girl students, especially to uncover their menstrual health practices and hygiene as well as their personal and cultural interpretations and beliefs). In addition, an open ended interview schedule was also prepared (25 items) for adults to understand their attitude towards healthy practices.

Data was collected from the tribal and non-tribal schools after obtaining consent from the heads of schools and after discussion and interaction with the local community. Parental consent regarding student participation in the study was obtained after Parent Teacher Association meetings. The teachers of the schools helped identify students who were willing to participate in the study. Rapport was established with students before administering the survey schedule. Students were requested to respond very genuinely to the questions and confidentiality of responses and anonymity was ensured. The data obtained were entered in data sheet and coded for further analysis. The responses of students were in the Yes/No format and the number of students who responded positively to an item was identified and expressed in terms of percentages. Student responses to the items in the survey schedule were considered as reflections of their understanding regarding different aspects of health. The number of students in both the categories, i.e., tribal and non-tribal groups, who responded positively to health-related matters were identified.

Results and Discussion: The results were obtained for both the tribal and non-tribal groups of students. There were 27 males and 45 items for each schedule. As mentioned earlier the areas covered in the schedule belonged to six areas, viz., personal hygiene, public hygiene, physical environment, personal health/fitness, home psychological environment, and personal self efficacy. The responses of both groups of participants, viz., tribal and non-tribal groups, are expressed in terms of percentages and are summarized in Table 1.

Table 1. Students' responses to questions in the survey schedule

Category	Tribal group (N=50) (in %)	Non-tribal group (N=60) (in %)
Personal hygiene	65	98
Public hygiene	61	98
Physical environment	57	96
Personal health	70	98
Home psychological environment	52	91
Personal self efficacy	43	98

The percentage values in Table 1 indicate the proportion of students who have a better understanding regarding health and hygiene related issues and psychological well being.

A comparison of the percentage values obtained by the two groups of students suggest poor facilities and practices in the case of tribal than for non-tribal students. A detailed analysis of results is made in the following sections.

a) Personal hygiene- Personal hygiene refers to the extent to which students engage in healthy practices such as maintaining oral/dental hygiene, bathing twice daily, cleaning hands with soap etc. It could be observed from Table 1 that only 65% of students belonging to tribal group have such habits compared to 98% of non-tribal students.

b) Public hygiene- The area of public hygiene covers items pertaining to the extent to which people use toilets, resort to proper waste management practices, take measures to control the spread of diseases etc. It could be noticed that the only 61 % of tribal students responded positively to the items in comparison to 98% of non-tribal students.

c) Physical environment- The area of physical environment is important in the sense that it covers items pertaining to the extent to which people have provision for healthy drinking water, electricity etc. Only 57% of tribal students have access to such facilities compared to 96% of non-tribal students.

d) Personal health- On aspects related to personal health such as the consumption of healthy, nutritious diet, exercise, sleep habits etc., it was found that around 70% of tribal students follow such patterns of behaviour in comparison to 98% of non-tribal students.

e) Home psychological environment- This area pertains to the mental health status of the family and it was found that only 52% of tribal students possess better mental health compared to 91% of non-tribal students.

f) Personal self efficacy- Regarding the extent of self confidence, ability to handle situations and goal orientation, only 43% of tribal students believe in themselves while 98% of non-tribal students have better feelings of personal self efficacy.

An examination of the above findings reveals the need for a valid discussion of the aspects of physical and mental health of tribal students. In addition to the 45 item survey schedule, another schedule s=consisting of 12 items were administered to the girl students belonging to the tribal and non-tribal category. The responses of students obtained in terms of percentage of positive responses are provided in table in Table 2.

Table 1. Girl students' responses to questions in the survey schedule

Category	Tribal group (N=23) %	Non-tribal group (N=30) %
Personal hygiene	60	96
Personal psychological environment	48	95
Personal/cultural beliefs	62	99
Self efficacy	43	99
Home psychological environment	30	96
School physical environment	100	100

The results obtained indicates the differences in the pattern of responses of tribal and non-tribal girl students to different aspects of menstrual health and hygiene practices as well as the extent to beliefs related to it. It could be noticed that tribal students tend to have lesser personal hygiene compared to non-tribal students. Similar is the case with personal psychological environment, personal and cultural beliefs associated with menstruation, self efficacy, and home psychological environment. The responses of students with respect to school physical environment were found to show a similar pattern.

Based on the open ended interview conducted on adults belonging to tribal group it was identified that their physical environment was so unhygienic that most of them don't have any toilet facilities and they use hidden bushes or forest for this purpose. This condition is highly risk bearing for children, women and elderly as they result in having skin infections, cholera etc. Based on the report by the School Head master, students as well as their parents were not bothered about students completing their schooling and should even be compelled to appear for examinations. The members of the tribal group was found to promote early marriage (13 to 19 years for girls and 19 to 22 years for boys) without any proper legal registration. This was found to result in risk of early pregnancy and child bearing of adolescents. It was also indicated that the regions near tribal schools were illegal drug zones and many students fall victims of drug use. Most of the parents are also addicted to substances such as alcohol and involved in illegal drug transportation.

Students in tribal regions were found to have poor health and hygiene practices, decreased oral hygiene, body hygiene etc. The public hygiene practices as well as the quality of physical environment were very poor. Many of the students reported that they receive no psychological support or care from their family or society to further go for higher education and boys were found to have no specific goals in their lives.

Conclusion: The present study provides understanding regarding the plight of the tribal group inhabiting the state of Kerala. Their physical and mental health practices and patterns were found to be poor when compared to that of non-tribal students. It is even disheartening to see the understanding of female students towards menstruation and related hygiene practices. These findings have implications for school based education and training programmes intended towards improving the health conditions of the population

Chapter Three

Existential Thinking and Posttraumatic Growth[3]

Introduction: Since many years, humans have been pondering on what makes the human life sustain even after experiencing many stressful life event's and trauma has become a shared human nature. (Skyle, 2014). Be it young age or old age, many individuals have experienced trauma in their life. Simple things such as illness of mother, breakup with a boyfriend, death or domestic violence, sexual assault or it might even include a bad childhood experience that has affected ones' lives in various ways. Trauma is usually associated with negative outcome as well as positive outcome. A large body of researchers have started to look at the positive aspect or growth followed by traumatic event. Also, many have suggested the potential for growth after experiencing a traumatic life event (Yalom, 1980; Maslow, 1954; Frankl, 1963 & Caplan, 1964). It is assumed that the experience of trauma often challenges one's belief system, reorganize one's schemas and involve in meaning making process (Calhoun & Tedeschi, 2006; Janoff-Bulman, 2004). The degree to which traumatic event challenges one's core beliefs is associated with greater posttraumatic growth. (Cann, Calhoun, Tedeschi, Kilmer, et al., 2010). Empirical evidences show how positive affect co-occurs with distress in stressful situation as well as class of meaning-based coping mechanisms are involved in the phase of post trauma

[3] **Sahana V,** Student, Jain University
Guneet Inder Jit Kaur, Ph.D., Asst. Professor of Psychology, Jain University

(Folkman & Moskowitz, 2000). In the book *Man's Search for Meaning*, Frankl suggests that we find meaning in life even when confronted with hopeless situation, and that searching for meaning is one of the basic and high-order need that every human goes through for optimal functioning (Frankl, 1984).

Traumatic events are different from stressful life events by their attributed seriousness (Krause, 2004). Wheaton (1994) defines trauma as events that are "…spectacular, horrifying, and just deeply disturbing experiences" (p.90). Traumatic experiences often involve a threat to life or safety, any situation that makes one feel overwhelmed and isolated even if it doesn't involve physical harm. Posttraumatic growth period is the most critical stage as it leaves one with distressing memories, emotions and anxiety that lasts for longer time (Robinson, Smith & Segal,2018). A number of studies and statistics have revealed that young adults are more susceptible to mental illness reasoning that young adults go through high stress and transition, where one is pulled away from their comfort zone and acquires new responsibilities (Grace, 2013). Posttraumatic growth is the positive psychological change experienced by the individual as a result of trauma. (Calhoun & Tedeschi, 1996). Calhoun and Tedeschi (2004) accentuated positive growth that occur in five domains: (1) Relating to others, (2) new possibilities, (3) personal strength, (4) spiritual change, and (5) appreciation of life. Greater appreciation for life following a trauma represents changes in priorities and taking pleasure in aspects that once were taken for granted. For posttraumatic growth to occur, many environmental factors such as support from family, interpersonal relationships, society as well as personal factors such as resilience, optimism, self-confidence and easy-going disposition plays a predominant role in the aftermath of the crisis (Schaefer & Moos, 1992). Also, trauma survivors ruminate more on traumatic experiences which makes them question, explore on concepts of human existence and their essentials (Calhoun et al., 2000).

Exploring on the concepts of meaning in life, existence, universe, and mysteries of life such as what happens after death, what is the purpose of life, and discussing about philosophy or beliefs. Is part of human nature and we all involve in thinking about these existential issues. *Allan and Shearer (2012) termed this tendency to explore the fundamental concerns of human existence and the capacity to engage in meaning-making process that locates oneself in respect to these issues as existential thinking.* The ultimate concerns of the human's existence relate to the one's relation to the grand organization of the cosmos, such as the nature of reality, as well as the most fundamental, inescapable parts of human conditions, such a s the meaning in life and the inevitability of death (Yalom, 1980). Thus, existential thinking is concerned with aspirations beyond the self (Hartelius, Caplan, & Rardin. 2007).

A large number of researchers have contributed in the study of meaning in life by attributing with posttraumatic growth and have used terminologies such as existential growth, existential meaning, and existential re-evaluation that contributes to posttraumatic growth (Kashdan & Kane, 2011; Calhoun et al, 2011; Janoff-Bulman, 2004; Reilly et al., 2017). These aforementioned information gives a vague idea about how posttraumatic growth and existential thinking are related to each other.

Posttraumatic growth literature has been rampantly explored since the initial formation by Calhoun and Tedeschi (1995). Most researchers on posttraumatic growth has conducted on adults (Helgeson et al., 2006; Linley & Joseph, 2004). A review of these have highlighted several factors associated with the development of posttraumatic growth including spirituality (Calhoun et al, 2004), demographics (Tedeschi & Calhoun, 1996), and Personality, (Prati & Pietrantoni, 2009). A large body of researchers have linked posttraumatic growth with existential thinking aspects in terms of meaning in life, meaning-making process, existential growth, existential meaning, and existential re-evaluation. (Calhoun et al., 2011; Janoff-Bulman, 2004; Kashdan &Kane, 2011; Reilly, 2017). As existential thinking is the tendency to explore around the concepts of existence and involves meaning-making process, it is essential to know how existential thinking plays a role in the phase of posttraumatic growth (Allan & Shearer, 2012).

The experience of finding meaning and thinking about the fundamental concerns of human existence during the crisis has been long seen in literature, philosophy, arts and religious teachings. In one of the study conducted by Yalom and Lieberman (1991) on bereavement and heightened existential awareness revealed that bereaved spouses showed varied degree of existential awareness.

Meaning-making is the central tenet of coping (Shaefer & Moos,1986; Park, Cohen, & Murch, 1996). Recognizing meaning amidst trauma and its aftermath may allow a person to experience emotional relief, lead to new philosophy of life (Janoff-Bulman, 1992; Taylor & Brown, 1988). Calhoun and Tedeschi (2004) gave five domains of posttraumatic growth among them, spirituality and philosophy change are somewhat similar to existential thinking. As after the traumatic event, one's existential awareness increases and one may reflect on meaning, purpose in life, and the individual may feel vulnerable and involves in ruminating about the traumatic event. Janoff-Bulman (2004) gave three explanatory models for posttraumatic growth. In her third model existential re-evaluation concerns about survivor's existential struggle to rebuild the inner world and there by comprehending the questions of trauma and involving in meaning-making process. Reilly, Lee, Laux and Robitaille (2017) led a study on finding existential meaning and growth through the creative arts in the face breast cancer survivors. Their study revealed that art-making created interstitial spaces that nurtured positive individual changes that consisted of existential and posttraumatic growth, that has implicated patents quality of life. Hefferon, Grealy and Mutrie (2009) conducted systematic review on post-traumatic growth and life threatening physical illness. The emerged themes were reappraisal of life and priorities; trauma equals to the development of self; existential re-evaluation and new awareness of the body.

Many factors have influenced posttraumatic growth, a large body of researchers have in fact suggested that it not one or two factors that contribute growth but multiple factors play a role (Cadell, Regehr, & Hemsworth, 2003; Schaefer & Moos, 1992; Calhoun et al., 2000; Schmidt, 2013). Jurisova (2016) conducted a study on coping strategies and post-traumatic growth in paramedic while examining the moderating effect of specific self-efficacy and positive/negative affectivity. The study revealed positive relations between coping, social support, emotional support, and posttraumatic growth. Similar study was conducted by Calhoun et al (2000), where factors such as religion and cognitive processing influenced posttraumatic growth. Another study by Prati and Pietrantoni (2009) revealed that optimism, social factors and coping strategies contributed to posttraumatic growth.

Friedrich Nietzsche (Twilight of idols, 1889) says "that which does not kill us, make us stronger" indicating that the adversity an individual endures during his life time, has in fact makes the person grow stronger. Suicide ideations are common during the period of trauma, this aspect is well researched. In one of the study conducted by Bush, Skopp, McCann and Luxton (2011) on posttraumatic growth as protection factors against suicide ideation after the exposure of combat and deployment. In fact, Albert Camus conveyed that individuals experience these when confronted with adverse or traumatic situation. Articulating that there is one serious philosophical question and that is suicide.

Camus argues that human beings cannot escape asking questions such as 'what is the meaning of existence?', it is observed in his book, *The Myth of Sisyphus* (1975), Sisyphus, who was punished by Gods to roll up a rock up the mountain, only to witness that it rolling back down, then descending after the rock to begin all over, in an endless cycle. Camus says that like Sisyphus, humans cannot help but ask questions about meaning of life. He writes, 'There is no sun without shadow, and it is essential to know the night' (p.123).

Stacey Kramer, a brand strategist shared her experience of posttraumatic growth in a ted talk 'The best gift I ever survived' (2010) conveying that when one is faced with 'unexpected, unwanted, and uncertain events in life, one must consider it as a gift'.

Jean-Paul Sartre (1946) proclaimed 'existence precedes essence' suggestive that the nature of the human being such as one's thought and emotions is fundamental than the mere fact of his existence. Implicating that one is involved in meaning making, and valuing one's acts.

Objectives: This study seeks to understand the relationship between post-traumatic growth and existential thinking. Also, to see if existential thinking plays a role in the phase of posttraumatic growth. Thereby, providing theoretical/ research base for developing clinical intervention to minimize the distress and promote well-being To see the link between posttraumatic growth with existential thinking aspects like existential re-evaluation, existential growth, meaning in life and existential awareness. To study the aspects of posttraumatic growth as displayed in religious texts, art and philosophy.

Results and Discussion: Upon reviewing the researches pertaining to posttraumatic growth and existential thinking, it is clearly observed that there is some relationship with posttraumatic growth and existential thinking. Let us look at some of the themes emerged from the review of literature:

- Presence of social support, optimism, spirituality/ religiosity, and coping strategies as contributing factors to posttraumatic growth (Prati & Pietrantoni, 2009; Jurisova, 2016, Calhoun et al., 1995, 2004)

- Meaning in life, existential re-evaluation, existential growth and meaning as some key themes emerged in the phase of posttraumatic growth (Triplett et al., 2011; Reilly et al., 2017; Hefferon, Grealy, & Mutri, 2009; Kashdan & Kane, 2010; Janoff-Bulman, 2004)

- Increased Cognitive appraisal and rumination about the traumatic event has revealed to have greater levels of posttraumatic growth (Calhoun et al., 2000, Linley & Joseph, 2004)

- Posttraumatic growth as a protection against suicidal ideation, posttraumatic stress disorder and depression (Bush et al.,2011; Segerstrom et al., 2007)

- Posttraumatic growth leading to positive affect, personality change and resilience (Jayawickreme & Blackie, 2014; Folkman & Moskowitz, 2000)

Overall, it is clearly seen that individuals who have experienced a traumatic event have involved in existential thinking process. Even though the level of existential thinking varies among people. The fact, that individuals ponder about the fundamental concerns of humans' existence and involve in meaning-making process determines existential thinking.

There are abundant anecdotal reports of people who feel that they have found benefits even amidst the most terrible of circumstances. What is less clear is whether this finding of benefit is independent of psychological well-being or it might lead to deleterious outcome. Even though Calhoun and Tedeschi (1995) have suggests that posttraumatic growth is independent and in some cases distress co-occurs with posttraumatic growth. Some of the challenges faced in the area of posttraumatic growth and existential thinking would be:

- Describing the concept of existential thinking and its difference from philosophical orientation of existentialism (Allan & Shearer, 2012)

- Differentiating between spirituality and existential thinking. Even though both the constructs have some similarity, as Allan & Shearer (2012) suggests that certain spiritual aspects of finding meaning and exploring on the energy and universe are components of existential thinking as it involves thinking pertaining to existence and meaning-making process

- Implicating the concept of posttraumatic growth and existential thinking in clinical interventions

- Some theorists are of the view that posttraumatic growth should be carefully perused, if implied in clinical setup. As Calhoun and Tedeschi (1995) suggests that posttraumatic growth is independent of psychological well-being, and if implicated, it should not harbour their process of growth.

Since posttraumatic growth and existential thinking are in the growing stages and have been defining themselves by linking with various variables. Maybe in the future much more understanding of the subject is conceptualized and might give more insights.

Conclusion: From the study, it is clearly observed that existential thinking plays a role in posttraumatic growth, even though the levels of existential thinking varies and is dependent on personality attributes. Posttraumatic growth and existential thinking are both positive aspects and have lead to personality change, life satisfaction, positive affect and coping. Studies of posttraumatic growth have displayed prevention of suicidal ideations and mental illness like posttraumatic stress disorder and depression. Implicating posttraumatic growth and existential thinking in clinical interventions would help many individuals who are not aware of these concepts. Many kids, adolescence and adults living in the border regions experience trauma, existential crisis and mayhem in life. Making them understand about these aspects and building hope in them, could bring about humanity among those who have lost. As Jean Paul-Sartre articulates existentialism is a humanism.

Chapter Four

Male Body Image[4]

Introduction: Research on female body image over the past few decades in the West has indicated an increase in body dissatisfaction, nut the corresponding research on men has thrown up inconsistent results (Grammas & Schwartz, 2009). Some researchers believe that there is an underreporting of appearance-related dissatisfaction amongst men, as most body image studies are designed with women in mind. (Grogan, 1999).

Studies which have been mindful of this have shown that concerns that men have regarding body image are different from those of women (Mishkind, Rodin, Silberstein, & Striegel-Moore, The Embodiment of Masculinity: Cultural, Psychological and Behavioural Dimensions, 1986). Metaanalyses of body image studies have concluded that women and men have become increasingly divergent in how they evaluate their physical appearance and that men's body images have worsened significantly (Cash, 2002).

Adhering to socially determined ideals for physical appearance comes with a host of positive outcomes ranging from being perceived as popular, stylish and friendly (Mishkind, Rodin, Silberstein, & Striegel-Moore, The Embodiment of Masculinity: Cultural, Psychological and Behavioural Dimensions, 1986), to being perceived as more qualified, and being more likely to be hired and receive higher salaries in professional settings (Shahani-Denning, Dudhat, Tevet, & Andreoli, Effect of Physical Attractiveness on Selection Decisions in India and The United States, 2010).

---

[4] **Paras Sharma,** Research Scholar, Tata Institute of Social Science

Although there is a growing body of literature showing a growing discontentment with physical appearance among men, there is a lack of cultural diversity among studies on male body image (Grammas & Schwartz, 2009)

Empirical data on male body image in India is scarce. Body dissatisfaction, eating disorders, and obesity, rather than body image itself, has been the focus of research in Indian settings. Studies on prevalence of obesity in urban Indian settings have shown high rates of obesity both among men and women (Deepa, Farooq, Deepa, Manjula, & Mohan, 2009). Children and adolescents with greater exposure to TV have a higher likelihood of being obese. At the same time research in the West indicates that increased exposure to media is tied with internalization of body ideals as propagated by the media, and thereby higher levels of body dissatisfaction among young men and women (Wykes & Gunter, 2005). A study by Singh and colleagues with Pre-University College Students (PUC) in South of India, indicated that 33 per cent of over 500 boys and girls, wished to be thinner than they currently were, and that there was a correlation between perceiving oneself as fat and having low self-esteem. (Singh, Ashok, Binu, Parsekar, & Bhumika, 2015)

Articles in prominent business newspapers and magazines, in India state that men's cosmetic products is a fast growing segment, with sales of some international brands in India being higher than the global average (Agarwal, 2014), (Mukherjee & Bailay, 2014), (Priyadarshani, 2014). This certainly points to an increased pre-occupation with looking better in India.

Factors Shaping Body Image The sociocultural perspective on body image states that there are societal ideals of beauty that get transmitted by a range of sociocultural channels, which are then internalized by individuals. One's body satisfaction or dissatisfaction then becomes a function of meeting/not meeting these ideals (Tiggemann, Sociocultural Perspectives on Body Image, 2011). In the case of men in particular, the ideal that seems to be perpetuated is that of a mesomorphic and muscular Vshaped body, wherein one has broad shoulders, chest and upper-body, but a narrow waist and hips. This ideal is transmitted through three chief sources, viz. the family, romantic/intimate partners, peers, and the media.

Though it may often be shown that body images are personal projects, and that one can design one's appearance as they please, writings on the inner workings of the fashion industry show that fashion trends are often decided months and years in advance through 'trend forecasting' that define the range of options from which one may 'choose' what to buy (Seto, 2017). The media can also cultivate exemplars of body shape in the public sphere which are designed to drive people to compare and evaluate their own physical shape in relation to that shape (Wykes & Gunter, 2005)

Similarly the expressed attitudes of family about physical appearance, as well as the way family members evaluate each other's physical appearance greatly shape the way people view their own physical appearances. Negative physical appearance appraisals from parents and family members can have a devastating effect on the physical appearance appraisals of individuals (Carlson-Jones, 2011) Being teased by peers is associated with heightened concerns about physical appearance as well as increased dieting behaviours among men and women. Lastly, when it comes to the opposite sex, men are likely to think that women prefer heavier and more muscular body types than women themselves have reported in research. (Tantleff-Dunn & Gokee, 2002).

Objectives: The present study aimed to form an understanding of what the concept of body-image means to young-adult males in the city of Mumbai, India; and how influences from agencies such as the family, peer groups, the opposite sex, the media shape this understanding. The present study is exploratory in nature.

Methodology: The current study was conducted in the year 2010 in Mumbai. It employed a concurrent mixed model design such that it was divided into two independent phases (Tashakkori & Teddlie, 2003). In the first phase, a pre-coded quantitative questionnaire was used to study the factors that influence the way men (i.e. consumers) understand and construct body images. The second phase used qualitative methods (semi-structured, in-depth interviews subjected to thematic analysis) to assess the opinions of expert professionals in the field of fitness, health and beauty (i.e. the market) to understand consumption patterns shown by men. Triangulation of methods in this manner allowed the researcher to confirm and corroborate the data collected. The sample for the quantitative study consisted of 103 males between the ages 21-25 years residing in the city of Mumbai, India. Only working men were a part of the study as this was a group with an access to income which is theirs to spend. The sample was obtained through non-probabilistic purposive sampling. The participants were graduates, employed in white-collar jobs, from a range of sectors, working in Mumbai. Descriptive analysis and cross tabulation of data was done to analyze the data quantitatively. For the qualitative phase of the study, the sample included four professionals viz. a freelance personal fitness trainer, a hair stylist from a popular salon, a dietician and personal trainer from a weight management clinic, and a dermatologist from a chain of skin clinics. Interviews were conducted either telephonically or personally, and the themes emerging were used to corroborate the findings from the questionnaire.

Results and Discussion: Data showed that the appearance-related concerns held by Indian men reflect some of the global trends observed in male body-image research. Height and weight All respondents were asked to state their height (in feet and inches) and their weight (in kg.); actual height and weight measures were not taken as a part of the study. The mean weight for the sample was 67.65 kg. (SD = 8.38). Sixty four per cent were within the normal range for weight; 21.4 per cent were underweight and 14.6 per cent were overweight.

The mean height for the sample was 5' 8" (SD = 2.45). It was seen that 76.7 per cent were within the normal range for height for the sample; 17.5 per cent were shorter than average, while 5.8 per cent were taller than average.

When asked about the ideal body type for Indian men, 86.4 per cent favored an athletic body type (which was pre-defined as 'Fit and flexible with well-toned muscles') over the other body types. The 'Macho' body type which was defined as 'Strong with Well Defined Muscles' was the least favoured body type. This is in agreement with research findings that state that extreme muscularity is perceived as unnatural and even repulsive (St Martin and Gavey 1996 as cited in Grogan 1999: 59). The sample rated balding, weight and height as the aspects of their appearance that they were most concerned with. Additionally, the professional hairstylist who was interviewed stated that an increasing number of men had started approaching stylists for tips on how to care for one's hair better and what products to (not) use to avoid hair fall and hair damage. 71.6 per cent considered height as an important determinant of physical attractiveness for men. The sample on an average wished to be almost 1.62 inches taller. However, it was seen that shorter than average individuals wished to be almost 4-5 inches taller, while taller than average individuals mentioned that they wished they were shorter. Therefore it cannot be said that men's desired height is unidirectionally tall. 75.7 per cent considered weight as an important concern when it came to body image. On an average the sample wished to be 4 kg heavier than the average weight reported for the sample (67 kg). However, as was the case with height, while nearly two-thirds wished to gain weight, nearly one-third wished to lose weight.

Lastly, nearly 45 per cent (or almost one in two) felt that complexion was an important determinant of physical attractiveness for men. The dermatologist interviewed for this study reported that popular celebrities endorsing skin products for men has resulted in increasing number of male clients comings for exfoliating and skin glow treatments.

Body-Modification Strategies Used by the Sample A high level of dissatisfaction with physical appearance was found among the sample. Nearly 90 per cent felt that physical appearance was something that could be modified to a great extent and felt that doing so would help increase confidence, fit in with others or to find partners.

These findings were supported by the data from the qualitative interviews. Nearly 50 per cent reported that they wished to change an aspect of their physical appearance. Overall body shape and muscularity, and weight were mentioned as the features that men wanted to modify with regard to their own physical appearance. Slightly more than 26 per cent had also tried to modify an aspect of their physical appearance in the past, with Hair, Body-shape and Weight being the three features that they had tried to modify. Exercising and dieting emerged as the most popular methods used to modify their physical appearance. The sample also reported using hair gels or creams, fairness creams and facial scrubs to improve hair and complexion. The dermatologist interviewed stated that most male patients seen by her came for skin glow treatments, peels (a dead skin removal treatment) and hair regeneration treatments.

Peer Influence More than 75 per cent felt that negative comments from peers could negatively affect men. It was also seen that men were likely to advise their overweight friends to lose weight (approximately 44 per cent said they had done so). The sample also reported that when they did so, their friends more often than not heeded their advice and made efforts to lose weight. This shows the hold that peers may have on the physical appearance of men.

The influence of the opposite sex was also considered an important, with men stating the finding partners and being able to live up to the standards of physical appearance expected by women as two main reasons for the increased attention to body image among men. The experts interviewed for this study concurred that romantic partners and spouses were often the ones who bought men to their facilities be it a hair salon, or a skin clinic. Nearly 71 per cent felt that comments from partners/spouses could influence the way men viewed their bodies and almost all these respondents felt that such comments could make men want to modify their physical appearance. While, a significant chunk (almost 32 per cent) felt that female peers exerted more influence over their physical appearance than male peers.

Nearly 39 per cent mentioned that their family members influenced their physical appearance with fathers being considered as the most influential followed by mothers, brothers and cousins. This is also in line with earlier research that suggests that children adopt several aspects of their parents' lifestyle and values towards the world (particularly the parent of the same-sex), including their attitudes towards their own bodies, as they grow older (Chernin 1985 as cited in Kearney-Cooke 2002). Results also showed that receiving physical appearance related criticism from parents can be a contributory factor behind having a poor view of one's own physical appearance. Lastly 61 per cent felt that siblings could influence physical appearance

Nearly 80 per cent felt that the media had a role to play in influencing beliefs and attitudes towards physical appearance, with dressing style, complexion, hair and muscularity being the physical features that the media most influenced. Nearly 76 per cent felt that the media promoted muscular, and appearance-conscious exemplars as the ideal body type for men over others. However, it is worth noting that this was not the body-type that the sample considered as the ideal body type for men. This indicates that there is some amount of discrepancy between media ideals and the ideals held by the sample. On an optimistic note, while over 83 per cent felt that their appearance did not match media ideals, 97 per cent felt they were more or less satisfied with their appearance, nonetheless.

Conclusion: The current study is one of the first and most comprehensive studies which not only talks to young men about what they consider as the ideal body type for men, but also talks about the factors that influence the shaping of these images as well. The findings indicate that not only are there distinct differences between the body image concerns of women and men, there are differences in the ideas of male beauty amongst men, as well. Most studies on the body image of men have focused on men's preoccupation with muscularity, and while the findings do indicate that men on an average do want to be taller, and heavier (closer to Caucasian ideals of male beauty), it must be noted that while men do want to be noticed by their peers and (prospective) partners, they do not want to stand out too much. Similarly, hair-loss and having a dark complexion being significant concerns is a finding that is unique to the Indian context. That peers and family appear to be influencing men's constructions of body image more than intimate partners and the media, shows that the primary agents of socializing men into masculine gender roles exert a greater influence on men's ideas of physical appearance. The study indicates that there are significant and distinct concerns surrounding body image amongst Indian men, and that men are willing to invest time and money address them. The breadth of appearance-related concerns brought forth by the current study underline the need for continual research interest in the area of male-body image, both in India and otherwise.

Chapter Five

Discrimination: A Case Study[5]

Introduction: The people from the North East (NE) in India reside in the eastern-most regions of India, compromising of the borderland states, also called 'Seven Sister and One Brother States' i.e Arunachal Pradesh, Assam, Manipur, Meghalaya, Mizoram, Nagaland, Tripura, and the Himalayan state of Sikkim (Maps of India). India's North East is popular for its varieties of rich heritage and culture, which also homes beautiful mountains, ranging from Kanchenjunga in Sikkim to Mount Saramati in Nagaland.

The NE of India also owns rich flora and fauna, where nearly about 220 languages are spoken exclusively only by the people of the North East of India (India net zone). India's NE are also very rich in agriculture, cultural handicrafts and delicacies of each state. Due to this factor, many people from other parts of India and all over the world visit the NE for their holiday tours and vacations (The green pastures). A bulk of folks from the regions of NE migrate to Bangalore for varieties of reasons and opportunities, majorly due to employment, educational opportunities and marriage etc.(Reimeingam, 2016; Chandra, 2010) and some of them also settle here and open their own businesses (Chandra, 2010). It is the unjustifiable negative behavior detected by instinct/inference rather than by recognized perceptual cues, based on the perception that an individual is a member of significant protected groups (age, gender, disability, migration, racial background, religion/faith and sexual orientation). Attributions to prejudice are more internal, stable, uncontrollable and communicate

---

[5] **Roshni Chhetri,** Research Scholar, Jain University
Lopamudra Goswami, Assistant Professor, Sampurna Montfort College, Bengaluru

excluding and devaluating messages to the disadvantaged groups, which results in significantly greater damage in the psychological well-being of the disadvantaged group's members (Branscombe, Schmitt, & Harvey, 1999). Due to rise of intolerance from the part of the oppressed groups, the need to explore and understand perception of discrimination is essential to understand discriminated groups (Dion, 2001).

The migration from India's NE to Bangalore is increasing every year to a great extent. Many people from the NE regions shift to metropolitan cities due to reasons like higher education (bachelors or masters), job opportunities and other significant reasons (Reimeingam, 2016; Chandra, 2011). There is also a vast increase on the issues of ethnic/racial discrimination, harassment, abuse and racial profiling against the people from the NE in the major cities (Delhi, Kolkata, Mumbai, Pune etc). A research by Chandra (2011) stated that '86% of NE Indians face racial discrimination in the Delhi and NCR, only 14% didn't face it but called 'Chinki, Chinese, Nepalis, Shaabjis' etc., 78.75% faced being treated like strangers in India, 22.5% physical attacks, 3.75% sexual assaults, 35% vulgar remarks, 41% cases of sexual abuse, 18% beating by locals, 12% rape cases, 9% killed in relation to sexual assault, 6% landlord harassment, 3% vulgar remarks, 3% eve teasing, 3% police harassment, 3% employer harassment, 3% media vulgar statements against North Easterners' (Chandra, 2011) focusing on the need for political aid and public sensitization required to bring the concerns/issues in the light of the Government authorities, to prevent/stop harmful behaviours intended towards NE people and for this, media and their involvement is very crucial (Chandra, 2011).

A study (McDuie-Ra, 2013) reports globalization of Delhi city in recent times and this has attracted a lot of people from the NE suburbs. Even though people of the NE are facing discrimination, harassment and sexual crimes beyond economic gains, but still people of NE do migrate to Delhi. Along with the opportunities, there is also a rise in terms of hate crimes, racism, harassment and violence and due to which the need to be sensitive to each other's culture is a must in the major metropolitan cities of India (McDuie-Ra, 2013). Studies (Mal, et. al., 2015) stress on the need for people of Delhi to change perception of other cultures along with sensitizing youths from NE India to be familiar with local cultures. Regarding issues, the national dailies didn't provide clear information on the abuses of NE people in Delhi, as in compared to the NE dailies that provided much clearer story. (Mal, et. al., 2015).

Objectives: To assess the Nature, Implications and Consequences of perceived discrimination of the North East people of India living in Bangalore. The brutal murder of Nido Tania, Richard Loitam, Ramchamphy Hongray, Dana Sangma suicide, rejection of filing an FIR for a molestation case (India Opines) arise questions—Do people of the NE perceive discrimination? If yes, in what ways do NE people perceive discrimination? These are the main questions that emerged before conducting the study and due to research gap, such a study is significant.

Methodology: This is a qualitative research, where phenomenological method was used. 10 participants from the North East of India (3 males and 7 males) either studying or working in Bangalore were interviewed, who have been living in Bangalore for two years or more, voluntarily participated in the research interview done in English. The convenience sampling method was used to include participants for the research interviews. Informed consent and demographic details were obtained from all the participants. Questionnaire method was used which consists of 13 open ended questions which attempt to understand the perceived discrimination of the people from the NE of India. The interview required about 45 minutes to an hour. After the interview, verbatim transcription was done of all the recorded interviews of the participants and following that, data was analyzed using thematic analysis and certain themes emerged out of the responses of the participants from which results were analyzed. Thematic analysis was used. First the data is coded and certain themes that emerged out of the data code were defined, interrelated and studied.

Results and Discussions: The results and findings were classified in three categories: nature, implications and consequences. From the 13 questions, 4 questions assessed the nature which is defined as the essential qualities or characteristics by which perception of discrimination (phenomenon) is recognized in the study, 6 questions assessed the implications which is defined as a meaning that is not overtly stated but is covert and 3 questions assessed consequences which is defined as the phenomenon that follows and caused by perceived discrimination (i.e the previous phenomenon).

In the terms of nature of discrimination, participants have perceived that many people are ignorant about the cultural ethos of NE states, due to which there has been misconceptions about people of the NE. As a result, participants were treated more as a foreigner in their own country. The participants perceived that their identity is diluted due to the numerous questions they face about NE states, that causes discontentment to the participants, since they feel that their identity as an Indian should be known to the nation. The participants felt that they are being considered as an outsider, not treated as Indian citizens despite having valid identity documents. As a result of such misconceptions and rising discontentment, it is creating a feeling of isolation in most of the participants, which makes them question their identity, found in other research studies 'Due to perception of a lost cultural identity, participants expressed feeling of no sense of belongingness with the in-group members'

(Baumeister & Leary, 1995). '64% respondents said the reason behind discrimination is lack of understanding/awareness about the people from the NE' (Bhattacharjee, 2014).

Secondly, participants experienced racist humor/ethnic jokes and have been victims of name calling (Chinki, Chinese) on a regular basis, common with other findings, 'For most respondents Racism in Delhi is reflected by the epithet "chinky"' (McDuie-Ra, 2013). 'The NE people are the only category of citizens to be constructed at a national level as a separate racial group with a dubious connection to the rest of the nation – mongoloides, chinkies, Chinese' (McDuie-Ra, 2015). Participants experienced name calling typically in a humorous manner by friends and strangers, perceived as an insult, consistent with other findings '56% respondents say that they were addressed by offensive names' (Bhattacharjee, 2014). Many participants have also perceived being mocked because of their Hindi language accent, which is different from other Indians.

The participants have also felt being inquisitively questioned about food habits (eating dogs, snakes etc.), creating a sense of anger as their self-esteem is effected by such enquiries, as they perceive it is done in a negative manner and to bifurcate between food habits of the two groups, resonating with a study finding 'Individuals lacking the resources to cope with negative events may experience increased feelings of inadequacy and hopelessness, negative self-perceptions, resulting in low self-esteem' (Abramson, Metalsky, & Alloy 1989). Many female participants have experienced being stared at, comments being passed more for them than other women in general, consistent with a finding, 'Women are doubly subjected to more discrimination through eve teasing' (Mal et al., 2015).

In terms of implications, many participants felt they are more likely to be taken for granted by other Indians in Bangalore because of the existence of assumptions about NE people, because of which they face issues like price hike by auto drivers, landlords and local shop vendors and at times by the police as well, similar to other finding 'Discrimination is felt most strongly in housing markets. Housing for North East migrants is expensive' (McDuie-Ra, 2013). At colleges, most student participants were given less preference than others (group work/class presentations). Others faced preference issues even in the government offices and during college applications. They felt that due to their linguistic barrier, assumptions about NE people exists, considering NE people intellectually inferior, similar to another study 'North Easterners are cast as backward and exotic; this is particularly true for tribal communities' (McDuie-Ra, 2013). This makes NE people feel insecure whereas some participants are able to understand that it stems from others' insecurities.

Majority of the participants felt they are looked as misfits in society because people assume they are frauds (asking for ID, driver's license), indulge in substance use, barbarians, resonating with another finding, 'One of the most worrying trends is that the respondents feel they are being looked upon with suspicion' (Bhattacharjee, 2014). While no participant has reported physical violence against them, they have heard from others which magnify the separation between them and other Indians. Participants working in Bangalore have not faced any personal implications related to preference issues at work, but they have heard about it through their NE counterparts.

In terms of language, participants felt that people of Bangalore are sort of compelling them to learn the local language i.e they perceive being forced. As a result, some participants have felt the need to make necessary social adjustments, to comply with other Indians in Bangalore. Female participants reported changing the way they dress (wearing more kurtis, salwars), whereas others put an extra effort in social circles for acceptance. Majority felt that people need to be more open minded and accepting towards minority cultures. Many participants perceived that they feel the sense of a collective identity in the environment of their NE counterparts because people gain a sense of positive self-esteem from their identity groups, which enhances a sense of community and belonging (collective identity).

In terms of consequences, most of the participants experienced negative prejudgements in terms of their lifestyle, values, ethnicity, race, culture, consistent with other findings, 'The study reveals that they faced ethnic or racial discrimination' (Bhattacharjee, 2014). 'Northeast migrants, particularly those with Mon-Khner, Tai, or Tibeto-Burman roots, are judged based on ascriptive notions derived from their physical features' (McDuie-Ra, 2013). 'Third, they are cast as immoral. North East women are cast as loose in morals and sexually promiscuous' (McDuie-Ra, 2013). 'Men are also subject to some of the loose and immoral assumptions but are also cast as heavy-drinkers, unpredictable, and potentially violent' (McDuie-Ra, 2013). The NE participants felt that the negative prejudgements are due to negative stereotyping, similar with other finding, 'These stereotypes feed discrimination' (McDuie-Ra, 2013). Many also perceived differences between the local people of Bangalore and the NE people due to negative stereotyping and prejudgements. Social support forums in college, progressive work cultures played huge roles in coping with prejudice, similar to a finding 'The major cause of discrimination that emerged from the survey was prejudice and lack of awareness about the northeast people' (Bhattacharjee, 2014). The emotional consequences faced by participants are fear, anger, sadness, frustration, helplessness and disgust, due to the inhuman incidents against NE people in Bangalore. Some find it difficult to describe their home state when asked by other

Indians due to their lack of awareness (e.g. say Darjeeling instead of Sikkim), whereas many confront/stand up for themselves when someone uses racial slurs or discriminate them.

Many participants felt that the government and the media isn't giving equal importance to the NE states and their people. They feel the media and the government trivializes the discrimination faced by people from the NE, common with other findings 'There is a general sense of apathy from the national media – print as well as electronic – by giving relatively lesser space to news involving North East States and its subject compared to other states that gets due share of reportage' (Mal et al., 2015). 'The Hindu did not cover the issues of the people of NE in Delhi-NCR' (Manukonda & Singh, 2015). Most participants voiced the need for change in governance system that offers equal treatment and which helps to bridge the gap in between, punishing racial offenders. Many participants felt less importance given to NE history and its contribution to India i.e. the educational system is to be blamed. A positive side was many participants expressing their openness for people to except them, hoping for a change, resonating with a finding, 'At-least 47% respondents have hope that this city can be free from discrimination in the future' (Bhattacharjee, 2014).

Some differential findings exist as well. Some participants believe that racism and prejudices go both ways, and if other Indians migrate to the NE regions, they may be looked as an outsider there and hence liable to face discrimination. One participant reported not experiencing much discrimination in Bangalore. One participant stated that because his facial features aren't like a 'North easterner', he passes as an 'Indian' to most of his colleagues around, similar to other findings, 'In Mysore, a Tibetan student was stabbed by two people who suspected him to be from NE India, indicating that his physical features would mark potential victims regardless from the place of origin' (McDuie-Ra, 2015).

Conclusion: India's NE people living in Bangalore do perceive discrimination in both covert and overt manner. If this trend increases, the rift between the two communities may continue to proliferate, so to avoid such problems for the NE people, a need to conduct group/ individual therapies and effective coping strategies for people who have been impacted or traumatized due to discrimination is necessary. An initiative to create an environment of awareness about the NE regions, culture and heritage may help in knowing about their forgotten compatriot. A need to build awareness and conduct workshops in schools, colleges and workplaces about multi-cultural diversity is also a possibility as such activities would be possible facilitators to familiarise and sensitise people with cultures across India.

Chapter Six

Soccer Fan Behaviour in India[6]

*"I have played for a lot of clubs in the country but haven't come across fans like the
ones in Bangalore. Where else have you heard fans chanting for 90 minutes?
We have an almost-packed house every home game and that says a lot about
what this club means to the fans. It's a pleasure to play in front of them."-Sunil Chettri*

Introduction: From Norman Triplett's experiment on bicyclists and later children
reeling fishing lines, it becomes clear that both the groups worked better in the
presence of others than when done alone. Although the concept of Social Facilitation
and this observation was restricted to athletes, it can be extended to that of a spectator.
Spectators make majority of the population in sports and allow for various activities
of a sport organisation and its continuation. From their initial awareness about a sport,
to forming allegiances with it, spectators gradually become 'fans' (Funk and James,
2001) and develop a level of psychological commitment to it. In other words, they
identify with a sport and a sport team which is called Team Identification (Wann,
2006) and consider the performances of the team as being self-relevant. Once their
loyalties are established, fans can be of many types. Various researchers have
identified multiple types of fans. Hunt, et.al., (1999) identified five types of fans;
temporary fans – who support a team only for a specific period, or depending on the
success or failure of the team and its performances; local fans – fans who are more
affiliated to a team that is from one's own geographical location, to name a few.

[6] **Aparna Ramaswamy,** Asst. Professor, Jain University
K.R. Santhosh, Ph.D. Asst. Professor, Christ University

Fans are devoted to the team they support and spend a lot of time, finances and energy towards them. They tend to gain more functional knowledge about the team, and develop more symbolic value for the teams (Funk & James, 2006). Along with this, fans also tend to show strong emotional reactions to the team and its performances. Similarly, Giulianotti (2002) identified four types of fans. On one end of the spectrum are supporters who are more traditional in their identification styles to a team, and on the other end are flaneurs who are more detached and consumer-oriented in their identification with a sport team.

In the recent years, football has been gaining popularity and is evident through the development of football leagues such as the *i-League* and *Indian Super League*. This promotes Indian football to a global level as well as allow many new teams to participate in national as well as international levels. In this light, The All India Football Federation (AIFF) has taken various measures such as youth coaching, coaching license, etc., to make football a more effective sport. This increasing popularity of the sport has also lead to an increase in the number of fans that associate themselves with the football teams. A precipitant of this is the interaction between the fans and the players within and out of the stadium. For example, in the *i-League*, a set of fans called the 'The West Block Blues' is the official fandom for the team *Bengaluru FC*. The team was formed in 2013, and although it has only been a short span of time, the team and its fans have set a benchmark in their engagement. Often, they are also known as the *twelfth man* and the fans have been credited by the team's players and coaches alike. Although the fans in this fandom identify themselves with Bengaluru FC, they also are fans of teams in leagues outside the country. This indicates a clear demarcation between a *local* fan and a *distant* fan and can be understood in terms of geographical location of team playing a role in any fan's level of identification with it and it can also be hypothesised that identification is higher when it is a local team than when the team is distant (Theodorakis, et.al., 2013).

There are about 83 million television viewers of football in the country as of 2011, and it is only probable that with more leagues, the number of viewers has increased. Viewership also increases with more fans attending matches in the stadia, and this is possible only if sport organizations know their fan base, understand and analyse the fans' different perspectives, and thereby making football accessible to the different types of fans in their fandom. Since fans in India also are fans of many international leagues (indicating fandom towards distant teams) such as the *English Premier League* (England), *La Liga* (Spain) & *Bundes Liga* (Germany) and are identified to specific clubs from these leagues, it can be interesting to see how the fans' identification is different for these leagues.

Objectives: Through literature review on football fandom in India, a deficiency in research on fan behaviours from the Indian context was observed. This study could diminish this gap in literature and lay a way for further development of research specifically in fan behaviours in the country, and globally. Why football fans affiliate themselves with a football team needs to be clearly understood; this gives rise to the need for understanding football fan behaviours. By conducting a research on a topic such as fan behaviours, fans themselves, sport organizations, as well as laypersons can understand how and why fans behave in certain ways and this can result in better interpersonal and intrapersonal relationships. This could also provide valuable insights to fans about their own behaviours and in relation with that of other fans and allow them to identify their adaptive and maladaptive behaviours and thereby act in accordance to what can make football experiences healthier for them.

Methodology: The present research paper adopted a Qualitative Research Design. The sample included 32 football fans by using a random sampling method, aged between 18-35 years from Bangalore, India. Using a semi-structured interview method, the data was collected on their behaviours before, during, and after a game of football involving the team that they are affiliated with. The data was analysed using Thematic Analysis. The five dimensions pertaining to need for fan behaviour research and functions of sport team identification were identified.

Results & Discussion: Based on the thematic analysis of responses from the fans, five themes emerged relating to the functions that sport team identification served, and summaries were drawn. The functions are:

Emotions – One of the most common responses provided by the participants when asked about why it is necessary to study fan behaviours was related to understanding the parallels between emotions and passions that fans exhibit during the course of a match. This could be possible because when they are affiliated to a team, fans are also emotionally invested in the progress of the team.

"The fans go through different emotions throughout the game and it might be difficult for a mere person to understand what they behave which usually occurs only during the game and its nothing but the passion"

Fans display a wide range of positive and negative emotions, and sometimes they could be overwhelming for people around them to understand why fans behave the way they do, and why the emotional connect with a team takes place. Therefore, it is important to understand the emotional function of affiliating with a sports team. This could allow prediction of behaviours associated with the emotion about the game and match outcomes; i.e., the difference in emotional expressions of the fans under winning or losing situations involving their favourite teams (Jones, et al., 2012; Wann & Branscombe, 1992; Leeuwen, Quick, & Daniel, 2002). In relation to the match outcome, emotional responses that the fans display, in a way allows for the understanding of the performance of a team. An insight about the way fans would then cope with these situations could also be gained, and recognize and prevent any form of aggressive or maladaptive behaviours, and enhance the match-viewing experiences. Fans express these emotions through their chants and vocalized behaviours, which could be seen as impactful on the players' performances.

Socialization – Absten (2011) found in her study that fans either associate with a team to feel assimilated or to feel differentiated from a group. This was also evident in the current research. It was seen that through football, fans opened up to many other fans (fans of the same team or rival teams, and individuals who are not fans of the sport) and this leads to social interaction.

"Games like football and cricket, when people watch them, they forget the boundaries, it is a great way to socialise I think."

Socialization can also be an important antecedent to fans identifying with a team (Melnick & Wann, 2011). This increases the scope for further growth of football fandom when there are conversations about the sport. Fans interact with one another either during a match, or over social media, and in doing so they maintain existing relationships and form new associations (Phua, 2012). This interaction is not merely restricted to fans, but through the advent of social media, athletes are also beginning to interact with their fans and this enables them to gain a better perspective of what the fans expect from their game and what makes their match experiences better. This indicates a mutual benefit of the fan and the organization. This can be summarised in the following quote by a participant: *"Athletes can become more interactive with the fans, and fans can motivate the team to do well through their chants and interactions." "Teams and their players can communicate better with their fans through this research. They will get the clear idea about what makes the fans happy and what disappoints them"*

In the current sample, fans believe that it is necessary for the sporting organization to know their fans, and know the differences in their behaviours as this would ease the administrative processes of the organization and act as 'damage prevention' and 'awareness' elements.

Economic Benefits – It became evident through the thematic analysis that fans are also considered consumers or customers of the sport that they follow. Many researchers have identified this characteristic of the fans in association with them purchasing team related official merchandises, and attending matches (Kwon & Armstrong, 2002; Sutton, McDonald, Milne, & Cimperman, 1997; Gau, James & Kim, 2009).

"If they find out that a particular sport is most watched, the broadcasting people can pay more attention to that sport, what attracts more audience, and based on that they can telecast. It also helps in club promotions – what fans expect from the team and they can do some interesting things and increase to their revenue, like purchase of shirts, sales, etc."

From the analysis of responses, it was seen that fans are revenue generators for the teams that they are affiliated with, and help in increasing sponsorships and marketing of a team through the fans' participation.

Motivation – From the analysis, it was evident that fans believe that they can motivate performances for athletes and teams. They believe that they can influence and drive the team forward with their support.

"Important to see how the fan behaviours develop, and how they influence players and vice versa, how do players influence fan behaviours".

An average team may also develop chances of winning a competition due to the motivation and inspiration of the fans. By making their opinions known to the sport team organisation and management, fans could also play a vital role in the team's administrative activities such as selling or buying of players to a certain team. The *home advantage* is created by the fans. This is especially in the case of fans who watch their team's matches at a stadium.

Introspection & Insight – The function of introspection and insight was seen as one of the most recurring theme in the responses by the participants. Through the investigation of various fan behaviours, fans could gain a deeper understanding of their own match-time expressions and those of the others. It was seen that the fans would then be able to find answers about where many of their behaviours stemmed from, and this could be related to the team's performance, the match climate, emotions associated with the team, irrational behaviours such as superstitions, etc. Fans also believed that there is a certain pattern in behaviours of fans of various teams, and that a thorough research of these fan behaviours could be an indicator of future behaviours and help in taking necessary measures under common situations.

This insight on behaviours is not merely restricted to fans that support the same team, but also that of fans who support rival teams. Through this insight, fans believe that they can be more tolerant in general, in the sense that they could become more accepting of outcomes and avoid unnecessary actions and reactions. This could be a result of various discussions that the fans have amongst themselves and the different perspectives that could be put forth and their acceptance of thoughts that are not always complying to a fan's own.

Conclusion: In conclusion, it is evident that understanding and researching on fan behaviours is important because it has multi-fold benefits not only to the fans, but also to teams, athletes and sports organizations. Therefore, the advantage of this research lies in its implications that could prove to be advantageous to sporting authorities in making football a healthy experience for the spectators as well as be benefitted with the knowledge of the types of fans and types of fan behaviours which allows them to make necessary amends in their management and administration.

Chapter Seven

Application of Military Psychology[7]

Introduction: We live in a world where one of the biggest industries is that of arms and where only 10 countries are actually free from conflict (Withnall, 2016). Regardless of the causes, reasons and justifications of why they are fought for, in any war it is mostly the lower-ranked soldiers battling in the front line, with their human sensitivity camouflaged behind the uniforms and weapons, their helpless families from lower middle classes left behind and the innocent civilians estranged amidst the barricades and refugee camps that suffer the most. The unseen wounds and scars of these victims are much deeper and painful psychological injuries triggered by numerous causes. In addition to this, all the physical and social trauma in a war setting also adds to the burden against the human mentality that is the most fragile and vulnerable of all. Thus, it is utterly impossible to ignore those unseen psychological wounds that are being left behind by any war. One evidence to prove this is the astonishing rise in the number of military deaths by suicide than during action in the past few years as reported by Daily Mail (2016, December 30). Therefore, it is high time to understand that military psychology has a long way to battle behind those front lines.

In view of such pathetic statistics and the lack of efficient attempts and intervention by the responsible authorities for the welfare of the returning military persons, their families and even the refugees that results in further trauma and destruction in their lives, the paper takes an eclectic approach to identify and to discuss risks in their already traumatized lives, the role of the intervention of the authorities and where it

---

[7] **M.M. Privini Devindi Sandanayake,** Student, Acharya Institute, Bangalore

has been failing drastically in many situations. Similarly, there is focus on exploring the triggering factors of war and conflict, through a psychological approach as an attempt to understand the potentiality to soothe the situations from there itself which would otherwise have turned into massively disastrous wars by eliminating those psychological causal factors.

This conceptual research is conducted for five purposes. First, to explore the numerous applications of psychology in military settings, its need and purpose. Second, to discuss the development of novel and further efficient applications of military psychology. Third, to detect where the whole system fails and deviates from an effective application of the same. Fourth, to explore deeper the triggering factors for wars and conflicts in a psychological outlook. Finally, to analyze the possibility to control such crisis situations with an ideal application of military psychology which if succeeds is powerful enough even in eradicating terrorism and warfare from its root causes itself. The proposed pathways also serve to highlight the need for further research on understudied resilience factors.

In view of the lack of empirically tested risk factors that explain the specific psychological causal factors in leading to terroristic behaviours (Sareen et al, 2007), the researcher has adopted an eclectic approach in identifying the potential reasons for higher levels of vulnerability and in exploring the prevention and the control of the shame. The researcher also looks forward for the indulgence of those who are better informed in the field in actualizing the ultimate purposes of the concepts explored in this paper and optimistically hope that thus it may serve as a vehicle for spreading transdisciplinary discussions on the topic.

The field of military is the pioneer in setting the example of application of psychology to various organizational functioning and it eventually led to the birth to the applied branch called 'industrial psychology' since as early as World War I itself (Bary, 2008). As defined by Wikipedia, military psychology is the research, design and application of psychological theories and empirical data towards understanding, predicting, and countering behaviours either in friendly or enemy forces or the civilian population that may be undesirable, threatening or potentially dangerous to the conduct of military operations (Military psychology, 2018). Furthermore, according to Melton's (1957) definition of military psychology, it must be accepted that military psychology is coextensive with psychology and is defined primarily by the context of application (Bray, 2008). Here lies the necessity to review the extent of application of military psychology in numerous war settings in the modern world, if it is efficient and sufficient as a universal and ubiquitous, living human science.

Application of military psychology: The application of military psychology can be numerous and commonplace in any war setting starting from the profit minded arms companies till the dumb walls of military hospitals. Its scope begins from prewar selection, training, organization, leadership and weapon, uniform and vehicle designing to in-action war tactics, attack plans, operation strategies, intelligent services, questioning and handling of the military captives to postwar rehabilitation, counselling, resilience and civil crisis resolution and much more. Basically, military psychology aims in providing effective guidance and psychological support in handling the numerous stresses in war settings, with its basic focus over the soldiers, their families and the civilians victimized by the military operations.

Nevertheless, the question if these goals of military psychology are effectively or perhaps universally achieved, especially in the third word situations where the necessity for the same is even higher and urgent, is often rhetorical in nature. "Suicide, not combat, is the leading cause of death of US soldiers deployed to the Middle East to fight ISIS", reports Daily Mail (2016, December 30). If this is the situation in the so called advanced USA, the situation in developing countries is therefore doubtlessly pathetic. This astonishing rise in the number of military deaths by suicide than during action proves that military psychology has a long way to battle behind the front lines. Further, it is the most urgent battle needed to be won first of all others as it is the battle against the fragile resistance of the most vulnerable from all its borders; the conflict within the human psyche which is irreparable once distorted. This is because of the higher risk factor and emotional vulnerability brought about by war mentality that often tend to blur the thin and absurd line between the normality and abnormality, the healthy and unhealthy and the favourable and unfavourable.

Within this context lies the necessity for the military psychologists as well as the military authorities to equip themselves with a sound understanding of the practical applications of psychology in military settings so that it may empower them to explore the potentiality within the field of military psychology to extend it further efficiently and sufficiently in further ubiquitous and universal modes of application.

The number of military deaths by suicide has increased drastically over the recent years (Wikipedia, 2018), as if to open the eyes and ears of the authorities to the more destructive mental warfare that the soldiers battle with daily, whilst in action battling on the frontline. The basic reason for all this trauma being the exposure to violence and bloodshed for longer periods also with both physical and emotional estrangement from one's secure environments, are of course difficult to be directly addressed in such extremely critical war settings yet there is always a scope for minimizing these or the effects of the same.

According to a recent research by APA, despite high needs to better understand the psychological impact of deployment on military personnel and families and to facilitate due support for them, rigorous research on the field is lacking(Adler, Bliese & Castro, 2011).

Regardless of the existing programs that are intended to help them, their effectiveness is found to be largely unknown (Acton, 2013). Here lies the need for better coordination, maximum outreach and optimal delivery of such programs at the level of individuals, families, and communities who are directly and indirectly involved or affected by war (Park, 2011).

New improvements are highly necessary in each level in the field of military. In the managerial level, the organizational policies have to be moulded in a far better way to minimize to the fullest the psychosocial risk and resilience factors and maximize the mental health conditions of military personnel and veterans deployed to war zones or other hazardous environments. Similarly, more number of regular supervisions and counselling sessions need to be conducted in order to regularly monitor the level of psychological wellbeing of the soldiers where the detection of those in risk conditions can be given further personalized support and guidance. The job of military has to be turned into more smooth flowing, by cutting short and taking away the unnecessary rigor and formalness whenever possible, thus encouraging the formation of informal groups within one's military unit and so on. This may eventually create a comfortable environment for the soldiers with enough of opportunity for self-expression that ultimately serves in the form of catharsis to ease their heightening stress levels at duty. Added to this is the necessity to further discourage any situations that may intensify their already heightening stress levels such as ragging, cornering, mocking and undue exploitation of any form by the superiors etc. The management may also keep updated records of their family conditions and facilitate the necessary to ease the torments of the families awaiting the living return of their loved ones away in front lines.

Even though similar procedures as those aforesaid are being followed in varying levels within certain countries with war, these need to be made more efficient and all-time, across the globe, together with further improvements.

Since every human being is unique and different from each other in their behaviours and responses to similar conditions at combat can vary drastically. For instance, murdering another human being, even though he is a terrorist and is done in the name of patriotism can lead to immense levels of guilt in the mindset of some soldiers, particularly within those naïve and the newly joined (Grossman, 1995). Whereas some may get used to this lifetime exposure to combat operations and witnessing atrocities or massacres (i.e, mutilated bodies, mass killings and so on) with time, some may fail in a quick adaptation to these experiences leading to numerous psychological vulnerabilities starting from conditions like depression to post traumatic stress disorder as well (Gold et al, 2007). In this manner it is difficult to predict about the particular moment or the exact situation that the fragile and vulnerable human psyche may cross the thin and absurd line between the normal and abnormal.

In order to support those with such potential risks, the provision of regular psychological guidance, therapy and counselling whenever necessary is as important as any other managerial supervision of the authorities. Thus, various attempts can be made to make the alienated soldiers feel at home amidst the battle field and to sense the togetherness within one's own military unit and troop. Such timely interventions can be extremely worthy, even in saving the precious lives of those who are willing to offer their lives for the sake of their motherland.

Here it is essential to apply the perspectives of an occupational health model. Thus, the military organizations may moderate such extreme impacts of wartime experience on their mental health through individual screening, training, peer support, leadership, and organizational policies. Due care and attention has to be projected on how to manage their mental health conditions during deployment to proposals for reconceptualising service delivery, the role of peers, and what it means to transition home. According to a recent research conducted by American Psychological Association (APA), it is proven that such systematic approaches for early interventions and psychological resilience training can be extremely supportive (Adler, Bliese & Castro, 2011).

Similarly there is a high need for transdisciplinary research on application of novel concepts and theories into the military setting such as "sport psychology research informing military decision training" (Ward et al., 2008). Such is the scope for the growth of the field and this has to be contributed by the military psychologists through further research in the field.

Military psychology in eradicating root causes of war: Be it the soldiers with patriotic feelings or the terrorists with separationist ideals, deep within those uniformed chests are the similar hearts pounding in the same beat. Nobody is born a patriot or a terrorist. The pure smile of a newborn child senses neither boundaries nor divisions to be fought for. But what leads to all these extremities and deviations from sensitivity to humaneness is worth questioning. The answer is simplified by the psychological theories like cognitive and behavioural perspectives which suggest that the experiences from the environment and the eventual societal demands lead to either the formation or the distortion of the cognition thus moulding personality and the shaping of the behaviour that ultimately transforms oneself into either of them, the patriotic soldier or the blood thirsty terrorist. Hence, it is one's society that is majorly responsible in cultivating the values within it. Here lies one of the root causes for the germination of the vicious seeds of terrorism and war when carefully analyzed. Therefore, the field of military psychology even has such high potentials as to attempt even in sweeping away the age-old curse of war from its root causes itself by attempting to heal such initial cognitive distortions leading to violent and antisocial tendencies in behaviour. For instance, one's own environment and society that surrounds him or her, starting from family, school, peer circle, neighbourhood, relatives to workplace, community and to the whole world around equally contribute in the shaping of such dangerous personalities as well as the germination of hatred and revenge leading to terrorism and warfare.

According to recent studies, it is found that poverty, lack of education and proper parental care are among the root causes for terrorism (Lee, 2011). This shows that a majority of terrorists had not had proper families, with caring parents or adult models who had succeeded in educating the child with proper moral education that instils more of sensitivity to humanity into their fast learning brains. Therefore, it is clear the everybody's social responsibility begins here, starting from due caring for one's family and children and this had to be continued upwards in the social hierarchy till reaching the macrocosm of the whole community, the society and the world.

Conclusion: Therefore, it is clear that apart from the present healing rendered to the burning world through its great intervention the field, military psychology also encompasses numerous new dimensions in its varying applications in military settings. These ideal applications of military psychology are so intense that it allows the world to visualize an optimistic future with the concepts of military psychology are productively applied to such extremes where there would be no wars or battles and the necessity for military psychology to exist would have completely be faded away. This way we may utilize military psychology to the optimal in order to revolutionize war for a better future!

Chapter Eight

Psychological Look at Goddess Renuka[8]

Introduction: As Charles Korte one of the student's of Stanley Milgram observes that his teacher's innovative ideas as the most significant influence in his career as a social psychologist. Milgram in his "Authority and Individual" raised a question if obedience would drop if the learner and teacher had shaken hands just before the research started, given the symbolism of a handshake? And within a week the students in Milgram's other course, "Urban psychology", shook hands with pedestrians on the streets of New York, just to learn how it would be received by strangers (Blass, 1999). Milgrams many questions on obedience were addressed with applied methods, though he was forceful in class at the same time brought unusually tolerant disagreements (Blass, 1999). His many experiments on obedience has thrown light on the different behavioural attitudes at different developmental stages.

The Indian system of thought believes in imparting knowledge and educates the student on a friendly landscape. The student and disciple share a very rare relationship which is a total balance of respect, friendship and obedience. The Upanishads themselves meaning to sit and listen near a master - the knowledge of the Self and often termed as 'mitra samhita' meaning 'an interaction made on a friendly note'. The Katha Upanishad elucidates the story of Nachiketa and Yama in the backdrop of

---

[8] **Vaishnaavi Chavan,** Student, Jain University

obedience. Nachiketa the little boy in the Upanishad exhibits the convention of obedience to a father even when the latter has lost his temper. (Nagler, 2007)

The Hindu mythology considers obedience as an act of merit and the foremost character of a righteous person. Obedience towards the parents, guru, elder siblings and elders in general was one of the first lessons of moral taught to a child. The Ramayana is an epic which illustrates many examples of obedience; obedience of Kausalya towards her husband Dasharatha; Lakshmana, Bharatha and Shatrughna displaying their obedience towards Rama in many instances and Rama himself stands as the best example for obedience by taking his father's orders to go to exile with no resistance (Klostermaier, 2007).

The guru who can be a teacher, spiritual guide or spiritual head of a Hindu tradition and practice of unquestioned obedience towards him is a mark of respect or reverence. (Werner, 2005) One of the important rules mentioned in the Ashtavarana of the Virashaivas, the eight-fold armour comprises obedience towards the guru. (Klostermaier, 2007) As Ananda Coomaraswamy puts it clearly "The Hindu religion is strictly speaking an obedience; and that this is a Hindu in good standing, not by what he believes but by what he does; or in other words, by his "skill" in well doing under the law." (Coomaraswamy, 2011) The Dharma shastra puts forth many laws which expect an enforcing obedience.

The Bhagavad Gita, in a dialogue between Krishna and Arjuna, stresses on obedience to dharma, selfless action, was more effective than sacrifice or mortification of the flesh. (Elgood, 2000) In the light of this paper, an attempt is made to rethink from psychological perspective of obedience with reference to Renuka, the mythic mother and goddess drawing a with her legend in which the obedience of the son towards his father arrives at an unethical stage much like Milgram's obedience experiments.

Legend of Renuka - the Mythic Mother and Goddess: Renuka the daughter of King Renu is wedded to one of the Saptarishis Jamadagni. Renuka had four sons and lived contented with her ascetic life discharging her duties to perfection. Her chastity was her penance and as a product of it she could collect water in an unbaked earthen pot which she made herself on the bank of the river; another version of the legend says she had the power of her chastity due to which she could gather water without a vessel but could form water into the shape of a pot and carry it home. (Pintchman, 1994)

One of the narrations says that one day on her way to the stream, she beheld Chitraratha the prince of Mrittikavati, with a garland of lotuses on his neck, sporting with his queen, in the water; and she felt envious of their felicity (Wilson,1868)

Another explains that she experienced adultery after looking upon a *gandharva*. Following this incident Renuka loses her power to collect water in the earthen pot or without a pot, she returns failing to fetch water for her husband's ritual. A furious Jamadagni raged by her temptations orders their son Parashurama to kill his mother. Parashurama assents on the condition that his father grants him a boon, which Jamadagni agrees to do. Parashurama obediently picks up an axe and chases his mother to kill her. Renuka runs and hides in the house of a washerwoman. Whilst the washerwoman tries to protect Renuka, Parashurama chops both of their heads. He returns back to his father and requests him to bring Renuka back to life in exchange to the boon. In a hurry to restore his mother to life, he exchanged the heads of the two women. Thus Renuka's head on Yellamma's body and Yellamma's head on Renuka's body. When he was realized Jamadagni accepted the woman with chaste head and high-caste body as his wife. The woman with the unchaste head and a low-caste body became a goddess. (Pattanaik 2000)

Conclusion: Stanley Milgram lived in many cultures in order to develop firsthand knowledge of two different cultures. Mythological stories consume a large chunk of our developmental stages, and inevitably, modulate personalities. Hindu households, in the researcher's perspective have always abided to authority, placed the value of obedience on the highest pedestal.

Renuka's life, in this aspect justifies the point stated above. Parashurama's actions based on blind obedience to his father speaks of the levels to which a person conforms to authority, especially if the authoritative figure is a family member. The outcome of the legend of Renuka brings the tragic story line of son beheading his mother upon the orders of his father, but at the same time exhibits his ardent love for his mother in his urgency to bring her back to life. The result of this episode of obedience transforms his mother Renuka into three goddesses who are relevant in the contemporary times also as goddess Renuka, Yellamma and Mariamma. They are propitiated for protection as village goddesses consecrated outside the village as a protector of all evils, ill health, and bad fortune. Each of the goddesses are cult figures by themselves popular in both rural and urban cities.

Chapter Nine

Internet Addiction and Social Functioning[9]

Introduction: Internet is being integrated as a part in our every day's life, because the usage of internet has been growing explosively throughout worldwide. Internet Addiction (IA) is an addictive disorder that has not seen as incredible amount of attention, yet it is the main cause for great concern in student's life (Hagedorn and Young,2011). Internet addiction was first proposed by Kimberly Young, and it has included in DSM-V. Internet addiction is also known by other terms "internet addiction disorder, pathological internet use, internet dependency, problem internet use, internet overuse and compulsive internet use". Earlier Research studies indicates that internet addiction is apparently associated to social aspects. This could be predominately true for adolescents who use the internet for interpersonal communication. (Fioravanti, dettore &casole 2012). Internet Addiction has been termed "Pathological Internet Use (PIU) or "Internet Dependency" and it is defined as the "inability to controls one's use of the internet which leads to negative consequences in daily life" (Li, O' Brien, Snyder &Howard 2015).

Self-compassion refers to kind and gentle towards oneself, and it mainly involved in

[9] **M.S. Sujamani.** Asst. Professor, Presidency College, Chennai
V. Ganesh, Research Scholar, Presidency College, Chennai
S. Usha Rani, Ph.D., Asst. Professor, Women's Christian College, Chennai

the face of negative experiences and perceived inadequacy and it requires to accept failures, distressful events and inadequacies which are the part of human condition (Neff, Kirkpatrick & Rude,2007). Research on several studies on self-compassion have demonstrated that self-compassion is a powerful predictor of mental health (Neff2003b). Social Functioning defines an individual's interactions with environment and the ability to fulfil their role within environment. Study conducted by Akini & Iskender (2011) examined the relationships between Internet addiction and social functioning. Results indicated that internet addiction is negatively correlated to social functioning. The above mentioned studies state a brief overview about the problems on internet addiction which affects individual's life. Interpersonal Relationship, social experience, social anxiety and self-efficacy also attained attention on Internet addiction.

Internet addiction has substantial adverse effects on physical and mental health, interpersonal relationship and academic performance levels of adolescents. Heavy internet users have numerous social contacts because of the internet use but they have reduced face to face contacts. Therefore, focussing on appropriate coping strategies is most important. This study is an attempt to evaluate the problem of Internet addiction and how does it affect self-compassion and social functioning among college students. It will enable to find the factors related to internet addiction which enables the teachers, counsellors, psychiatrists to recognize the association of self-compassion, social functioning and psychological problems faced by the students on internet addiction.

Objectives: The study has twofold objectives. i) To investigate the levels in self-compassion and social functioning due to Internet over usage. ii) To find the Gender difference in self-compassion and social functioning due to Internet addiction.

Methodology: The research design adapted for the present study is Ex-Post Facto research design. Purposive sampling method was used with total of 160 participants selected from four different Engineering college students in Chennai. The data was collected using survey method through questionnaire form. A demographic profile and consent form along with the questionnaire was distributed to the college students, those who signed the consent form were included in this study. He following tools were used: Internet Addiction Test (IAT) developed by Dr. Kimberly Young to measure Internet Addiction. It consists of 20 items that measures Mild, Moderate and Severe level of Internet. Scoring: A 6-point scale response from "Does not apply" to "Always". Higher the score, the greater level of addiction. Self-Compassion Scale - Short Form (SCS-SF) developed by Dr. Kristen Neff's to measure self -compassion. It consists of 12 items that measures Low, Medium and High level of self-compassion.

Scoring: A 5- point scale response from "Never" to "Always". Higher the score, higher level of self-compassion. Social Functioning Scale (SFS) developed by Dr. Max Birchwood to measure social functioning. It consists of seven sub Areas. Scoring: A 4- point scale response from "Never" to "often". Higher the score, lower the social functioning.

Results and discussion

Table 1 Comparison of Internet addiction, Self- compassion and Social Functioning among male and female college students

Variable	Male N=91 Mean + SD	Female N=69 Mean + SD	t (df=159)
Internet Addiction	41.7 + 14.8	38.7 + 14.9	0.21**
Self-compassion	38.0 + 6.9	38.5 + 5.7	0.60**
Withdrawal	11.3 + 2.8	11.1 + 2.3	0.68**
Interaction	13.8 + 4.1	14.0 + 2.7	0.77**
Pro-social	27.4 + 9.0	27.1 + 8.0	0.84**

** Significant difference at p<0.01

Table 1 shows the comparison of Internet addiction, Self-compassion and Social Functioning (withdrawal, interaction and pro-social). The calculated t-value was less than that of the table value at 0.01level. There was significance difference between Internet Addiction, self-compassion and social functioning.

Table 2 Association between Internet addiction and self-compassion, social functioning (withdrawal, Interaction & Pro-social) among college students.

Variable	N	r
Self-compassion	160	-0.129
Withdrawal	160	-0.027
Interaction	160	0.009
Pro-social	160	0.177*

* Significant difference at p<0.05

Table 2 shows the association between internet addiction and self-compassion, social functioning (withdrawal, Interaction & Pro-social) among college students. In pro-social domain of social functioning. Calculated 'r' value is greater than that of the table value at .05 level of significance. In other domain of social functioning and in self -compassion calculated 'r' value is lesser than that of the table value.

In this study the sample consists of 160 students from four different Engineering colleges in Chennai. Among the total sample of 160, there were 91 male students and 69 female students. Comparatively, male students scored (41.7+14.8) (Table 1) higher than female students (38.7+14.9) in Internet Addiction, over all it showed that male students internet usage is higher than female students. The score of male students in self-compassion (38.0 + 6.9), withdrawal (11.3+2.8) and pro-social (27.4+9.0) were slightly higher than female students who scored in self-compassion (38.5+5.7), withdrawal (11.1 +2.3) and pro-social (27.1 +8.1). Thus, it is interpreted as even though the male scores are higher there is no much difference in self-compassion and social functioning (withdrawal and prosocial). In interaction domain male students scored (13.8+4.1) lesser than female students (14.0+2.7) which shows that female students have difficulty in interaction with others. This study also examined the association of internet addiction on self-compassion and social functioning. In (Table 2) Association between internet addiction and self- compassion revealed that there was almost negligible relationship and Association with internet addiction and domains of social functioning, withdrawal (-0.027) interaction (0.009) and prosocial (0.177) also showed almost negligible relationship with Internet Addiction. In the association between internet addiction and social functioning domain (pro-social) there was significance at .05 level.

Conclusion: Based on the above findings it is concluded that there is a difference in the level of Internet Addiction and Interaction between male and female students. However, the results do not clearly indicate any difference with other variables (self-compassion, withdrawal and prosocial) between male and female students. Also, the study does not suggest any clear relationship between the variable internet addiction and other variables (self-compassion and social functioning) which is contradictory to the available literature. This might be due to the daily routine of Engineering students who use internet for projects and also for other academic purposes. Therefore, further research can be done with the variable of Internet Addiction with other educational background students and it also forms the limitation of this study.

Chapter Ten

The Effects of Dance[10]

Introduction: Dance is a discourse of the body. It is a form of art that involves the rhythmic or non-rhythmic movement of the body to music. Dance is also referred to as a form of expression that can convey varied messages through movement or utilization of the body. According to Merriam Webster (1828), dance is the rhythmic movement to a particular style of music that can be performed or even done with a guide. People from different walks of life are the students or the learners of various dance forms and are taught by the trainers. Each form has its own ethic of teaching, learning, initiation and termination. The effectiveness of learning or teaching, on different aspects of life, can be explained by the mind body connection.

According to Demelius (1940), the sentient body is an extension of the Self that can feel and communicate. Movement contains a symbolic function and as such can be evident of unconscious processes (Jones, 2013). It is not just the unconscious, but movement in general can originate from and affect both the mind and body. It could either be representative of the mind or a manifestation of the bodily state. Meekums (2015) defines the mind and the body as interconnected entities where movement has a symbolic meaning and is known to represent unconscious material or processes. It can also express the different aspects of personality. Kate Toohil (2014), emphasizes that, dance helps aid the mind body connection by either, stimulating the body and thus may have a relaxing, distracting, touching effect on the mind or originating from the mind in the form of expression and aiding the process of communication of thought to the self or the world at large.

---

[10] **Sukriti Dua** & **Kishor Adhikari,** Christ University, Bengaluru

Any mind-body therapies focus on becoming more conscious of mental states and using this increased awareness to guide our mental states in a better, less destructive direction (Hart, 2015). Dance movement therapy is the therapeutic use of movement to further the emotional, cognitive, physical and social integration of the individual, based on the empirically supported premise that the body, mind and spirit are interconnected (ADTA, 1992). Various studies have been conducted to study the benefits of this therapy on different clinical populations In various research by Jeong et al (2005), Sandel et al (2005) and Erwin-Grabner et al (1999), dance and movement therapy was found to have a positive effect on different variables under measure for people having mild depression, cancer and anxiety.

Aspects of self like self-esteem, body image, optimism and the like are known to be the most effected since various movement activities are based on them. The group format of sessions works a lot on the social skills of an individual through self-confidence and self-esteem based activities. The medial prefrontal cortex is known to be associated in memory, decision-making and cognition, which are known to be the basis of formation of the different aspects of self. The prefrontal cortex also contains the motor cortex, which is associated with movement (Gabbott et al., 2005; Heidbreder and Groenewegen, 2003; Hoover and Vertes, 2007). While dancing, there are new connections established in the brain, as is the case with new learning. According to Dr. Lovatt (2011), these connections tend to establish or develop new neural pathways in the brain, in the motor and pre-motor areas, thus reflecting in the medial prefrontal cortex, and leading to surrounding changes in aspects of memory and cognition that are known to be the basis of aspects of the self.

Objectives: This study aims to identify the effect of dance on the self-esteem, body image, optimism, mental well-being and quality of life of individuals. The main goal is to identify the differences in these factors (if any) among dancers and non-dancers and also among trainees and special children in the dance therapeutic setting.

- Are there any significant differences in aspects of self (like self esteem, body image and optimism, well-being and quality of life) among dancers and non-dancers?

- Are there any significant differences in aspects of self (like self esteem, body image and optimism, well-being and quality of life) among those in training to become dance/movement therapists?

- Are there any significant differences in aspects of self (like self esteem, body image and optimism, well-being and quality of life) among children with childhood disorders, undergoing dance/movement therapy sessions?

Methodology: This research study is essentially quantitative in nature. The first part of the study is experimental, drawing a comparison among dancers and non-dancers. The second part is intervention based, drawing a comparison between the same sample's scores on different variables related to self. Lastly, the third part is intervention based as well, drawing a comparison on the basis of the observational technique.

In study 1, a comparison was drawn between dancers and non-dancers whereas in study 2 and 3, the intervention effect was differentiated with. Study 1 analysis was done using independent samples t test whereas study 2 analysis was done using paired samples t test. Both of these were done on SPSS version 22. Since study 3 involved an observation checklist, it was converted into an interval scale of scoring for quantifiable items. Negatively and positively scored items were identified and total scores for each of the factors on the observation checklist was obtained. A dependent samples t test was then done for each of the factors individually.

Results and Discussion: The normality testing for all three parts of the study was done using SPSS and the Shapiro Wilk test was used. The scores of 100 individuals in Study 1 and 18 trainees in Study 2 were normal on all the different variables under measure. The scores for 20 participants in Study 3, were also normal on all four variables. In Study 1, the t test yielded a significant difference for only one of the variables among all five under evaluation, i.e. body image. The sample including the dancers was found to have a mean score of 71.64, which was higher than non-dancer sample mean score, 67.36. The mean difference was statistically significant at the .05 level. According to the given analysis, the hypothesis H1a, H1b, H1c and H1d are retained or there is failure to reject the null hypothesis, as there is no significant difference among the scores on the factors of self-esteem, mental well being, quality of life and optimism. Hypothesis H1e stands rejected, as there is a statistically significant difference among the mean scores of both the groups on body image.

In Study 2, the t test yielded significant results for two variables and three domains of a third variable, between the pre and post test. A significant difference was found in the self-esteem scores. The sample mean score of 31.16 changed to 34.50 in the intervention scores. A significant difference was also found in the body image scores where the sample mean score of 70.27 changed to 74.94 post the intervention. The mean difference for both of these was statistically significant at the .001 level. Significant differences at were also found for the physical (.05 level), psychological (.01 level) and social (.05 level) domain scores on the quality of life scale, between the pre-test and post-test evaluation.

According to the given analysis, the hypothesis H2b and H2d are retained or there is failure to reject the null hypothesis as there is no significant difference among the pre-test and post-test scores of the trainees on the factors of mental well being and optimism. Hypothesis H1a and H1e stands rejected as there is a statistically significant difference among the mean scores of pre-test and post-test rating on self-esteem and body image, likely brought about by the intervention.

There is a failure to reject hypothesis H1c, as one of the domains of quality of life does not yield a significant difference among pre-test and post-test scores. There are statistically significant differences in physical, psychological and social domains of the quality of life but there isn't an overall state of difference.

In Study 3, the t test yielded significant results for all the factors on the observation checklist. Significant differences (.01 level) were found in the scores of physical, emotional, cognitive and social factors between the pre-test and post-test evaluation.

According to the analysis conducted, hypothesis H3a, H3b, H3c and H3d stand rejected indicating a visible difference on these factors, post intervention.

The results from Study 1 suggest that by just pursuing dancing, there could be an increased sense of body image for an individual. Some research studies from around the world, done with ballet dancers, have found results of pre-occupation with the body image (Eg: Ravaldi, Vanacci et al, 2006). Other studies with ballet dancers have also found elevated rates of body image associated traits, with respect to controls (Elisana, Bakali et al, 2010). In another study by Radell (2012), body image was studied with different levels of dancers in the context of mirrored and non-mirrored classes where high performing dancers had an increase in the body image satisfaction, as opposed to lesser change for non-mirrored classes. These studies, even though done in the non-Indian context, reflect how dancing at a normal class or basic professional level can bring about changes or alleviation in the body image, supporting the results found out by current study. This result paves way for further research on how dance can be therapeutic for people that have body image issues or eating disorders. Since no studies have been done in the Indian context, this study lays the basis of the same as it includes dancers from various Indian and western forms.

With respect to Study 2, there is a dearth of literature regarding how training affects the trainers' mental frameworks, which speaks volumes about the need and significance to focus on this completely new area. Qualitative feedback from trainees though, in response to changes experienced, expressed a heightened level of awareness that could be bodily and sensational or even an increased understanding of themselves and their actions. Movement becoming a mode of expression and being less conscious of their own body and movement, were also few thoughts brought out. These subjective findings seem to validate the findings at the surface level. These are mostly representative of the characteristics of self-esteem, body image and even the physical and emotional factors of the quality of life. A few of them also mentioned that they have gained clarity with regard to themselves and a greater understanding of others around them. This may be reflected in the changes on the social dimension of quality of life.

The different children observed in study 3 had various childhood problems like mental retardation, autism, ADHD, learning disability and even physical disability. Since there have been significant changes in scores of physical, emotional, cognitive and social factors; it seems that movement therapy, in a continual format, may have a positive effect on the growth of these children across the observed factors. Feedback from teachers corroborated the same, where they noted positive changes in students who were completely reserved. Katherine Ann (2012), in a case study, described a narrative of how dance and movement therapy helped build a connect and establish better rapport with a child having autism, only across five consecutive sessions where the child became relatively receptive and mostly complying with instructions given. There also seemed to be an increase in the motor functions and certain amount of control in terms of behavioural and emotional symptoms in two young boys who went through 10 sessions of movement therapy (Gronlund, Renck & Weibull, 2005).

These studies indicate that there is a growing need of research to be done in this field, as there are some impressive implications visible, of dance and movement therapy, with respect to children and childhood disorders.

A few of the items on the observation checklist that could not be quantified, like "splits in body part coordination", "self stimulatory behaviours and tense body parts" did not seem to change for most of them. Items on "physical contact", "eye contact" and "touch" seemed to have changes for some only. The item on "body image" was removed, as most of the children were too young to have an understanding of this, express it outwardly or be observed on it.

Conclusion: This study aimed to note the effect of dance in a holistic manner by understanding, how dance, at a normal, therapeutic and clinical level effects certain aspects of the self. Evident from the results and discussion, dance is likely to be beneficial in a holistic way. The results from study 1 state that, the effect of dance at a basic level in normal population involved in professional dancing (teaching, learning, performing) leads them to have a higher body image with respect to a control population that is not associated with the field of dance. At a therapeutic training level (study 2), dance seems to have brought an increase on scores of self-esteem, body image and physical, emotional and social domains of quality of life; after a three-month intervention. At the level of therapy for children (study 3), there seems to be observed changes on all factors - physical, social, emotional and cognitive, associated with the movement therapy interventions that took place for a period of four months. This speaks volumes about the effects of dance on different aspects of the self. This multi-level approach to study dance and its effect has been beneficial understanding how the self may be regulated through the medium of dance.

Chapter Eleven

Mindfulness Training[11]

Introduction: The word mindfulness has derived from the word *Sati* which means awareness, attention and remembering. It involves intentionally bringing one's attention to the internal and external experiences occurring in the present moment (Baer.2003). Mindfulness is paying attention to a particular way on purpose, in the present moment and non-judgmentally. The primary interest of this tradition is the quality of the consciousness in the present moment. Effective mindfulness can be done anytime, anywhere because it is all about observing, not judging and about living in the moment without focusing on negative things that have happened in the past or worrying about the things an individual would want to have, or do in the future. Mindfulness is all about the mind, body and spirit. It is not a religious practice, but it is spiritual. Mindfulness is not about removing thoughts or preventing your feelings to appear. It is observing them from a detached place, it is about not judging them but about acknowledging the presence and just letting go. Practicing of mindfulness, in time, thoughts will appear less and less, stories of life experiences will become more positive.

Mindfulness helps to become more engaged in our activities, being more present in everyday life and everyday experience, has better connection with people, improves

---

[11] **Chitaranjan Khuman,** Student, The Oxford College of Arts, Bangalore

relationship and focused. It can improves physical well being by reducing stress, lowering blood pressure, alleviating gastrointestinal difficulties, improves sleep and boost working memory. And also helps in decreasing anxiety, worry, fear, low self esteem and emotional reactivity. It can improve whole well-being and quality of life. According to Anna Fox (2017) in her book *Mindfulness for the Everyday Life*, mindfulness is a way of perceiving the world. It includes living in the moment being now, but also, it is the we look at emotions, thoughts, event, that are happening, and the circumstance around the world. Mindfulness includes viewing all of those things non-judgmentally acceptance and neutrality. Mindfulness is all about the mind, body and spirit. It is not a religious practice, but it is spiritual. Davis and Jeffrey (2012) define "mindfulness" as a psychological state of awareness and defined mindfulness as a moment-to-to awareness of one's experience without judgment. It can be promoted by certain practices or activities, such as meditation, yoga, tai chi and qigong. Most of the practices are focus on training attention and brings mental process under greater voluntary control and foster general mental well being and development such as calmness, clarity and concentration. Researchers found that mindfulness meditation promotes meta-cognitive awareness, decrease rumination via disengagement from preservative cognitive activities and enhances attention capacities through gains in working memory.

In one study, Chambers et al. (2008) asked 20 novice mediators to participate in a 10-day intensive mindfulness meditation retreat. After the retreat, meditation group had significantly higher self reported mindfulness and decreased negative effect compared with a control group. They also found less rumination. And also have better able to sustain attention during a performance task compared with control group.

Jon Kabat-Zinn, creator of the research-backed stress-reduction program Mindfulness-Based Stress Reduction (MBSR), explains how mindfulness lights up parts of our brains that aren't normally activated when we're mindlessly running on autopilot.

Objectives: To study the effect of Mindfulness Training among Under Graduate students. Specifically, the study explores, What is the effect of Mindfulness Training among Under Graduate students?

Methodology: Convenient Sampling Technique was used and 15 Under Graduate Students were selected. The following tool was used: Mindfulness Training model was developed by the scholar. The training Model includes Mindfulness exercises, videos related to mindfulness and open ended questions. The Open ended questions were selected under the scrutiny of three experts. The study was executed in 5 sessions. Each session was designed by the scholar. The sessions included mindfulness exercises, a video related to mindfulness and the scholar asked few open ended questions based on the training and mindfulness.

Session 1: Mindful Gratitude- Scholar facilitated mindful gratitude to the samples. Explained about gratitude and mindfulness. The scholar also emphasized on daily practice of mindful gratitude. A video related to gratitude was shown to the samples. Samples were asked to answer the open ended questions given to them.

Session 2: Listening to Music Mindfully- Scholar executed training on mindful listening to music. Samples were asked to listen to music for 5 minutes. The scholar also emphasized on daily practice of listening to music mindfully. A video related to music was shown to the samples. Samples were asked to answer the open ended questions given to them.

Session 3: Mindful Meditation- Scholar trained samples about meditation and later asked samples to meditate for 5 minutes. The scholar also emphasized on daily practice of meditation. A video related to meditation was shown to the samples. Samples were asked to answer the open ended questions given to them.

Session 4: Mindful Rest- Scholar trained about mindful rest and spoke about rest and mindful rest. Samples were asked to have mindful rest for 5 minutes. The scholar also emphasized on daily practice of mindful rest. A video related to rest was shown to the samples. Samples were asked to answer the open ended questions given to them.

Session 5: Mindful Eating- - Scholar spoke about eating and mindful eating. Samples were asked to eat mindfully during session. The scholar also emphasized on daily practice of mindful eating. A video related to eating was shown to the samples. Samples were asked to answer the open ended questions given to them.

Results and Discussion: Mindfulness is way of perceiving the world. It includes living the moment, being in now, but also, it is the way of looking at our emotions, thoughts, events that happening around us. Mindfulness is a skill very much needed to be learned. We cannot let something stuck in our life, they come, and goes as like the nature rivers flowing from the streams. Mindfulness gives you the understanding that each and every problem you faced in your life will not stay the same. It will go like the clouds they never stay. Present study aimed at training samples in conscious practice of mindfulness, bringing awareness about mindfulness and explaining the practicality of practicing mindfulness in various aspects of life. Responses given by the samples in each session was recorded. Themes have been identified based on the responses to understand the impact of mindfulness training.

Mindful Gratitude: The samples expressed their opinion about Mindful Gratitude that they see things from a different perspective and enhance life with healthy thinking. "We need Mindful Gratitude to blur the greed and negative things that we waste our time focusing on" said by one of the sample. "Once in a day just close your eyes, focus on your breathe & try listening to heartbeat and smile for that" reply from one of the sample on how they can practice Mindful Gratitude.

Mindful Gratitude helps to live life more satisfied because we are grateful for what we already have and forget what we don't have. We should be grateful for each and every moment of our lives. We should be happy of who we are and what we have.

Listen to Music Mindfully: The samples expressed their opinions after the Training that Listening to Music Mindfully takes them to the different world where they feel good and happy by enjoying each and every piece in the music and forget every past life for a while. "If I listened to Music Mindfully I feel like I'm the happiest person in the world" told, one of the sample.

We should listen to Music Mindfully to relax, calm and to bring peace in our mind. Sometimes when we listen to music mindfully you tend to hear your inner voice and giving your ideas about the things you really focused on.

Mindful Meditation: Samples gave their opinions on Mindful Meditation after the training that they feel more relaxed and lighter than before about the stress and problems they have. Consistent practice of meditation will help them to increase their concentration level, memory and can focus more into study. They expressed the feel of relaxation of mind and body.

It helps to focus our task and finding inner peace. Mindful Meditation is now being examined scientifically and has been found to be a key element in stress reduction, short temper and overall happiness.

Mindful Rest: After the training of Mindful Rest, samples gave their opinion that they felt very relaxed, peaceful, calm and energetic. In day to day life they face many tensions and struggle at work. In this busy schedule of life everyone should have rest i.e. not normally but mindful.

Resting for 5 minutes mindfully is more effective than resting for 1 hour without mindful concentration on resting. It helps them to do daily activities more effectively. It improves the capacity of our brain to think and work more, have stress free day and more relaxed. It plays an important role in our day to day life.

Mindful Eating: After the Training subjects shared their opinions that it helps them to eat what their body required and they are more aware of the foods they ate. They tend to realize which food is good for their health and which one is bad. They increase their tasting skills. One of the sample told "Eating Mindfully by knowing the taste of the food makes me feel more appetite". "Mindful Eating also enables our mind to be grateful for everything that we eat" added by one of the sample.

People often eat without even tasting the food. They are not aware they are really hungry or what their bodies need and want to eat. Mindful eating means to pay attention to the food we are eating, before and during the meal. It helps from over eating, making person healthy and reduce health issues.

After the end of the training sessions the samples began to feel more calmness, peace, more grateful of what they have and they completely change their perspectives of seeing things. They become more enthusiastic, self motivated and live a quality life. Quality life is not only having a fancy clothes, big house, expensive cars and wallet full of money but it is something that we really are grateful for the things we already have and live each and every moment happily. They are more aware of the things happening around them. Training had a positive impact on the feeling expressed by the samples. Making people understand mindfulness would be the first challenge, but it would definitely be attained through rigorous training. Applying mindfulness in all aspects of life is the other challenging task. Daily practice of mindfulness would become a habit later. Mindful practice of each activity will then become easy. Research shows that practicing Mindful exercises regularly improves overall well-being.

Conclusion: The average human life expectancy is 75 years. Studies have proven that human live only the 7 years of life. That is average person sleeps almost 25 years of life. 12 years of life spend looking at cell phone, TV, computer etc. 14 years of life spend in school and at work. 6 years of life spend on drinking, eating and preparing for foods. 11 years of life spend early childhood, travelling from one place to another, driving, doing household activities, shopping, doing bathroom activities, cleaning and grooming. And in total we remain only with 7 years of life. But most of the people live their life by worrying about the past, future and they missed the present moment. We should live each and every moment happily. So, the practice of Mindfulness can really help someone's life by living the moment.

According to the findings of Mindfulness Research, people who practice mindfulness tend to be more aware of the present moment. We are living in the society, interacting with the people, each and every chores of life. Mindfulness is something that can change someone's life how they think, act, and react to a situation and live life by aware of the present moment happily.

Chapter Twelve

Psychological Wellbeing and Personality Traits[12]

Introduction: Food is the basic need of every human being. As we mature our food preferences also changes so does our behaviour. Different people prefer different kinds of food based on many factors like environmental, cultural, genetic, religion etc. As per many studies it is proven than the food we eat to an extent determine our state of wellbeing and personality. The study aims at determining the dominant kind of personality trait among the big five personality traits in vegetarians and non-vegetarians. In this era of many personality disorders the study help in understanding which group (Vegetarian or non-vegetarian) is more prone to personality disorders.

Adulthood is the period in the human life span in which full physical and intellectual maturity have been secured. Adulthood is also the phase in which food preferences take a distinguished shape in an individual's life. There are multiple parts in an adult's life that can affect their preferences in food, Environment, mental, physical, health and life style choices are all contributing factors to the way a person decides on what food they like or dislike. In India, when it comes to food preferences, we can mainly see two categories – vegetarians and non -vegetarians. A person who does not eat animal products especially for moral or religious reasons is called a vegetarian. Different factors which results in vegetarianism include health, political,

---

[12] **Jasmin, Krishna Ramachandran, Farha Pallikamath Moidu, Ligi George,** LISSAH, Calicut

environmental, cultural, aesthetic, economic or personal preference. Non vegetarian is used to refer to a person who consume meat as a major source of nutrition. "We are what we eat" is an old saying and it is scientifically proven fact that our food choices affect our health. In the same way, there can be a link between our psychological wellbeing, personality traits and food choices. Psychological well-being consists of positive relationship with others, personal mastery, autonomy, a feeling of purpose and meaning in life and personal growth and development. Psychological wellbeing attained by achieving a state of balance affected by both challenging and rewarding life events. The big five factors of personality are five broad domains which define human personality and account for individual differences.

Wellbeing is the state of being comfortable, healthy or happy. It is the general term for the condition of an individual or group. There are multiple factors for wellbeing or wellness. Wellness refers to diverse and inter connected dimensions of physical, mental and social wellbeing that extend beyond the traditional definition of health. It includes choices and activity aimed at achieving physical vitality, mental alacrity, social satisfaction a sense of accomplishment and personal fulfilment.

Psychological wellbeing has been the focus of intense research attention. Psychological wellbeing resides within the experience of the individual. It may be defined as the state of feeling happy and healthy having pleasure satisfaction, relaxation and peace of mind. It deals with people's feelings about everyday experiences in their life. Such feelings may range from negative mental states such as in frustration, emotional exhaustion and depression to a state which has been identified as positive mental health. Psychological wellbeing is deeply related to individual's religious beliefs.

Carol Ryff and her colleague Keyes conceptualized psychological wellbeing as a theory based upon the literature on positive psychological functioning of individuals. Ryff and Keyes proposed a new definition and model of psychological wellbeing based on several theoretical approaches proposed by renowned psychologists. According to Ryff and Keyes (Ryff -1989 and Keyes – 1995) psychological wellbeing refers to the existential challenges that an individual face in his or her life and how and to what extend he or she overcomes those existential challenges. They presented the view that the real meaning of psychological wellbeing should be the full development of an individual's potential. The psychological wellbeing model proposed by Ryff and Keyes indicates that psychological wellbeing consist of six elements. The six dimensions that constitute psychological wellbeing are autonomy, environmental mystery, personal growth, positive relation with others, purpose in life and self-acceptance.

One of the most important assets of a person is the character or the personality he holds. Personality is an individual's unique and relatively stable pattern of behaviour thoughts and emotions. Personality is explained by many theorists. The psychodynamic theory proposed by Sigmund Freud explains that personality is divided into three significant components - id, ego and superego. The behaviourist theory of personality developed by B F Skinner, social cognitive theory proposed by Albert Bandura, humanistic theory put forward by Abraham Maslow and Carl Rogers have made major contributions in understanding human personality.

The five factor theory emerged to describe the essential traits that serve as building blocks of personality. The relevance of big five personality trait theory has been growing over the past 50 years. Beginning with the research P.W. Fiske (1949), this initial model was advanced by Earnest Dupes and Raymond Crystal in 1961, Goldberg (1981) and McCrae and Costa (1987). These dimensions are considered to be the underlying traits that make up an individual's overall personality. The big five factors are openness to experience, conscientiousness, extroversion, agreeableness, and neuroticism or OCEAN. It is important to note that each of the five personality factors represents a range between two extremes.

Extraversion is a personality trait which is characterized by excitability, sociability, talkativeness, assertiveness and high amounts of emotional expressiveness. People who are high in extraversion are outgoing and tend to gain energy in social situations. People who are low in extraversion tend to be more reserved and have to expand energy in social settings.

Agreeableness is another personality trait which includes attributes such, trust, altruism, kindness, affection and other prosocial behaviours. People who are high in agreeableness tend to be more competitive and even manipulative.

Conscientiousness in the big five personality trait include high levels of thoughtfulness with good impulse control and goal directed behaviours. Those who are high on conscientiousness tend to be organized and mindful of details.

Neuroticism is a trait characterized by sadness, moodiness and emotional instability. Individuals who are high in this trait tend to experience mood swings, anxiety, moodiness, irritability and sadness. Those who are low in this trait tend to be more stable and emotionally resilient.

Openness to experience features characteristics such as imagination and insight and those high in this trait also tend to have a broad range of interest. They tend to be more adventurous and creative. Those low in this trait are often much more traditional and may struggle with abstract thinking.

Objectives: To find out the relationship between the psychological wellbeing and the big five factors among vegetarians and non-vegetarians. To know the difference in the big five factors and the psychological well-being among vegetarians and non-vegetarians

Methodology: 80 adults (age 20 to 60) consisting of 40 vegetarians and 40 non vegetarians of Calicut and Wayanad districts of Kerala were selected for study. Purposive random sampling method was used for sample selection. In the present study 2 tools were used: the big five inventory scale. developed by Goldberg in the year of 1993. It is a five pointer scale containing 44 questions. The internal consistency and reliabilities were adequate for all five BFI scale (mean values were .77, .78 & .81. Ryff psychological wellbeing scale, the test – retest reliability coefficient of psychological wellbeing scale (RPWBS) was 0.82.

Result and Discussion: To verify the hypothesis 1, whether there is any relationship between psychological well-being and big five personalities among vegetarians, is tested.

Table 1: Correlation between Psychological Wellbeing and Big five factors among Vegetarians

	A	E	O	C	N
Pw	.094	.133	.172	-.020	-.411[**]

     **. Correlation is significant at the 0.01 level (2-tailed).
     *. Correlation is significant at the 0.05 level (2-tailed).

From table 1, it is clear that there is no significant relationship between psychological well-being and major 4 personality traits , but there is a negative correlation between psychological well-being and neuroticism in vegetarian which means as psychological well-being increases , neuroticism decreases and vice versa. From this study, it can be assumed that vegetarians experience less stress and tension due to their good nutrition style as vegetable food sources are more compatible to human body for digestion and absorption.

Hypothesis 2, whether there is any relationship between psychological well-being and big five personalities among non-vegetarians.

Table 2: Correlation between Psychological Wellbeing and Big five factors among Non -Vegetarians

	A	E	O	C	N
PW	.546**	.334*	.232	.478**	-.172

From the table 2, it is clear that there is a positive correlation between psychological wellbeing and agreeableness, conscientiousness and extraversion of big five personality in non-vegetarians.

From the study, it can be concluded that non vegetarian show more pro-social behavior, tend to be more organized and sociable with others due to wide variety of food they consume .

Hypothesis 3, whether there is any difference in psychological well-being among vegetarians and non-vegetarians.

Table 3: Mean, Standard Deviation and t value of Psychological Wellbeing with respect to group

Variable	Group	N	Mean	SD	t value
PW	Veg	40	70.65	6.776	-1.291
	Non	40	72.90	8.693	

p>0.05

From table 3, it is clear that there is no significant relationship between psychological wellbeing of vegetarians and non-vegetarians. From this, it can be concluded that food choices doesn't have a significant influence on our state of wellbeing. So other than the food preferences, the way people are brought up, their past experiences, and mind set may be the contributing factors for psychological wellbeing.

To verify the hypothesis 4, whether there is any difference in agreeableness among vegetarians and non-vegetarians, it is tested.

Table 4: Mean, Standard Deviation and t value of Agreeableness with respect to group

Variable	Group	N	Mean	SD	t value
A	Veg	40	35.02	4.698	0.382
	Non	40	34.60	5.246	

p>0.05

From the table 4 it is clear that there is no significant difference for agreeableness in both vegetarians and non-vegetarians.

This concludes that food choices doesn't have any notable role in shaping our personality of agreeableness. It may be due to many other factors like, cultural genetic or environmental differences.

The hypothesis 5, whether there is any difference in extraversion among vegetarians and non-vegetarians was tested.

Table 5: Mean, Standard Deviation and t value of Extraversion with respect to group

Variable	Group	N	Mean	SD	*t* value
E	Veg	40	26.47	5.028	-1.810
	Non	40	28.62	5.582	

p>0.05

From the table 5 it's clear that there is no significant difference for extraversion in both vegetarians and non-vegetarians.

This concludes that individual's food preference has a significant role in shaping personality of extraversion. The way an individual is nurtured, his/her genetic nature, past experiences and complex may be the reasons for different level of extraversion in different people other than food choice.

Hypothesis 6, whether there is any difference in openness to experience between vegetarians and non-vegetarians.

Table 6: Mean, Standard Deviation and t value of Openness to experience with respect to group
p>0.05

Variable	Group	N	Mean	SD	*t* value
O	Veg	40	36.62	7.594	1.024
	Non	40	35.02	6.322	

From the table 6 it is clear that there is no significant difference for openness to experience in both vegetarians and non-vegetarians. So it may be predominantly influenced by the genetic factors and exposure rather than individual's food preference.

Hypothesis 7, whether there is any difference in conscientiousness among vegetarians and non-vegetarians.

Table 7: Mean, Standard Deviation and t value of Conscientiousness with respect to group

Variable	Group	N	Mean	SD	*t* value
C	Veg	40	33.32	6.039	2.203*
	Non	40	29.92	7.667	

p<0.05

From the table 7 it is clear that vegetarians have more amount of Conscientiousness than the non-vegetarians. This may be due to the difference existing in the nutritional level of vegetarians and non-vegetarians. As the vegetarians tend to have more balanced diet they may have more controlled emotional status and goal oriented life than the non-vegetarians. Therefore, according to this study, food choice along with socioeconomic status, living in urban or rural areas, educational level etc can also influence one's conscientiousness.

Table 8: Mean, Standard Deviation and t value of Neuroticism with respect to group

Variable	Group	N	Mean	SD	*t* value
N	Veg	40	23.57	5.261	-1.118
	Non	40	25.25	7.882	

p>0.05

From the table 8 it is clear that there is no significant difference for Neuroticism in both vegetarians and non-vegetarians. It can be concluded that more than the food we consume, genetics, social interactions, hormonal stability, responsibilities can etc., influence one's trait of neuroticism.

Conclusion: Thus from the whole study, it can be concluded that as the psychological well-being increases neuroticism decreases in vegetarians whereas as the psychological well-being increases agreeableness, conscientiousness and extraversion among non-vegetarians increases simultaneously. When looked at the areas of difference in big five personality traits among vegetarians and non-vegetarians, what was found was that conscientiousness in vegetarians were higher than the non-vegetarians .The rest of the personality traits remained   same for both the groups.

Chapter Thirteen

Hope, Optimism and Resilience Among College Students[13]

Introduction: In the study of human behaviour, there has been an unbalanced emphasis on how mental illness and deviance occur in individuals. While these investigations came up with good results in terms of learning about the origins and treatment of psychological disorders. Until now, the field has not concentrated on how people maintain good mental health. Moreover, a balanced focus on the positive, as well as negative, aspects of human psychological functioning has been lacking until recently. However, there is a growing movement in psychology associated with the scholarship of Martin Seligman, Mihalyi Csikszentmihalyi and Ed Deiner known as "Positive Psychology" that revolves around the ways in which people can remain psychologically healthy and lead fulfilling life's. It is the theme that has spurred continued scholarly research into such topics as creativity, 'flow' experiences, subjective wellbeing, happiness, hope and optimism. The domain of research has also lead to the development of this project which focuses on understanding the relationships and correlates of three specific constructs within 'Positive psychology', mainly hope, optimism, and resilience.

There has been considerable recent attention given to the topic of optimism. Definitions of optimism and its measurement have been stated (Peterson. 2000;

---

[13] **Anunanda, S, Maneena James, Athulya Jose, Athira Aneesh,** LISSAH, Calicut

Scheier & Carver, 195; Seligman, 1990). While Scheier and Carver (1985) define optimism as a 'generalized expectancy for positive rather than negative outcomes, Seligman (1990) specifies optimism as an attribution style characterized by unstable, specific and external attributions for the causes of negative events as well as stable, generalized and internal attributions for the causes of positive events. Optimism has been found to be important to healthy psychological functioning in both lay (Norman Vincent Peale, 1952) and academic circles (Seligman, 1990; Scheirer, Carver, & Bridges, 1994). There have also been demonstrated links between optimism and maintenance of healthy physical functioning (Segerstrom, Taylor, Kenmeny, & Fahey, 1998, Aspinwall & Taylor, 1992). A sense of optimism has also been shown to have indirect benefits in terms of an individual's personal success during difficult times and coping (Carver, Scheier, & Weintraub, 1989; Cozzarelli, 1993; Weintraub, Carver, 1986).

Depression is becoming a fashion among the youngsters. In this present situation hope, optimism and resilience has an important role in their success of life.

Optimism is a form of positive thinking that induces the belief that you are responsible for your own happiness and that more good things continue to happen to you in the future. It is the key to success and gives meanings to our lives. Optimism, on one hand allowing one to have an optimistic outlook on lives, lets a gain confidence. On the other hand, it brings positive changes to one's mind. So that we can overcome our problems successfully.

Hope is an optimistic state of mind that is based on an expectation of positive outcomes with respect to events and circumstance in one's life or the world at large. The hope can be defined in the modern aspects as the wish for, to expect, but without certainty of the fulfillment; to desire very much, but with no real assurance of getting your desire. Hope is not only an attitude that has cognitive components. It is responsible to facts about the possibility and likelihood of future events.

Psychological resilience is defined as an individual's ability to successfully adapt to the life tasks in the face of social disadvantage or other highly adverse conditions. Adversity and stress can come in the shape of family and relationship problems, health problems or work place and financial worries, among others. It means bouncing back from situations which cause anxiety, stress and other negative experience. Optimism is ability of a person to encounter every life experience with a positive outlook. This positive attitude develops a thought in their mind that everything happens, happens for a reason and somehow will lead to a good outcome in their lives. This positive experience develops a sense of hope in them which may or may not be fruitful. Both these hope and optimism adds up to person's resilience, capacity to overcome a problem. For a college student who had to adapt to a new situation has a hope in their mind that coming days will bring a good change in my life: this hope leads them to optimism. Both these factors point out to resilience. Hope, optimism and resilience all has been a focus of increased interest. These variables play an important role in the life of college students from their adaption to the new place and the performance they exhibit.

Objectives:

1. To understand the relationship between hope-optimism and resilience among college students.
2. To understand the difference between female and male in terms of hope-optimism.
3. To understand the difference between female and male in terms of resilience.

Methodology: The sample consisted of 100 under graduated students (50 females and 50 males) from Calicut and they were drawn by simple random technique. The data were collected by using questionnaires ensuring confidentiality of the responses. Instruments used: Time Horizon Questionnaire. This scale was reproduced with permission of Jeralad J.S Wilde. This scale is developed for the general adult population, including adolescents. This scale contains 40 items with all 5 alternative responses as strongly disagree, disagree, unsure, agree and strongly agree. The total score is calculated by finding some of the all items and also negative scores were assigned for certain questions.The scale has sati factionary internal reliability indices as given by a Cronbach alpha 0.76.

The Time Horizon Questionnaire is correlated with hope, optimism, future orientation, success and efficiency.Resilience Scale (Annalakshmi, 2009) consists of 30 likert type items. The scale is used to measure 7 domains of Resilience including duration forgetting back to normalcy, reaction to negative events, response to risk factors in life, perception of effect of past negative events, defining problems, hope or confidence in coping with future and openness to experience and flexibility. All the 30 items in the scale are in the form of personal statements. The responses of the participants for all 30 statements in the scale are summed up to yield a single score on the scale representing the level of psychological resilience of the individual. The high score on resilience scale indicate high resilience. The Cronbach Alpha for the scale was found to be 0.82. The scale had significant positive correlation with Freiburg resilience, 0.349* and bells adjustment scale 0.382*.

The needed data were collected from undergraduate college students from Calicut, Kerala. The tools to measure the variables under the study were administrated to the subject's individuality by the investigator. The statistical analysis was done by using Karl Pearson's correlation and t-Test. Karl Pearson correlation coefficient, often referred to as the Pearson r-test, is a statistical formula that measu.re the strength between variables and relationship. To determine how strong the relationship is between two variables, you need to find the coefficient value, which can range between -1.00 to +1.00. The t-test is any statistical hypothesis test in which the test statistic follows a student's t-distribution under the null hypothesis.

Results and Discussion: The correlation between hope-optimism and resilience among college students is 0.135. It was found that hope –optimism and resilience have weak positive correlation. As the hope-optimism increases, resilience increases. Thus the hypothesis 'there will be relationship between hope-optimism and resilience among college students' is accepted.

Table 1: Mean, SD and t value of hope-optimism with respect to gender

Variable	Gender	N	Mean	SD	t value
Hope	Female	50	130.62	12.697	
	Male	50	128.92	11.938	0.690

p>0.05

From Table 1, the mean and SD in hope-optimism among female was found to be 130.62 and 12.697 respectively. The mean and SD in hope-optimism among males was found to be 128.92 and 11.938 respectively. The t-value was found to be 0.690. Thus the hypothesis 'there will be no difference between female and male in terms of hope-optimism' is accepted.

Table 2: Mean, SD and t value of resilience with respect to gender

Variable	Gender	N	Mean	SD	t value
Resilience	Female	50	84.24	17.671	-3.553*
	Male	50	95.44	13.582	

p<0.05

From Table 2, the mean and SD in resilience among females is found to be 84.24 and 17.671 respectively. The mean and SD in resilience among males is found to be 95.44 and 13.582 respectively. And the t-value is -3.553*. Thus the hypothesis 'there will be no difference between female and male in terms of resilience' is rejected. From the results we can conclude that there is correlation between hope-optimism and resilience. When hope-optimism increases, resilience also increases, as well as when hope-optimism decreases, resilience also decreases. The coefficient of correlation is 0.135, this indicates a weak positive correlation. This result supports our study which states that there is relationship between hope-optimism and resilience. When analyzing table 1 we reach in a conclusion that there is a significant difference between female and male in terms of hope-optimism. Here the t-value is 0.690. This indicates that gender difference do influence their hope-optimism. This result also supports our hypothesis that inspect the relationship between female and male in terms of hope-optimism. From table 2 we arrived at a result that there is a significant difference between male and female in terms of resilience. The t-value -3.553. This indicates that the result supports our study which deals with the relationship between female and male in terms of resilience.

Conclusion: From the study we could find that hope-optimism and resilience are interconnected When hope-optimism increases resilience also increases and vice-versa. The result we could obtain were 'The gender difference influences hope-optimism whereas gender difference does not influence resilience'

Chapter Fourteen

Playing, Watching Videogames and Academic Achievement[14]

Introduction: Videogames have become a ubiquitous part of children of all age groups and the interests towards gaming are very prominent among adolescence also. Decades of research already exists on the effects of violent videogames on children and adolescents and its negative impact on their physical and mental health. More balanced perspective is needed for the negative effects of videogames and should throw more lights on the benefits of playing these games. Many researches that have done earlier on violent video games have deleterious effects (Anderson & Bushman, 2001; Anderson et al.). Contrary to conventional beliefs that playing video games is intellectually lazy and sedating, it turns out that playing these games promotes a wide range of cognitive skills. Evidences prove that skills that are important can be built or reinforced by videogames, like, playing games can improve the spatial visualization ability. This research study is focused on the positive effects of videogames on classroom attention and prosocial behaviour.

Most of the studies on video game focused on the effects of violent form of video games on aggression. Aggression is defined as any behaviour directed towards another individual that is carried out with the proximate intent to cause harm. In addition, the perpetrator must believe that the behaviour will harm the target, and that the target is motivated to avoid the behaviour (Anderson and Bushman, 2002). Since

---

[14] **Smitha Baboo, Ph.D.,** Asst. Professor of Psychology, Jain University

it is unethical and inappropriate to induce violent behaviour in an experimental setting, the milder forms of aggressive behaviour is used as the outcome variable of interest in most of the researches in the effects of violent video.

Logical conclusion on the effect of a given stimuli (video games) relies upon the ability for the effect of that stimulus in order to generalize throughout various measures that leads into the same conceptual construct (behaviour intended to harm another person). Due to this reason, researches based on the effects of violent video games make use of other measures and establish relationship between violent video game play and verbal aggression, delivering painful electrical shocks to another person (Sakamoto et al.,2001), children's peer rating of aggressiveness, getting into arguments with teachers, getting into physical fights(Anderson et al.,2007; Moller & Krahe,2009), children's aggressive behaviour observed during free play(Silvern and Williamson, 1987).

As educational video games is used as a learning tool for the school children, employees and physicians likewise violent video games can teach aggression (Weber et al., 2006). A comprehensive review of media violence effects on aggression and aggression related variable found unequivocal evidence that media violence increases the likelihood of aggressive and violent behaviour in both immediate and long term contexts (Anderson et al., 2003). This report also found that aggressive behaviour is positively associated with the real life violent video game play and laboratory exposure to graphically violent video game (Anderson,2004; Anderson and dill,2000). Meta-analytic reviews of the video game research literature reveal that violent video games increase aggressive behaviour in children and adults (Anderson, 2004; Anderson & Bushman, 2001; Sherry, 2001). Various researches has also found that violent video games can also increase physiological arousal and thoughts and feelings related to aggression.

Swing et al., (2010) explore that there is an increase in classroom attention problems among student because of rapid pacing, or the natural attention-grabbing aspects that television and video games use. It suggest that video games are changing the conventional trends of education and games are more like a simple form of entertainment (Shaffer, Squire, Halverson,& Gee,2005). It explains that student learning can be enhanced by the experiences of vast virtual world. Virtual world are useful because they make it possible to develop situational understanding (Shaffer, Squire, Halverson, & Gee, 2005).

Chambers and Ascione (1987) studied the effects of prosocial video games on the giving and helping behaviours of elementary and middle school children in two ways: by counting money donated to a charity and by counting the number of pencils sharpened for the research assistant. They found no significant positive effects of the video game play compared to the negative control (no game play). However, they neglected to take into consideration the kinds of prosocial behaviour that takes place among video game players when they play.

Objectives: In the present era, the need of studying the potential benefits of the videogames is more important as from all the age groups; from children to adults playing videogames is an important part of their life because the nature of the video game has changed dramatically in the last decade which is becoming increasingly complex, diverse, realistic, and social in nature. The current research is to provide strong enough evidence and a theoretical rationale to inspire new programs of research on the largely unexplored educational and mental health benefits of the video gaming. The researcher is focussed on the current study to explore the following research questions: Is there any difference with regard to the educational and social outcomes while playing or watching videogames? Whether there are any differences while playing and watching videogames on the classroom attention and prosocial behaviour among experimental group I, experimental group II and control group?

Methodology: The goal of the study was to analyse the effect of an independent variable on the dependent or an outcome variable within a population. The researcher has adopted an Experimental pre-post design method to find the cause effect relationship between the variable used. The independent variable used for the study is playing and watching videogames and the dependent variable is the effects on classroom attention and pro social behaviour.

The experimental method adopted for the current research explores the previous usage level of videogames, the addiction factor, time spent in playing in a daily or hourly basis through a personal interview with the samples taken. The researcher used three questionnaires to assess the effects of videogames on the variables used like classroom attention and pro social behaviour both in the Pre-test and Post-test level. Videogames of different levels and types is used to assess the cause and effect. The participants selected for the present study were middle school children between the age group of 10 to 13 years. The participants were randomly selected by using lottery method and finally the total numbers of participants selected were forty five boys and forty five girls from different sections of grade 5, 6 and 7.

The researcher used twenty five desktop computers with the key boards given in the computer lab to show videogames of different content and different levels of difficulty. Speakers were also used for the purpose of study. Different videogames were used to measure the effects of playing and watching videogames on the classroom attention and prosocial behaviour. The researcher employed three questionnaires for the study which will be used in the pre assessment and post assessment level of the experiment. The questionnaires used were adopted a Likert scale method. The questionnaires used for the study were Classroom Attention Scale and Prosocial Behaviour Scale.

Results and Discussion: Paired Sample t-test was conducted to compare the differences in the mean scores between pre-test and post-test group of Experimental I, II and Control Group with regard to the Classroom *Attention*. The results show that there is a significant difference in the mean scores between pre-test and post-test group of Experimental I,II and no significant difference in Control Group with regard to the Classroom *Attention*.

Attention can get diverted for any area of work or any area of interest, for some it will be watching television, for others it will be talking with friends. The interest can vary from one individual to another. In the context of middle school children the curiosity to know something, fun and the nature to challenge something new is inbuilt in their behaviour. Since video games gives a lot of fun and thrilling experience their thought processes will be always dwindling about their winning and losing events in the play. The researcher was giving hands on experience of the selected videogames for every day for nearly an hour to the participants. During this time a naturally occurring neurotransmitter in the brain called dopamine is released which is largely responsible for reward driven behaviour.

Findings suggest that the release of dopamine will be high who play videogames as it is reward motivated. This is the reason why children play with the intention of gaining reward, be it advancement in the game, rising up a ranking board or badges and trophies. Children who played more videogames at the beginning experienced increased attention problem towards the end. This was true even after controlling for prior student attention problems (Swing et al., 2010).

In this current research the focus was on to whether the participants who passively watch the videogames have any effects on the attention level. As the results shows passive participants also has a greater influence in the classroom attention, this highlights that videogames are so powerful for and the thoughts of it can haunt for a passive player also. Moreover, they experienced more stressed than the active participant as they were not able to express their ideas and moves.

Bushman & Anderson (2009) have found correlations between attention problems and video game play. High excitement and Rapid changes of focus that occur in many video games may weaken children's abilities to maintain focus on less exciting tasks (eg; school work) and shorter they are attention spans. In a longitudinal study on video game use and attention problems, video game play predicted children's attention problems 13 months later, even while controlling for other relevant variables (Swing et al., 2010). A three year longitudinal study of more than 3000 children found evidence of a bidirectional relation between attention problems and video game playing and found a stronger relation between the amount of gaming and later attention problems than for the content of gaming (Gentile et al.,2012).

Paired Sample t-test was conducted to compare the differences in the mean scores between pre-test and post-test group of Experimental I,II and Control Group with regard to the Prosocial Behaviour. The result shows that there is a significant difference in the mean scores between pre-test and post-test group of Experimental I, no significant difference in the Experimental II and Control Group with regard to the prosocial behaviour. Very few researches have been done to highlight the effects of videogames on the prosocial behaviour, Gentile et al., (2009) compared to participants who had played either the neutral or the violent video games, participants who had played the pro social video game shows significantly lower levels of aversive noise, thereby indicating lower levels of aggressive behaviour. Moreover, these results remained significant even after controlling for levels of trait altruism, aggression, arousal and mood.

Whitaker and Bushman (2012) examined the effects of videogames on prosocial behaviour and also on positive mood. The study compared to participants who have played either the neutral or the violent video game, participants who had played the relaxing video game reported greater positive effect and displayed greater helping behaviour and there was a mediation effect of positive mood also. Saleem, Anderson & Gentile (2012) found out that the pattern of increased helping behaviour after playing a pro social video game has been consistently demonstrated. Whitaker and Bushman (2012) study shows that those who had played the pro social video game choose significantly less difficult puzzles for their partner to complete than did those who have played either the neutral or the violent video game. As they were not actively or physically playing the videogames the skill of prosocial behaviour that developed in the playing participants was not seen in the participants who were watching the videogame played by the others. The passive group or watching participants were stressful as they were not allowed to take the moves because they were a passive observant.

The current research has found out that prosocial behaviour is developed in the players who were actively playing and not for the passive players this could be due to the time constraint and the involvement that the passive players lack.

Conclusion: The research study found out that in experimental group I there is a difference in the classroom attention and prosocial behaviour and in experimental group II there is a difference in the classroom attention and no difference in the prosocial behaviour whereas in control group there is no difference in all the variables. This shows that there is a strong impact of videogames on the classroom attention and prosocial behaviour.

Chapter Fifteen

Anxiety among Female College Students[15]

Introduction: Anxiety is a necessary part of life and it is a motivational factor to complete the important tasks, it has been proved that women are more prone to have higher anxiety levels than men. Sometimes the duration or severity of an anxious feeling can be out of proportion to the original trigger or stressor, when it is out of proportion to what might normally be expected in a situation, these responses move beyond anxiety into an anxiety disorder. Anxiety disorders can be classified into six main types viz., Generalized anxiety disorder (GAD), Panic disorder, Phobia, Social anxiety disorder, Obsessive-compulsive disorder (OCD), Post-traumatic stress disorder (PTSD) and Separation anxiety disorder. Some studies suggest that females will have more anxiety compared to males.

In spite of a few studies failing to find significant sex differences in the prevalence of anxiety disorders, clinical and community studies have generally reported higher rates of panic disorder (PD), agoraphobia (AG), specific phobias (SP), generalized anxiety disorder (GAD), separation anxiety (SA), and both acute and posttraumatic stress disorder (ASD and PTSD) in females compared to males.

Sex differences are less pronounced for social anxiety disorder (SAD) and obsessive-compulsive disorder (OCD), and sex differences in the prevalence rates of these two

---

[15] **Veolene Elizabeth Jacob**, Student, Teresian College, Mysore
Nasreen Afza, Faculty, Teresian College, Mysore

disorders are not always significant. It has been suggested, that sex differences in the development of internalizing and externalizing disorders may be partly attributable to differences in socialization processes that are intensified during adolescence and activate concepts of masculinity and femininity. Such gender roles are likely to affect sex differences in anxiety. Due to the risk of having high anxiety among females, it is also many a times been proved that the opposite gender also have a role as to how their affecting the females consciously or unconsciously.

It is hypothesized that when girls are provided an environment where they can interact with all, especially in student's life. High school and college is a critical time in a person's life. It's the time when you are trying to find yourself and build a strong personality with respect to the relationships you create with your peers, teachers, and parents. When females interact with opposite gender persons that gender anxiety will be reduced i.e. when they study in co-education system. If they are isolated from the opposite gender the level of anxiety will be higher.

Objectives: In this present study, investigator is interested to check the level of anxiety among female students in co-Educational and single sex College system because, this is a time when puberty occurs and everybody's bodies are changing and developing. It's also a time when you start to notice the opposite sex (Alexa Guglielmi). It's also a stressful time academically when grades and test scores have the power to make or break your future endeavors. All these factors have the ability to affect your level of self-esteem. The objective of the present study is to compare the level of anxiety of female student who study in single sex college system with co-education college system.

Methodology: In this study, the sample involved 80 female students, selected randomly, 40 from single-sex colleges, 40 were from co-educational colleges in Mysore, Karnataka. Administered the Taylor's manifest anxiety questionnaires with proper instructions. The main purpose of the study is to identify whether the levels of anxiety in girls of co-educational colleges is higher compared to girls of single-sex colleges. This study was carried out in colleges in Mysore, Karnataka. The female students were from different colleges. The Taylor's manifest anxiety questionnaire (1953) It consists of about 40 true or false questions in which a person answers by reflecting on themselves in order to determine their anxiety levels. Data collected was analyzed using SPSS 16 version. Descriptive analysis was first conducted to calculate mean and standard deviations and later independent sample t test was applied.

Results and Discussion: The objective of the present study was to explore the level of anxiety among female students in co-educational and single sex college system.

Table 1 Mean, standard deviation and significant value of anxiety

Groups	Mean	Standard Deviation	Standard Error Mean	Df	t	Sig
Single-Sex	21.9250	4.33464	0.68537	78	-2.100	0.039
Co-Education	23.8250	3.73403	0.59040	76.327	-2.100	0.039

Table 1 shows that Mean score of female students who study in single sex college system is 21.92, Standard deviation is 4.33 and Mean score of female students who study in Co-Educational colleges system is 23.82 and standard deviation is 3.73. The significant value is 0.039; hence there is a significant difference.

The purpose of the study is to analyze the Anxiety level's of girls in single-sex colleges and girls in co-educational colleges by using Taylor's Manifest Anxiety questionnaires (1953). There is a significant difference in the Mean and standard deviation between girls studying in single sex colleges (Mean- 21.92, Standard deviation- 4.33) compared to girls in Co-Educational colleges (Mean- 23.82, Standard deviation- 3.73).The value of t shows a significant difference of 0.039.

In general, very limited resources were found that has examined the effect of the opposite gender on female student's anxiety levels. The National Association of Single-Sex Education states "because girls are so diverse and boys are so diverse, single-sex schools offer unique educational opportunities for girls, and for boys." Single sex colleges increases the opportunities as well as increases the self esteem of individuals. Girls in general can take part in many of the extracurricular activities as well as the academic activities provided by the institutions. Women empowerment increases and there is a definite confidence boost without the constant fear of being you. It helps girls find themselves and become more active with their surroundings which makes them adapt easily and reduces the risks of having high levels of anxiety.

Conclusion: In conclusion, the purpose of the current research was to analyze the levels of anxiety among girls studying in co-educational colleges compared to girls studying in single-sex colleges. The hypothesis states that the anxiety levels of the girls studying in co-educational colleges will be higher compared to the girls studying in the single sex colleges. The results state that there is a significant difference, hence accepting the alternative hypothesis.

𝕮𝖍𝖆𝖕𝖙𝖊𝖗 𝕾𝖎𝖝𝖙𝖊𝖊𝖓

Premenstrual Syndrome and Spiritual Intelligence[16]

Introduction: Premenstrual syndrome (PMS) is a condition that affects a woman's emotions, physical health, and behaviour during menstrual cycle days. It encompasses an amalgamation of physical and emotional symptoms which occurs during the luteal phase of the menstrual cycle and Spiritual intelligence is one of the multiple intelligences one possesses and it can develop independently also. It is believed to be an integration of the mind and spirit along with the outside life in the world.

PMS is a very common condition that affects up to eighty five percent of menstruating women. PMS symptoms usually start five to eleven days before menstruation and typically go away once menstruation begins but in some females it continues during the menstruation days also. A lot of researchers believe that it's related to a change in both sex hormone and serotonin levels at the beginning of the menstrual cycle. It is believed that the levels of oestrogen and progesterone increase during certain time of the month. An increase in these hormones leads to mood swings, anxiety and irritability which are few of the affective symptoms. The symptoms of PMS are usually mild or moderate with nearly eighty percent of women have reported one or more symptom that does not substantially affect daily functioning, according to the Journal of American Family Physician.

[16] **Anshika Sharma,** Student, Christ University, Bangalore
Satheesh Varma, Asst. Professor, Christ University, Bangalore

Twenty to thirty two percent of women report moderate to severe symptoms that affect some aspect of their lives. The symptoms of PMS are abdomen bloating, sore breasts, acne, food cravings, headaches, constipation, irritability, fatigue, emotional outbursts, depression, anxiety to name a few. Women who suffer from PMS are approximately nine times more likely to report impairment in the quality of life which includes social activities, hobbies, and work productivity than the ones who don't suffer from it (Robinson & Swindle, 2000; Winter, Ashton, & Moore, 1991). Research has shown that women who suffer from PMS have higher levels of absenteeism than women without PMS (Robinson & Swindle, 2000). It has also been observed to have an effect on the daily life activities of women (Pal, Dennerstein & Lehert, 2011).

A study was done to examine symptom severity in the women suffering from premenstrual syndrome as well as how severe symptoms are associated to functional impairment. It was seen that tension and irritability were the most severe symptoms of all the symptoms whereas other symptoms like headache, irritability, self depreciating thoughts, and depressed mood were seen as burdensome. In terms of functional impairment, there was a significant relationship between the severity of symptoms and the social and occupational impairment (Johnson, 1987; Robinson & Swindle, 2000). It was also observed that women who suffered from severe symptoms were nine times more likely to report impairment in their social activities, hobbies, and work productivity (Robinson & Swindle, 2000; Winter, Ashton, & Moore, 1991). Women with PMS also were seen to be more absent than women without PMS (Robinson & Swindle, 2000). Research data of another study provide evidence that premenstrual symptoms hamper the daily life activities of women with PMS (Pal, Dennerstein, & Lehert, 2011).

Spiritual intelligence is one of the multiple intelligences one possesses and it can develop independently also. It is believed to be an integration of the mind and spirit along with the outside life in the world. It is used for making spiritual choices which will result in psychological well being and overall human development. Wisdom and compassion in the person are the two ways through which one can express it. It can be infused in oneself through questioning, inquiry and practice. Spirituality is something that exists everywhere, within traditions and cultures and independently of traditions and also in men and women. Emmons's (2000) thought-provoking article defined a spiritual intelligence that involves five characteristics:

- The capacity to transcend oneself.
- The ability to reach higher spiritual states of consciousness.

- The ability to invest everyday activities, events, and relationships with a sense of the sacred and purity.

- The ability to utilize spiritual resources to solve one's everyday problems.

- The capacity to engage in behaviour which is virtuous to oneself and to others. (To show forgiveness, to express gratitude, to be humble, to display compassion).

It is seen that the quality of life is affected because of the interaction of an spirituality, individual's health, mental state, their relationships and elements of their environment around them (WHOQOL, 1996). Various researches have shown that the spirituality helps in lowering down rates of depression, lower rate of death, better mental and physical state and eventually higher quality of life. Vaughan (2002) believes that one's understanding of himself or herself is one of the important factors of spiritual intelligence because our emotions are regulated by it. It can be considered that different consequences of health including life quality, happiness and non-depression are often affected by spiritual intelligence and religion (Bagheri & Hatami, 2011).

Piedmont (1999) stated that spirituality is comforting during the stressful and anxiety provoking situations. It is also believed that people who have spiritual tendencies respond better to such situations and also help in making health better (Denise & Walt, 2006). Also spiritual qualities of a man such as kindness and compassion helps to endure the hardships of the life therefore people who are inclined towards spirituality have greater adaptability and are less prone to anxiety (Elkins, 2004). A lot of studies have reported consistent results on how spiritual intelligence is positively related mental health. People with high inclination towards spirituality have shown to have lower levels of depression with greater longevity and less infliction by the diseases (Elmer et al. 2003).

It was seen that the PMDD results in substantial burden on both physical and mental health of a person. In a research spirituality was seen to improve the quality of life in persons with cardiovascular diseases. Religious involvement and spirituality have been associated with better quality of life and effective coping in people (Mueller, Plevak, & Rummans, 2001). Different studies have also talked about how spiritual intelligence is positively associated with resilience and helps to cope with everyday's problems (Dale & Cohen, 2014). This study aims to find out if there is any relationship existing between the symptoms of the premenstrual syndrome and spiritual intelligence.

Objectives:

- To explore if there is a correlation between the symptoms of premenstrual syndrome and spiritual intelligence in college going girls.

- To explore if there is a correlation between the symptoms of premenstrual syndrome and spiritual intelligence in working women.

Methodology: The research design used for this study is survey research in the form of mailed questionnaires. Survey Research selects a sample of respondents from a population and administers a standardized questionnaire to them. The questionnaire, or survey, can be a written document that is completed by the person being surveyed, an online questionnaire, a face-to-face interview, or a telephone interview. The two questionnaires were distributed and mailed to the respondents as a part of this design.

The sample used for this study is females between the age group of 18-26 years which includes 30 college girls and 30 working women who are unmarried. The sampling technique employed is purposive sampling because only females who suffer from symptoms of premenstrual syndrome are considered in this study. Females who were working part time were excluded from the study.

The tools used for this study are Roqan Spiritual Intelligence Test and a Premenstrual Syndrome Questionnaire. The Roqan Spiritual Intelligence Test (Zainuddin & Ahmad, 2005) is used to measure the spiritual intelligence in the females. The Roqan Spiritual Intelligence Scale was constructed by Prof. Roquiya Zainuddin and Ms. Anjum Ahmad from Aligarh Muslim University. This test consists of 78 items and it measures Spiritual Intelligence. The test- retest reliability was calculated and Cronbanch's Alpha coefficient computed is .73 and Guttmann Split-Half Coefficient calculated is .70. The validity of this test is .85.

The questionnaire is designed by taking a section of Women's Health Questionnaire (1992) by Myra Hunter at London University. It is designed for women who are experiencing premenstrual, menstrual, menopausal, or gynaecological health concerns. The premenstrual syndrome questionnaire is expert validated and is used to record the symptoms of the premenstrual syndrome. It is expert validated by the two faculty members of psychology who had completed PhD's in their respective fields. Only one section of premenstrual syndrome symptoms was considered for the research because the other sections were not required for this study and the number of items of this questionnaire is 10. To check the normality Shapiro Wilk's test was used which showed that both the variables were normally distributed and therefore Pearson's correlation was run to find out the strength and direction of association between two variables.

Results and Discussion

Table 1 *Mean standard deviation and median of premenstrual syndrome symptoms and spiritual intelligence*

	N	Mean	Std. Deviation
PMS of C	30	56.63	50.91
SI of C	30	51.16	10.76
PMS of W	30	57.06	16.95
SI of W	30	52.85	8.41

The population of this study consisted of 30 college going girls and 30 working women between the age group of 18 to 26 years. The table above is the descriptive data of the two variables chosen for this study.

Table 2 *Shapiro-Wilk test for normality*

	Statistics	Df	Sig.
PMS of C	.963	30	.361
SI of C	.968	30	.494
PMS of W	.974	30	.654
SI of W	.957	30	.254

*Significant at 0.01 level

Table 2 shows the Shapiro- Wilk test for normality. Since the significance of PMS for college going girls (p = .36), PMS for working women (p = .65), SI for college going girls (p =.49) and SI for working women (p =.25) were more than 0.05, therefore the data is normally distributed. Hence Pearson's Correlation was used to find out the correlation between PMS and SI of college going girls and working women.

Table 3 *Relationship between Premenstrual Syndrome of college going girls (PMS) and Spiritual Intelligence of College going Girls (SI)*

		PMS of C	SI of C
	Pearson's Correlation	1	.174
PMS of C	Sig.		.359
	N	30	30
	Pearson's Correlation	.174	1
SI of C	Sig.	.359	
	N	30	30

This table shows that there is no correlation between the two variables in college going girls because the sig. Value (p>0.05) is .359

Table 4 *Relationship between the Premenstrual Syndrome of working women (PMS) and Spiritual Intelligence of the Working women (SI)*

		PMS for W	SI for W
PMS for W	Pearson's Correlation	1	.260
	Sig		.165
	N	30	30
SI for W	Pearson's Correlation	.260	1
	Sig	.165	
	N	30	30

To test if there is any significant relationship between symptoms of PMS and SI in the college going girls and working women, Pearson's correlation was done.

Table 3 and 4 show that there is no significant correlation between the two variables in the college going girls (*r=.174, p=.359*) and working women (*r=.260, p=.165*). Thus the hypotheses for this study are accepted.

The purpose of this study is to explore if there exists a relationship between premenstrual syndrome symptoms and spiritual intelligence in college going girls and working women. The results of the study indicate that spiritual intelligence is negatively associated with premenstrual syndrome symptoms in both college going girls and working women. These findings don't contradict the general assumption that spiritual health is significant to managing one's stress (Greenberg, 2002). But however it directly states that spiritual intelligence does not guarantee any immunity against stress. Stress being one of the important symptoms of premenstrual syndrome, it is very important to manage one's stress to cope with the syndrome. Coping with stress does not only require spiritual intelligence but also other psychosocial and socio cultural factors and social support.

Thoresen (1999) has cited psychosocial mechanisms that were pointed out by other researchers -- mechanisms that could possibly explain a spiritual/religious-health connection. These could include cognitive/motivational processes such as self-perception of worth, perceived self-efficacy beliefs about competence against the odds, locus-of-control beliefs, and optimistic explanatory style behavioural; interpersonal processes such as group meditation skills, spiritual help-seeking through prayer or personal religious counsel, opportunities for fellowship, involvement in formal social programs, and companionship; and socio-cultural processes. These factors may decrease the chance of major overwhelming stresses and also might help to lower the symptoms but these were not included in the scope of this particular study.

As far as the limitation of this study are concerned, it could be mentioned that the research was conducted in a limited area in Bangalore because of which the results cannot be generalised to the females of the entire country and also a lot of females didn't respond to the questionnaire. Also the sample size for this research was only 60 females which are very small to attribute the findings of this study to other females.

Conclusion: Further research should include a larger sample size and also there should be prospective studies done on the different dimensions of spiritual intelligence. Various psychosocial and socio cultural factors should also be included while studying the relationship between these two variables.

Chapter Seventeen

Attitude Towards Counselling[17]

Introduction: Emotional Intelligence is now believed to be more important than their IQ and is certainly a better predictor of success, quality of relationship and overall happiness. A high level of emotional intelligence directly correlates to a positive attitude and outlook on life. By better understanding and managing our emotions, we are better able to communicate our feelings in a more constructive way. Self – Awareness is a way for us to explore our individual personalities, value system, beliefs, natural inclinations and tendencies. Self-awareness is the first step towards setting goals for ourselves. An attitude is an evaluation of an object or a person(s). It shapes our social perception and behaviour and it can be positive, negative or neutral. The expressed intent of the counselling is oriented to personal growth or oriented to the resolution of problems. Self awareness and Emotional intelligence plays a vital role in counselling. Teachers play a major role in the overall development of the students. So teachers should have better understanding of themselves and positive attitude towards counselling so that they can understand and help the students.

Upadhyaya Pratik (2013) conducted a study on "The Relationship between Emotional Intelligence and Academic Achievement among Student- Teachers", The aim of the study is to explore the relationship between emotional intelligence and academic

---

[17] **V. Selva Meenaksh**, Asst. Professor, Manonmaniam Sundaranar University

achievement among student-teachers. The sample for the study comprised of 97 B. Ed. students of Allahabad city. Test of Emotional Intelligence (Student-Teacher Form) developed by K. S. Misra was used as a tool for the study. Thus, the findings of the study imply that EQ training programme with the help of an instructor is essential for the improvement as well as for assuring the success of any teaching-learning activity (Tucker et al. 2000).

Salami (1996) University of Ibadan conducted a study on "Attitudes towards counselling among rural college students in Nigeria". The purpose of the study was to investigate the attitudes of students towards counselling at the college of education, Oro. The subject of the study consist of a total 208 National Certificate of Education (NCE) students randomly selected from I, II, III students at the college of education Oro. Attitudes towards guidance and counselling Inventory (ATGCI).was used to collect the data for study. The results obtained indicated that the students have positive attitude towards counselling; their disposition to seek counselling depends on the types of problems they have.

Objectives: To study the level of Emotional Intelligence, Self Awareness and Attitude towards Counselling among B.Ed students

- To find out the level of Emotional Intelligence, Self Awareness and Attitudes towards counselling among B.Ed students
- To know the relationship among Emotional Intelligence and Self Awareness and Attitude towards Counselling

Results and Discussion

Table 1 Frequency Distribution for Level of Emotional Intelligence, Self Awareness and Attitude towards Counselling

Variables	Low		Moderate		High	
	Frequency	Percent	Frequency	Percent	Frequency	Percent
Emotional Intelligence	108	28.0	179	46.4	99	25.6
Self Awareness	107	27.7	189	49.0	90	23.3
Attitude towards counselling	105	27.2	184	47.7	97	25.1

Table 2 t test for significant difference between Male and Female with respect to their Emotional Intelligence, Self Awareness and Attitude towards counselling

Variables	Gender				t value	P value
	Male		Female			
	Mean	SD	Mean	SD		
Emotional Intelligence	119.44	16.01	122.23	15.59	-1.290	0.198
Self Awareness	26.83	3.25	28.18	3.95	-2.562	0.011*
Attitude towards counselling	50.54	8.87	50.65	6.09	-.125	0.902

: * Denotes significant at 0.05 level

It is concluded that there is a significant difference between Male and Female with regard to their Self Awareness. Females are very expressive than Males and good in maintaining their relationship with others. They are able to be more aware of their feelings than Male and thus Females are high in self aware than male.

Table 3 Chi-square test for Association between level of Emotional Intelligence and level of Self Awareness

Level of Emotional Intelligence	Level of self awareness			Total	Chi-square Value	P value
	Low	Moderate	High			
Low	31 (28.7) [29.0]	63 (58.3) [33.3]	14 (13.0) [15.6]	108		
Moderate	56 (31.3) [52.3]	78 (43.6) [41.3]	45 (25.1) [50.0]	179	13.815	0.008**
High	20 (20.2) [18.7]	48 (48.5) [25.4]	31 (31.3) [34.4]	99		
Total	107	189	90	386		

Note: 1. The value within ( ) refers to Row Percentage

2. The value within [ ] refers to Column Percentage

3. ** denotes significant at 1% level

Students those who are having high emotional intelligence they are high in self awareness. Self-awareness is all about recognizing and understanding how thier own emotions both affect their interactions with others and impact on others' emotional state. This involves being conscious of their own emotional state and thus students high in Self Aware are high in Emotional Intelligence.

The statistical analysis of the data was done by applying 't' test, Chi Square and. The findings revealed the following conclusion:

1. The level of Emotional Intelligence, Self Awareness and Attitude towards Counselling are moderate among B.Ed. students.

2. There is no significant difference between Male and Female with respect to Emotional Intelligence, Attitude towards Counselling and there is significant difference between Male and Female with respect to Self Awareness

3. There is no association between Emotional Intelligence and Attitude towards Counselling.

4. There is no association between Self Awareness and Attitude towards Counselling.

5. There is association between Emotional Intelligence and Self Awareness.

Conclusion: The present study reveals that female students are more self aware than male students. There is significant relationship between self awareness and emotional intelligence. Students of B.Ed. have moderate attitude towards counselling. So far it has been observed that importance of counselling for student – teacher has not been given much importance.

Implications for Education

1. B.ED students should be given importance of counselling so that the future teachers can help students.

2. Every School and College should have the counselling cell and it is important to have positive attitude towards counselling.

3. In educational institutions the individuality of the students should be respected and given opportunities to develop confidence, cooperation etc.

4. Teachers working in B.ED colleges should be properly trained through orientation and refreshing programs for developing their skill in developing their counselling skills.

𝕮𝖍𝖆𝖕𝖙𝖊𝖗 𝕰𝖎𝖌𝖍𝖙𝖊𝖊𝖓

Concept of Health Among Women[18]

Introduction: The status of Indian women has radically changed since the independence of the country. Both the structural and cultural changes provided equality of opportunities to women in education, employment and political participation. With the help of these changes, exploitation of women, to a great extent was reduced. More freedom and better orientation were provided to women to pursue their interest. Presently, most women are not limited to giving birth, nurturing their young, performing daily chores, etc., rather, they are now out of this and have taken over the work force to show their potential, and prove that they are equal to men. Women are working outside the house and have acquired almost all fields like politics, science, defense, etc. As centuries passed, the number of roles has increased and it is hypothised that, because of the different roles and high expectations from women as a homemaker and employee they are both physically and psychologically exhausted and have poor general health. According to WHO, general health is *'a state of complete physical, mental and social well being and not merely the absence of disease and infirmity'* (WHO, 1948)

A study conducted by Usha R. Rout (1997) included 101 sample. 78 per cent were working mothers and 22 per cent non-working mothers. Researcher assessed the stress and depression experienced by working and non working women and also how they cope with it. The results revealed that the working mothers had better mental health and reported less depression than the non-working mothers.

---

[18] **Dania Muhammadi Nayyar,** Student, Teresian College, Mysore

103

Revati R. Dudhatra and Dr. Yogesh A Jogsan (2012) conducted a study to find out the mean difference between working and non-working women in mental health and depression. The total sample consisted of 80 women. The research tool for mental health was measured by Dr. D.J. Bhatt and Gita R. Geeda (1992). The tool for depression used was by Beck (1961). The results showed that non-working women have better mental health compared to working women.

With reference to the above mentioned review, results are not unidirectional and more empirical studies need to understand this, hence out of curiosity the researcher has undertaken a small research using 70 participants 35 (married working women) and 35 (married non-working women).

Objectives: The main purpose of the study was to identify whether the general health of working women was different from non-working women due to the numerous roles played by the working women.

- To assess the General Health of working and non-working women
- To study the General Health of working women
- To study the General Health of non-working women

Hypotheses

- The general health of working women will be poor compared to non-working women.
- Non-working women will have good psychological health compared to working women

Methodology: In this study, 70 participants were randomly selected 35 (married working women) and 35 (married non-working women) participants were in the age range between 30 to 40 years. All participants were from Mysore, Karnataka.

Tools: *General Health Questionnaire,* (Goldberg 1970). A 28 item self report questionnaire designed to assess four aspects of distress. It is suitable for all ages from adolescent upwards.

Numerous studies have investigated reliability and validity of the GHQ-28 in various clinical populations. Test –retest reliability has been reported to be high (0.78 to 0.9) (Robinson and Price 1982) and interrater and intrarater reliability have both been shown to be excellent (Cronbach's 0.9-0.95) (Falide and Ramos 2000).

Scale is having a four point rating scale with the categories "not at all", "no more than usual", "rather more than usual" and "much more than usual". The items are scored with the values 0,0,1,1. There are 4 domains and each domain has 7 statements. If the score of each domain is 4 and above, then the subject is susceptible to the symptoms and if the overall score is 16 and above, the subject's psychological health is not good. The independent t test method was used to ascertain whether there was a significant difference in the general health of working and non-working women.

Results and Discussion: The data was analyzed using the independent t test. The data was analyzed using all four dimensions and also each dimension was analysed separately.

Table 1 - Mean, Standard deviation and significant value for all four domains of GHQ N=70

Variables	Mean	Standard deviation	Standard error mean	df	t	Sig
Working (35)	5.0000	5.23000	.88403	68	-.320	.750
Non-working (35)	5.4000	5.21423	.88137	67.999	-.320	.750

Table 1 shows the overall general health of working and non-working women. The mean of working women is 5.00 and the mean of non-working is 5.40. The standard deviation of working women is 5.23 and for non-working women is 5.21. There is a slight difference in the mean score and standard deviation between working and non-working women. The significant value is .750; hence there is no significant difference.

Table 2 - Mean, standard deviation, significant value of Somatic Symptoms of GHQ

Variables	Mean	Standard deviation	Standard error mean	df	t	Sig
Working (35)	1.4286	1.63214	.27588	68	-.152	.879
Non-working (35)	1.4857	1.50238	.25395	67.539	-.152	.879

Table 2 shows the results of the somatic symptoms between working and non-working women. The mean of working women is 1.42 and the mean of non-working women is 1.48.The standard deviation in working women is 1.63 and the standard deviation of non- working women is 1.50.

There is a slight difference in the mean score and standard deviation between working and non-working women. The significant value is .879; hence there is no significant difference.

Table 3 - Mean, standard deviation and significant value of Anxiety and Insomnia of GHQ N=70

Variables	Mean	Standard deviation	Standard error mean	df	t	Sig
Working (35)	1.8000	2.27260	.38414	68	.000	1.000
Non-working (35)	1.8000	1.90664	.32228	66.006	.000	1.000

Table 3 shows the result of anxiety and insomnia between working and non-working women. The mean of working women is 1.80 and the mean of non-working women is 1.80.The standard deviation in working women is 2.27 and the standard deviation of non- working women is 1.90. There is a slight difference in the mean score and standard deviation between working and non-working women. The significant value is 1.00; hence there is no significant difference.

Table 4 - Mean, standard deviation and significant value of Social Dysfunction of GHQ N=70

Groups	Mean	Standard deviation	Standard error mean	Df	t	Sig
Working (35)	.8286	1.01419	.17143	68	-.921	.360
Non-working (35)	1.1143	1.52954	.25854	59.054	-.921	.361

Table 4 displays the result of social dysfunction between working and non-working women. . The mean of working women is .82 and the mean of non-working women is 1.11.The standard deviation in working women is 1.01 and the standard deviation of non- working women is 1.52. There is a slight difference in the mean score and standard deviation between working and non-working women. The significant value is .360; hence there is no significant difference.

Table 5 - Mean, standard deviation and significant value of Severe Depression N=70

Groups	Mean	Standard deviation	Standard error mean	Df	T	Sig
Working (35)	0.9417	1.70614	.28839	68	-.072	.943
Non-working (35)	1.000	1.62698	.27501	67.847	-.072	.943

Table 5 shows the result of severe depression between working and non-working women. The mean of working women is .94 and the mean of non-working women is 1.00.The standard deviation in working women is 1.70 and the standard deviation of non- working women is 1.62. There is a slight difference in the mean score and standard deviation between working and non-working women. The significant value is .943; hence there is no significant difference.

The main purpose of the present study was to assess the difference in general health among working women and non-working women. The hypothesis states that the general health of working women will be poor compared to non-working women.

The results presented in Table 4.1 reveal that there is no significant difference in the general health of working and non-working women when data of all domains combined were analysed. However, this is not in support with the results from the studies carried out by Usha R. Rout which suggests that working mothers had better mental health and reported less depression than the non-working mothers.

The present study does not agree with Revati R. Dudhatra and Dr. Yogesh A Jogsan's study which claims that non-working women have better mental health compared to working women. Also there was no significant difference when data was analyzed separately for each domain viz., Somatic Symptoms, Anxiety and Insomnia, Social Dysfunction and Severe Depression. However, in one dimension i.e. Severe Depression, with reference to the mean and standard deviation there is a slight difference

So the present study reveals that that there is no significant difference in general health of working and non-working women, thereby rejecting the alternative hypothesis.

Conclusion: There was no significant difference when data of the four domains were analyzed together. There was no significant difference when data of each domain was analysed separately. In one dimension i.e. severe depression, there was slight difference.

Chapter Nineteen

Organizational Commitment[19]

Introduction: In the present era, many people spend a major portion of their daily lives in organizations. Organizations are defined as groups of individuals who work in collaboration with each other towards some goal (McShane, Glinow, Sharma, 2012). The functioning of an organization can be attributed to various factors. The most essential factor among them is organizational commitment. The topic organizational commitment has become a key topic in organizational research and in understanding the behaviour of employees towards their workplace. It has been extensively discussed in print media, social media as well as in formal workplace groups. The term organizational commitment is defined as the psychological attachment of an employee towards his or her organization and its respective objectives (Jayakumar & Ranjan, 2011).

The phenomenon of organizational commitment is distinct from two related concepts such as organizational citizenship behaviour and organizational identification. While the concept of organizational commitment refers to psychological attachment towards an organization, the term organizational citizenship behaviour refers to behaviours that employees display out of their own willingness rather than with the expectation of being rewarded externally by an organization (Velickovska, 2017). The meaning of the terms organizational commitment and organizational citizenship behaviour differ from the meaning of the term organizational identification which refers to a sense of oneness with their organization (Jayakumar & Ranjan, 2011).

---

[19] **Shruti Jayakumar**, Research Scholar, Jain University
S. T. Janetius, Ph.D., Professor, Jain University

Organizational commitment can be enhanced through three categories of factors namely personal factors, social factors and organizational factors. Personal factors include age and growth needs. As far as age is concerned, it is inferred that older employees are more likely to be committed towards their organizations because they have more responsibilities, challenges and more opportunities to satisfy their growth needs unlike younger employees who mostly hold entry-level job positions that are less stimulating and challenging. This could be a plausible explanation for a recent finding in a survey conducted by Tech Mahindra company which indicates that Millennials or individuals who have reached young adulthood in the twenty-first century often retain in a specific organization for a maximum average period of a little over 3 years (Gupta, 2017). The growth needs of various employees depend upon their job characteristics such as stimulation, autonomy, variety and feedback received from authorities (Jayakumar & Ranjan, 2011). As far as the social factors are concerned, it has been observed that employees who work in groups show a higher level of commitment than employees who work alone. (Jayakumar & Ranjan, 2011).

With respect to organizational factors that contribute to the level of organizational commitment among several employees, job enrichment, the opportunity to use their skills and the level of commitment displayed by their employers towards themselves play a major role in exhibiting their level of commitment towards their respective organizations. The extent to which employers exhibit commitment towards their employees can be gauged is through organizational support. (Jayakumar & Ranjan, 2011).

Employees engaging in organizational commitment can lead to both positive and negative outcomes for themselves. Many employees who rise to the management-level in huge multinational corporations are strongly committed individuals who stay with their company throughout their occupational life. However, the adverse impact at an individual level could be a source of discomfort experienced in case of a failure to establish strong commitments and ignorance of attractive job opportunities outside their organizations. The level of commitment exhibited by employees in their organization can also benefit employers since several studies have indicated a negative correlation between organizational commitment and variables such as employee absenteeism, employee attrition and employee turnover. Other scientific research studies have also indicated a positive correlation between organizational commitment and employee productivity.

A plethora of western approaches towards organizational commitment have been formulated since the early twentieth century. Nevertheless, one of the most dominant and popular models that has been extensively used to study this topic in several South

Asian and South-Eastern cultures include the three-component model of commitment proposed by Natalie Allen and John Meyer from the University of Western Ontario in the early nineties. According to this model, organizational commitment can be categorized into affective commitment or emotional attachment and identification with an organization, continuance commitment or a sense of attachment towards an organization due to the fear of losing individual gains such as promotions, pension, friendship with co-workers and normative commitment or the sense of attachment based on an employee's obligation to remain in an organization due to the internalization of its goals and values (McShane, Glinow, Sharma, 2012).

Post Allen and Meyer's model, several models of organizational commitment arose in South -East Asian countries such as China which focused on including an employee's values, training opportunities and career development opportunities. The latest model of organizational commitment that is being studied in the Asian context was proposed by researcher Yingyan Wang who elucidated that in addition to employees remaining committed to their organization for affective reasons and reasons for being afraid of foregoing individual benefits, employees remain committed to their organizations due to the availability of on-the job or off-the job training opportunities, challenging job opportunities ,promotions and non-availability of better work opportunities outside the organization. Wang categorized the initial three reasons for organizational commitment as active continuance commitment and the latter three reasons for organizational commitment as passive continuance commitment (Wong, 2014).

Customer -focused professionals refer to those working in organizations that emphasize on delivering their performance to meet the wants of clients or companies affiliated with them for achieving profits. These professionals primarily focus on improving their technical and persuasive strategies to ensure that they capture clients or client companies at a rapid pace and ensure speedy delivery of performance to achieve targets set by these organizations. Therefore, customer-focused professionals ensure that they are consistent in meeting and exceeding the expectations of their clients to ensure that clients do not remain disappointed and hamper their process of achieving monetary targets of their respective organizations (Bacon, 2017). Customer-Service representatives, Behavioural Intake Counsellors, Tax-associates, Technical Consultants are examples of professionals in customer-focused organizations.

While customer-service representatives are main points of contact for customers handling requests, inquiries and other types of duties that vary depending upon the type of business, Behavioural Intake counsellors work for mental health providers and substance abuse health providers to obtain in-depth information about a client to help psychologists and psychiatrists understand the prognosis and suitable interventions for the client (Christensen, 2018; Scottsdale, 2018).   While tax associates help individuals and businesses with central and state income tax compliance and preparation in self-employed or private financial services companies and accounting firms, technical consultants are professionals who conduct trouble-shooting functions and attempt to resolve issues faced by clients about technical products and processes. These consultants are highly knowledgeable about their respective company's products and applications so that they can assist their clients as well as other employees with any concerns related to these products and appliances (Florida Tech, 2017; "technical job description", 2017) Several research studies have been conducted regarding the level of organizational commitment among customer-focused professionals in certain industries.

Guha and Barua (2017) conducted a literature review of several studies to understand the level of organizational commitment of customer-service representatives in India according to the three-component model of organizational commitment proposed by Allen and Meyer. They discovered that majority of the participants were committed towards their organizations due to affective and normative reasons and negatively correlated to continuance commitment. This finding is contrasted with the results obtained by Jayakumar and Ranjan in the year 2011 whereby the Organizational Commitment questionnaires by Allen and Meyer were distributed among software engineers in a service industry to explore the gender differences among 20 male and 20 female service engineers using this phenomenon, In contrast to the previous findings, results of this study indicated that both male and female service engineers displayed affective, continuance and normative levels of commitment around similar rates (Jayakumar & Ranjan, 2011).

As far as the application of Wang's model of commitment to the Indian context is concerned, a recent qualitative research study conducted among customer-focused professionals in several multinational companies of the Information and Technology Service Sector based on the framework of ground theory indicated that majority of the employees at higher level positions such as managers often reported remaining committed to their job opportunities due to passive type of continuance commitment or a lack of better opportunities outside their organizations. However, unlike the results observed in the previous study published by Jayakumar and Ranjan in the year 2011, the level of normative commitment or being committed to the organization due to internalization of company values or norms was not prevalent among these employees (Aswathy, Gupta, Rajen, 2010).

Newman, Thanacoody and Hui (2011) have conducted a research study on examining the relationship between organizational commitment and employee turnover in Chinese Information and Technology Service Industry using Farh's Scale and concluded that the higher the level of training opportunities available for employees, the more committed they tend to remain towards their organizations or engage in active continuance commitment which in turn will drastically reduce the measure of employee turnover in this industry. The results of this study are contradictory to the results mentioned in a previous study conducted among Indian managers whereby individuals exhibited a passive rather than an active form of continuance commitment (Aswathy, Gupta, Rajen, 2010). Nevertheless, Similar results of the previous study conducted in the Chinese Information and Technology Service sector was also observed among customer-focused Information Technology service professionals in Pakistan whereby the results obtained from 200 professionals, who were given a self-developed questionnaire, indicated that the affective level of commitment among these professionals were directly linked to a healthy organizational learning culture (Malik & Danish, 2010).

As far as the level of organizational commitment among customer-service representatives are concerned, a recent quantitative research study conducted among 133 customer-service professionals in Pakistan have revealed an indirect relationship between emotional exhaustion and affective organizational commitment. On the Allen and Meyer's Organizational Commitment Scale (Rehman, Karim, Rafiq, Mansoor, 2012). The finding in this study regarding the phenomenon of an affective organizational commitment to similar studies conducted among these professionals in the Indian environment.

Saxena and Rai (2015) attempted to explore the level of organizational commitment among 107 financial service professionals across different companies in the financial service industry and inferred that individuals scored high in the level of continuance commitment rather than other levels of commitment among these professionals in India. These results are further supported by the findings of a research study conducted among 286 employees in the financial services industry in China which indicated that employees are closely linked with continuance commitment for the sake of receiving rewards from their respective organizations (Newman & Sheikh, 2012). On the contrary, empirical research studies conducted among 215 employees in the financial services industry in Pakistan indicate that employees tend to have a high level of organizational commitment due to higher job security rather than owing it to the recognitions made by an organization externally (Abdullah & Ramay, 2012).

One of the major concerns faced by customer-focused professionals across the world is employee attrition. The term employee attrition is referred to the loss of employees due to various reasons such as resignation or retirement (Farkiya, 2013). According to recent surveys conducted to examine the attrition rates among employees in different job sectors every year, the business processing outsourcing industry experiences around 60 % of employee attrition rate per year, Information and Technology Service Industry experiences around 26 % of employee attrition rate per year and the Financial Services Industry experiences around 17.4 % of employee attrition rate per year (McShane, Glinow, Sharma, 2012; Gupta, 2017; Rhattigan, 2016). Hence, it becomes imperative to examine the meaning of organizational commitment among customer-focused professionals in these industries.

Objectives: The purpose of this qualitative research study is to develop indigenous theories of organizational commitment among each of these types of customer-focused professionals such as Behavioural Intake Counsellors and Customer Service Representatives from the Employee Assistance Program Industry (EAP), Technical Consultants belonging to the Information and Technology Service Industry and Tax associates belonging to the Finance Industry.

The following broad research questions will be explored initially as a part of my qualitative study based on the framework of Ground theory. Specific research questions will be arrived at a later stage during the process of analyzing data and collecting data from the samples.

Q1. How are the different processes and actions specific to behavioural intake counsellors contributing to our understanding of the meaning of organizational commitment?

Q2. How are the perceptions of behavioural intake counsellors regarding different processes and actions exhibited by their employers contributing to our understanding of the meaning of organizational commitment?

Q3. How are the different processes and actions specific to customer-service representatives contributing to our understanding of the meaning of organizational commitment?

Q4. How are the perceptions of customer-service representatives regarding different processes and actions exhibited by their employers contributing to our understanding of the meaning of organizational commitment?

Q5. How are the different processes and actions specific to technical consultants contributing to our understanding of the meaning of organizational commitment?

Q6. How are the perceptions of technical consultants regarding different processes and actions exhibited by their employers contributing to our understanding of the meaning of organizational commitment?

Q7. How are the different processes and actions specific to tax associates contributing to our understanding of the meaning of organizational commitment?

Focus of the Study: By developing indigenous theories of organizational commitment among customer-focused professionals such as Behavioural Intake Counsellors and Customer Service Representatives from the Employee Assistance Program Industry (EAP), Technical Consultants belonging to the Information and Technology Service Industry and Tax associates belonging to the Finance Industry, we can understand the meaning of organizational commitment attributed by these customer-focused professionals. This, in turn, will help employers and human resource professionals to implement various strategies to minimize attrition rates and enhance employee retention in these sectors. Further research topics include exploring gender differences and differences among senior-level employees and junior-level employees in views regarding the meaning of organizational commitment among these customer-focused professionals

Conclusion: This paper aims at introducing the meaning, causes and consequences of organizational commitment traditionally and the theoretical approaches of measuring organizational commitment among customer-focused professionals in certain sectors in three Asian countries namely India, China and Pakistan. The purpose of developing indigenous theories of organizational commitment among four types of customer-focused professionals namely such as Behavioural Intake Counsellors and Customer Service Representatives from the Employee Assistance Program Industry (EAP), Technical Consultants belonging to the Information and Technology Service Industry and Tax associates belonging to the Finance Industry was discussed along with the rationale to understand the meaning of organizational commitment among them so that employers and human resource professionals can take suitable steps to minimize attrition rates in these industries by developing suitable retention strategies to motivate employees to deliver their best performance at work.

Chapter Twenty

Burnout Among Employees[20]

Introduction: With the advent and awareness about psychology at workplace or what is commonly called as Industrial psychology, lay men are understanding the concept of job performance, satisfaction, stress and burn out in a detailed manner, thanks to the world wide web. In lay man's terms, burn out is physical or mental collapse caused by overwork or stress. With reference to Counselling psychology and the field of helping professionals, burnout is a prolonged response to chronic and emotional stressors at job or workplace that renders a person to feel worn out easily, exhausted and emotionally numb. (Oser B, Pullen, & Harp, 2013)

Burnout is a concept that has been studied since the 1970s and predominantly gained significance because of the works of Freudenberger (1975) and Maslach (1976). Burnout, initially, was being studied extensively in mental health practice especially with psychiatrists and social workers. Later on, it gained momentum and research was done in serveral other areas including in the field of medicine and education. The origin of the word goes back to the 1960s, in a book called "A Burnt-out case" by the English author called Graham Greene, which is about an architect who quits his job due to his condition of leprosy which then leads to disillusionment and lack of content in life, and moves to the jungles of Africa. Earlier writing about burn-out focuses largely on fatigue, and loss of passion of job. Burn out was unique as a concept as it

[20] **Sumithra Sridhar**, Research Scholar, Jain University
Madhurini Vallikad, Ph.D., Asst. Professor, Jain University

117

did not use a particular theory, rather it was derived from people's experiences regarding their work and workplace.

Freudenberger characterized burnout by a set of symptoms that includes exhaustion resulting from work's excessive demands as well as physical symptoms such as headaches and sleeplessness, "quickness to anger," and closed thinking. He observed that the burned-out worker "looks, acts, and seems depressed". Burn out is felt and expressed in many ways. People usually express that they are drained and tired. They see no meaning in the work that they do and they also don't feel valued for the work that they do. They feel unimportant and unrecognized. People, who go through burn out or experience burnout, feel that there is an issue within the work system.

Corey (1996), suggests that burn out is a syndrome that can feed off itself. Hence practitioners feel more and more isolated. Burn out is something that goes beyond physical exhaustion from all the over work and the stress. Burn out occurs because of the distance that the person starts making, as a response to the issues faced at work. Hence, since burn out is about understanding the "external" world and the effect it has on us, it also puts the blame on the environment. Job burnout is induced by distress. "It is majorly characterized by some degree of physical and emotional exhaustion, socially dysfunctional behaviours, strong negative feelings about oneself, low self-esteem, constantly talking ill about oneself and lastly, organizational inefficiency through decreased output and poor morale. "(Cedoline, A. 1982)

Objectives: The aim of the paper is examine the concept of burnout. The objectives of this paper are:

- To examine the historical development of concept of burnout
- To examine the different models of burn out

Methodology: The study used reviews and evaluation of existing literature Different data bases were used access theoretical papers (listed in the references). In addition, the researcher has also made reviewed the book titled "Burnout: The Cost for Caring" by Maslach (1982).

Results and Discussion: The findings with respect to the first objective of examining the historical development of the concept of burnout, are presented and discussed below. The history behind the concept of burnout can be understood through two phases, the pioneering phase and the empirical phase. The pioneer phase gave us a basic understanding of the concept of burnout and normalised the term as something that people go through, hence not giving it a badge of illness. The 1st psychiatrist to study this phenomenon was Freudenberger (1974) who noticed that in the mental agency he was employed at, the volunteers started showing signs of not being motivated or they were constantly feeling drained out. This process occurred a year after their work had started and was followed by a variety of physical symptoms that included ulcers, headaches, stomach diseases etc. He came up with the word burnout and used it to refer it to this state of mental exhaustion. The term was earlier used to denote a sign of drug abuse. At the same time, Christina Maslach, a social psychology researcher was studying how people cope up with emotional arousal at job, which she analysed using interviews.

Early literature on burnout was mostly non-empirical in nature. In the 1980s, close to 50 articles that were published, out of which only five provided empirical evidence. The rest of the papers predominantly focussed on suggestions, causes of burnout, hence serving a theoretical purpose. Most papers followed a similar pattern where they spoke about the stressful nature of the job due to which burnout occurred, followed by a case study to illustrate the issue further and concluded with preventive strategies and recommendations. When compared to other aspects, burnout research was comparatively low key as it only triggered the interest in practitioners, who were bound to face it, but it never captured the attention of the researchers, because it was considered to be more "pop psychology" due to the lack of theoretical evidence behind the concept of burnout.

The empirical phase happened in the 1980s where the work was more focused on evidence-based research and was more constructive in nature. This was the time, models of burnout were being made by different practitioners to give it a theoretical background. What was initially studied only in the United States spread to Canada and Great Britain as well. During this period, the Maslach Burnout Inventor (MBI; Maslach, 1981) was being used a scale to measure burnout. The scale gained popularity in Europe as well, where it was translated into the major languages such as French, Spanish, German etc. Burnout literature during this period included the topic to be studied among the professions that were human services related. Another common factor that was seen, was that the research focused on the job and the environmental factors and not about the person's personality or resilience. Most of the studies conducted were mostly on stress, job environment, workload, lack of support at work etc.

Another evident factor was that the researchers used the MBI extensively, which is a self-measure inventory, hence the authenticity and reliability of the person's answers was doubtful. The empirical phase started developing theoretical frameworks to study burnout as there was initially no theory attached to the concept. But in recent times, due to the development of several models, burnout has been studied through a conceptual framework. In literature, there are four well-known developmental models of burnout, which explains about how burnout develops over a period of time, as a process. Currently, burnout is theoretically grounded and has been researched. Models of burnout have been developed, to understand the process of burnout and the implications it holds in that particular area of work. From the previously conducted researches, burnout has been operationally defined as a "psychological syndrome in response to chronic interpersonal stressors on the job" (Maslach, Schaufeli & Leiter, 2001)

According to Christina Maslach's multidimensional theory of burnout, which is viewed as the first model of burnout, there are three dimensions of Burnout, which are, 1) emotional exhaustion- the person becomes overly involved in emotions and later feels overwhelmed by the emotional demands that are imposed by other people, sometimes making them less sociable and more prone to depression. 2) Depersonalisation- It refers to a negative, cynical or an extremely detached response to people. It is developed or is formed due to the extreme level of emotional exhaustion. It is a form of protecting oneself as a barrier, by distancing themselves from people and their issues, but after a point of time, it could lead to dehumanization. (Maslach, 1981). 3) Reduced personal accomplishment- the person begins to feel inadequate and keep assessing himself/herself as failures. His/her self-esteem might be at stake, which also has a high chance to leading to depression in some cases and reduced personal accomplishment. Hence, it can be understood from this model that Maslach believed that the process of burnout occurred in a pattern, where emotional exhaustion leads to depersonalisation which then leads to reduced personal accomplishment. This model has been criticised over the years. Some conceptualize burnout as multidimensional construct, while other researchers propose that it is a unidimensional construct, which means that it is viewed only with regard to the symptom of emotional exhaustion. Others argue that burn out involves all three aspects which happens sequentially. Leiter (1993) criticised the works by stating that emotional exhaustion occurs in isolation and is not associated with the other two factors. Maslach (1993) acknowledged that there are newer ways of perceiving the model of burnout and proposed that some burnout components develop in parallel, rather than in sequence, because they are reactions to different factors in the work environment.

The second model of burnout was developed in 1980 by Cherniss and his associates, who interviewed 28 professionals from 4 different fields of mental health, poverty law, public health nursing and high school teaching. This model proposes that individuals who possess certain career orientations interact with the work settings.

They usually possess their own idea of demands and supports which in itself leads to high levels of stress. They cope with the stress by undertaking positive way of problem solving and getting out of the mode, while some people resort to pessimism and exhibit negative attitude changes. For Cherniss, burnout is something that happens over time and it is a process. It represents how one adapts or copes with the particular sources of stress that are both present in the environment and internalised. This model was criticised as it overlooked the possibility of burnout being caused due to the work environment and role ambiguity as well, along with the individual characteristics of the person. The sample size used by Cherniss was too small to generalise the results and make a model, based on it.

The third model was proposed by Golembiewski and his colleagues in 1983 which stated that burnout can be examine as a process. They made use of the Maslach Burnout Inventory that has three subscales, each measuring a dimension of burnout namely, emotional exhaustion, depersonalization and reduced personal accomplishment. Using the scores, they came up with eight phases of burnout, which have been arranged theoretically in a sequence that ranges from a positive to a negative experience spectrum. This model states that the individuals who belong to the advanced phase ideally report more negative work experiences and express more negative outcomes when compared to the ones who belong to a lesser advanced phase.

The criticism of this model is the ambiguity of the phases and the way how the scores around the mean, determining which phase a person would be in. It is difficult to understand the effect of interventions using this model, because even if a person's score increases slightly post-intervention, he could still be in the same phase or the phase that is slightly less advance, hence it would not be viewed as "progress" in its actual sense.

Leiter proposed the fourth model of burnout based on two assumptions. He stated that three components of burnout as proposed by the Maslach Burnout Inventory influence each other and that they have a distinctive relationship with the environment factor and with the individual's personality as well. This model places the dimension of "Emotional exhaustion" in the central position, meaning this developed first, hypothesising that people tend to depersonalise only after they feel exhausted emotionally. As they begin to depersonalise and lose out on their relationships, their sense of personal accomplishment diminishes as well. This model states that emotional exhaustion is caused due to stressors such as work overload, conflicts with peers, which will later have an effect on their level of depersonalisation and personal accomplishment too. The weakness of the model is that the stressors are not clearly defines. How these are developed? At what level do they become problems? Coming up with interventions for them is a difficult process.

Although each of these models focus on the problem of burnout in a different way, they are similar in the way they provide interventions, that will help reduced workers burnout and help increase in productivity by proposing ideas to help bridge the gap between employer-employees. They also talk about how organizations can make certain changes in their work plan to cater to the mental and emotional needs of the workers. At the same time, enough focus was laid on giving individuals solutions to understand how burnout is affecting their personal and professional lives.

Conclusion: Burnout has been a topic of study for practitioners and researchers since the 1970s. With the advent of Industrial psychology, it can be said that people who belong to any field of work can empathise and understand the concept of burnout, because after a point of time, they all go through it, in a way. Burnout in this study has been limited to understanding it from a "helping profession" or a "social interaction procession's" point of view. This paper aimed at explaining the concept of burnout in detail, using the history and models, using a theoretical framework rather than empirical researchers. Most researches in the past decade have not developed the theoretical construct further.

Chapter Twenty One

Employability of Graduates[21]

Introduction: Higher education is experiencing a time of rapid change in which the traditional picture of a college-aged student sitting in a large lecture hall is no longer. The students complete their education in a variety of formats and sometimes from multiple institutions with the focus on educational technologies that can provide solutions for classroom management, assessment, micro-learning, affordability and collaboration. The areas of need for higher education lead to many quality educational technology tools and apps for leading the way in an era of rapid change. In the recent years, there had been many initiatives that advocated for the development of employability for young and unemployed people in the India by various agencies of Public & Private. This schemes and policies incorporate skills in both academic and general education (secondary, higher and tertiary) and vocational education and training. These employability skills had been emphasized with skill development and enterprising skills development/education.

Employability is a term that has multiple definitions for instance employability is about skills, preparing individuals for employment. The Skills, understandings and personal attributes, which will make the graduates more likely to gain employment and be successful in their chosen occupations' (Knight and Yorke, 2003: 5). Knight and Yorke (2004: 25) identify seven employability definitions with numbers 5 to 7 having the 'greatest appeal to us':

---

[21] **C. Swapna**, Department of Education, IASE, Osmania University

1. Getting a (graduate) job.
2. Possession of a vocational degree.
3. Possession of 'key skills' or suchlike.
4. Formal work experience.
5. Good use of non-formal work experience and/or voluntary work.
6. Skillful current career planning and interview technique.
7. A mix of cognitive and non-cognitive achievements and representations.

The call for the value and relevance of these skills has been led collaboration with Education and Employment that focused upon:

- Effective communication—including written skills

- Application of numbers—the ability to work with numbers

- The use of information technology.

- Working with others—how you work with others when planning and carrying out activities to get things done and achieve shared objectives

- Improve self-learning and performance—how you manage your self-personal learning and career development

- Problem solving—about recognizing problems and doing something about them

Objectives

1. To know the perception of student's occupational choices.
2. To understand the teaching and learning in higher education yielding employability.

The following research questions are framed for the study:

1. Is curriculum embedded with career and employability?

2. Is University focusing on understanding, analysis, synthesis and creativity, and evaluation for the student's employability?

3. How might the University ensure that each (and every) student is fully exposed to each skill area?

4. Should skills be assessed separately from the general curriculum? How should the skills be assessed?

5. Does the University providing vocational education and training and giving proper employment for the students?

Methodology: Focused group discussions, interviews and surveys were used to collect data from the students of higher education of Osmania University Campus by the researcher.

Results and discussion: Skills and is felt by all those responsible for (or subject to) teaching, learning or assessment. Each of the key players - lecturer, student and examiner is obliged to act in a manner which may be somewhat different from that which was previously regarded as the norm. The interacting work of these three players is also seen to change as the employability skills are emphasized. Employability skills are grouped under four main headings:

1. Information retrieval and handling.
2. Communication and presentation.
3. Planning and problem solving.
4. Social development and interaction.

For each skill area (above) the specific descriptions should be phrased to take account of the progressive development of the students from Level I through to Level 3.

For each level, the descriptions give details of the University's expectations in respect of the context of learning-, the degree of student responsibility for their own learning, and the ethical frameworks within which learning is to take place.

Student motivation to go to university careers services for support, physically or online, will be low unless they are aware of the opportunities.

Work placements and experience appear in many university strategies with different emphases reflecting the nature of the institution. The relevance of work placements in non-vocational degrees is always a source of debate. Pressure to include such experiences comes in part from government initiatives. 'Work experience, either as part of a programme of study, or as an external extracurricular activity, should be recognized in some way and formally accredited where possible'. Most students have paid employment in term-time and vacations; many have undertaken voluntary work at home and increasingly abroad during gap experiences. There is plenty of material for these students to reflect upon and trawl for examples of employability skills and attributes.

The world of educational technology changes constantly. There are new platforms and promises of transforming education. It is important for online higher education leaders to think critically about how to serve their students with appropriate technology solutions. Thinking back technology designed to improve online learning or reduce the cost for students are strong areas to explore and utilize.

The depth of engagement with employability taken by a member of staff will vary depending on the nature and level of a module, and the activities that students undertake in other modules. What follows are possibilities to prompt further engagement. It was not long ago that virtual reality was cost prohibitive and caused nausea for many people. However, the technology is rapidly advancing, and virtual reality is now feasible for use in the classroom and beyond. Students can create 3D videos and watch them through an app on their phone using Google Cardboard. Virtual reality has endless applications and can be used with any subject to superimpose a simulation into the physical environment. While some of the simpler attempts became a worldwide phenomenon with the technology.

Making the link between personal reflection and workplace application is easier for students who encounter personal development planning in their vacation or term-time employment. Where students struggle to see the relevance of reflection, tutorial activities that begin with interviews with people who use personal development planning at work may be helpful as would ask students to read and reflect. Giving students the opportunity to practise making personal evaluative statements, before encountering them at work, is an employability skill in its own right. The lack of confidence of both students and academics with personal development processes exists partly because they are asked to articulate in unfamiliar language information about which they feel self-conscious. Finding the language to make employability links clear to students, and to expand their employability vocabulary, it is suggested that the skills and competency terms and synonyms employers use should also be used in module descriptors and outcomes. If this seems to be pandering to the employment agenda, it is worth remembering that these terms are commonly used in research and academic job advertisements.

Conclusion: This paper has emphasized the benefits to students of being consciously aware of how they approach tasks as well as the knowledge that they gain from them. It argues that the ability to reflect on how you operate will both benefit current degree performance and build lifelong learning skills. It suggests that tuning the curriculum through many small-scale, awareness-raising activities and employability-aware reflection can be very powerful. In addition, specialist modules may be offered. As curricula evolve vulnerable as staff move to other projects, whereas embedded discussion and reflection on learning processes and skills are likely to survive for the long term. University learning may be moving in ways that help employability, but do students realize that there is a change, and do they appreciate the value of reflecting on how they learn as well as what is learned? Methods for integrating engagement must be backed up by positive support from the teaching community. Also there should be amalgamation of both traditional and non-traditional techniques for the betterment of the output wherever necessary.   The following recommendations are made from the study:

- Encouraging more young people to take non-traditional routes in their working lives.

- Colleges should provide appropriate support to young people who are interested in traditional jobs. Also there should be amalgamation of both traditional and non-traditional techniques for the betterment of the output wherever necessary.

- Overall developmental careers guidance including class-based practical exercises and project work to increase young people's understanding of the realities of job tasks, pay and the lifestyle.

- Placements could play an important role in students if they are adequately organized and funded to a level where they were able to give meaningful work experience in their interest area.

- Parents should support their children to undergo occupational choice courses and so they need to be provided with better information and support and guidance in order to enable them to help their children make the best possible choices for their futures.

- Advice and guidance to students should include details about the pay, the work-life balance and lifestyles associated with different kinds of jobs.

Chapter Twenty Two

Personal Effectiveness, Psychological Wellbeing and Quality of Work Life[22]

Introduction: A good life is directly connected to well-being and a happy life. Some workers work for more than 60 hours a week. As a result of this, their personal hobbies and interests may clash with their work. Life is a bundle that contains all the strands together and hence the need to balance work life with other related issues. Quality of work life signifies the favorableness or unfavourableness of a job environment for the people working in an organization. The period of scientific management which focused solely on specialization and efficiency, has undergone a revolutionary change. In the present scenario, needs and aspirations of the employees are changing employers are now redesigning jobs for better quality of work life.

Personal effectiveness is the ability to make a positive and energetic impact on to others by conveying ideas and information clearly and pervasively, involves planning prioritizing available means by using interpersonal skills to help build effective working relationships with others and reduce personal stress. It encourages managers to develop self-knowledge and apply this to their behavior, both in relation to their own job performance in the role of leading and managing others. The barriers of personal effectiveness include lack of self-discipline lack of will power, inability to take responsibility for one's destiny, lack of information procrastination and lack of time management skills.

---

[22] **Minnu Thomas, Daya K.S, Keerthana Sivan V.K., Shibymol, C.B.,**
LISSAH, Calicut

Being psychologically well is the simple notion of a person's welfare, happiness, advantages, interests, utility and quality of life. Psychological well-being consists of positive relationship with others, personal mastery, autonomy, a feeling of purpose and meaning in life, and personal growth and development. Psychological well-being is attained by achieving a state of balance affected by both challenging and rewarding life events.

Quality of life is the degree to which a person enjoys the important possibilities of his or her life. It refers to level of happiness or dissatisfaction with one's career or quality of work life refers to then favorableness or unfavorableness of the job environment of an organization for its employees. Factors that play a role in quality of life vary according to personal preference but they often include financial security, job satisfaction, family life, health and safety.

The employees working in a multinational company faces many issues which affect the work life of an employee. Some of them include work place stress, motivation, job satisfaction etc. In this study we measure the personal effectiveness and psychological well-being on quality of work life. By organizing programs and activities that leads to increase the personal effectiveness and psychological well-being to increase the quality of work life of a person. By appointing psychologists in an MNC most of these issues can be solved. A psychologist can directly deal with the problems of employees and can be able to motivate them.

Jain, Shahnawaz, Gupta and Bhatta (2013), had done a study on "Personal Effectiveness of Public Health Management Personnel in South East Asia Region". The result showed that more than three-fourths of the public health management personnel in SEAR were found to be 'high' on openness to receiving feedback followed by three- fifths who have 'high' perceptiveness. However, less than one-half have 'high' self-disclosure. The compositions of the three dimensions of personal effectiveness of all the respondents suggested that about one-fourth were 'effective'. Nearly one-third of the respondents were found to be 'secretive". One out of every ten respondents was found to be "ineffective". Pathak and Srivastava (2011), had done a study on "Variables Affecting Personal Effectiveness: An empirical study on B-School Students". The findings of this study indicate that personal effectiveness among students is closely related to the internal locus of control. Students with internal locus of control were found to be higher on personal effectiveness.

Paul and Amato(1994) conducted a study on "Father-children relations, Mother-child relations, and offspring psychological wellbeing in early adulthood". The results showed that parental divorce weakens the salience of the father-child relationship for adult children's life satisfaction. Similarly, marriage, parenthood and full-time employment diminish the salience of both the mother-child and the father-child relationship for offspring wellbeing.

Armsden and Mark and Greenberg(1987), conducted a study on, "The inventory of parent and peer attachment: Individual differences and their relationship to psychological wellbeing in adolescents". The results showed perceived quality of both parent and peer attachments were significantly related to psychological wellbeing. Adolescents classified as high securely attached reported greater satisfaction with themselves, a higher likelihood of seeking social support, and less symptomatic response to stressful life events.

Payne and Pheysey (1971) in the light of an interesting study conducted on "organizational climate" came to conclusion that job satisfaction is an indicative of positive Quality of Work Life. This was to highlight qualities of employee's work life. Job satisfaction is an indicative of positive quality of working life. Sayeed and Sinha (1981) examined the "Relationship between Quality of Work Life dimensions, job satisfaction and performance". The result revealed that Quality of Work Life dimensions are related to job satisfaction in both the types of organizations. The result indicated that, organization with low Quality of Work Life tended to yield comparatively better relationship between Quality of Work Life dimensions and performance measures than the organization with high Quality of Work Life.

Objectives: The study is focused on identifying relationship between personal effectiveness, psychological wellbeing, work-life balance among employees from MNCs. It also studies the gender differences among these variables.

Methodology: This study used a descriptive research design. Survey and interview method were used for the collection of data. A total of 40 employees in MNCs were selected as the sample of the present study. Among them 20 were males and 20 were females. Random sampling technique was used to draw the sample from the population. The following Instruments were used: Personal effectiveness scale (Pareek (2012). Psychological well-being Ryff scale (1989) WALTON's Quality of work life questionnaire (1975).

The data was collected by survey and interview methods. At first, the investigators randomly selected 40 employees (20 males & 20 females) from different MNCs in Calicut. For the consolidation of the data, inventories provided were scored according to the scoring procedure. Total score of each were taken for the analysis. Karl Pearson correlation was used to find out the relationship between the variables and independent sample t-test was used to compare the groups of the present study.

Results and Discussion

Table.1 shows the *r-value* and level of significance between personal effectiveness and psychological wellbeing among employees.

Variable	r-value	Significance
Personal effectiveness	.169	.298
Psychological wellbeing		

The coefficient of correlation and level of significance between personal effectiveness and psychological wellbeing was found to be .169 and .298 respectively which shows no correlation, which means both the variables are independent each other. One variable doesn't have any influence on the other.

Table. 2 shows the *r-value* and level of significance between personal effectiveness and quality of work life among employees

Variable	r-value	Significance
Personal effectiveness	-.244	.130
Quality of work life		

The coefficient of correlation and level of significance between personal effectiveness and quality of work life was found to be -.244 and .130 respectively, which shows no correlation, which means both the variables are independent each other. One variable doesn't have any influence on the other.

Table. 3 shows the *r-value* and level of significance between psychological wellbeing and quality of work life among employees

variable	r-value	Significance
Psychological wellbeing	-.221	-170
Quality of work life		

The coefficient of correlation and level of significance between psychological wellbeing and quality of work life was found to be -.221 and .170 respectively, which shows no correlation.

From the results of table 1-3 it is clear that the variables under the present study has no influence on others, which means each variables are independent each other. All the three variables, personal effectiveness, psychological wellbeing and quality of work are independent each other.

Table. 4 shows the mean, standard deviation, *t-value and p-value* of personal effectiveness between male and female employees.

Variable	Group	N	Mean	SD	t-value	p-value
	Male	20	34.45	9.43	-.123	.902
Personal effectiveness	Female	20	34.75	5.39		

p>0.05

The mean and standard deviation in personal effectiveness among male was found to be 34.45 and 9.43 respectively. The mean and standard deviation among female was found to be 34.75 and 5.39 respectively. The t- value and p-value of the 2 groups in personal effectiveness was found to be -.123 and 0.902 respectively.

From table. 4 it is clear that personal effectiveness does not differ with the group (male and female) which means both male and female have almost the same level of personal effectiveness. In the present scenario regardless of the gender they are getting equal stress from there authorities when considered their work life. Since both males and females are having equaled burden of work, the level of responsibility also the same. Working hours are assigned regardless of the gender and as a result, they may experience the same level of stress and anxiety. Therefore the present result is relevant.

Table. 5show the mean, standard deviation, *t-value and p-value* of psychological wellbeing between male and female employees.

Variable	Group	N	Mean	Standard deviation	t-value	p-value
Psychological wellbeing	Male	20	72.10	14.11	-.409	.685
	Female	20	73.50	5.96		

The mean and standard deviation in psychological wellbeing among males was found to be 72.10 and 14.11 respectively. The mean and standard deviation in psychological wellbeing among female was found to be 73.50 and 5.96 respectively. The t-value and p-value of the 2 groups in psychological wellbeing was found to be -.409 and .685 respectively.

From table 5 it is clear that psychological wellbeing does not differ with in the group (male and female) which means both male and female have almost the same level of psychological wellbeing. In the present scenario the work stress as well as all other burdens are equally shared and affect both male and females similarly, hence the psychological problems which they face are also equal.

Table. 6 show the mean, standard deviation, *t-value and p-value* of quality of work life between male and female employees.

variable	group	N	Mean	Standard deviation	t-value	p-value
Quality of Work life	Male	20	123.20	31.806	-.007	.995
	Female	20	123.25	10.06		

The mean and standard deviation in quality of work life among males was found to be 123.20 and 31.806 respectively. The mean and standard deviation in quality of work life among female was found to be 123.25 and 10.06 respectively. The t-value and p-value of the 2 groups in quality of work life was found to be -.007 and .995 respectively. From table 6 it is clear that quality of work life does not differ with in the group (male and female), which means both male and female have almost the same level of quality of work life. Both men and women seem creative enough now a day, because both gets equal exposure to all life aspects.

Table. 7 shows the mean and standard deviations obtained by the two groups on the variables under the study

variables	groups	N	Mean	SD
Personal effectiveness		20	34.75	5.39
Psychological wellbeing		20	73.50	55.96
Quality of work life	Male	20	123.25	10.06
Personal effectiveness		20	34.45	9.43
Psychological wellbeing	Female	20	72.10	14.11
Quality of work life		20	123.20	31.80

The mean and standard deviation of personal effectiveness was found to be 34.75 and 5.39 in males and 34.45 and 9.43 in females respectively. The mean and standard deviation of psychological wellbeing was found to be 73.50 and 55.96 in males and 72.10 and 14.11 in females respectively. The mean and standard deviation of quality of work life was found to be 123.25 and 10.06 in males and 123.20 and 31.80 in females respectively. From the table it is clear that the groups didn't show much difference in the in their personal effectiveness, psychological wellbeing and quality of work life.

Conclusion: In the present study we conclude that there is no relation between personal effectiveness, psychological wellbeing and quality of work life. And the result showed that personal effectiveness, psychological wellbeing and quality of work life does not differ with respect to the group. The men and women possess equal level of personal effectiveness, psychological wellbeing and quality of work life.

Chapter Twenty Three

Visual Media's Portrayal of Suicide: Counsellor's Perspective[23]

Introduction: Suicide is the act of taking one's own life voluntarily and intentionally, most often as a result of depression or other mental illness. Suicidal ideation or suicidal thoughts means thinking about or planning suicide. These thoughts can range from a detailed plan to a fleeting considerations. In most of the cases, these are temporary and can be treated, but in some cases, they place the individual at risk for attempting or completing suicide (Nordqvist, 2018). More than one lakh lives are lost every year due to suicide in India. In the last three decades (from 1975 to 2005), the suicide rate increased by 43%. Majority of suicide (37.8%) in India are by those below the age of 30 years imposes a huge social, emotional and economic burden on society (VijayKumar, 2008). The current study is based on how these media portrayal of suicide can influence people. The current study focused on the series called '13 reasons why', which was a very popular show in the Netflix. Evidences show that the rate of suicide has increased after the streaming of the show. The current study is based on how the portrayal of suicide in media can influence people to take drastic steps. In order to tap into that aspect, this study focused on interviewing Bangalore-based practising counselling psychologists, clinical psychologists and psychotherapists who deal with suicide and depression in their clients to find out their perspective on the series '13 Reasons Why'. Series like this

---

[23] **Zeina Sravya Ahmed, Deepthi M. Pandit, Minee Jha**, Student, Jain University
Guneet Inder Jit Kaur, Ph.D., Asst. Professor, Jain University

could be very damaging and scarring for those who are battling mental illness on a daily basis.

Media is one of the most powerful and important resource for the communication. The role of media is becoming increasingly relevant. Social media are web-based communication tools that enable people to interact with each other by both sharing and consuming information. Social media is becoming an integral part of life online as social websites and applications proliferate. Everything looks and feels easier to do with social media. It plays a vital role in broadening social connections and learning technical skills. Media is being used in ways that shape politics, business, world culture, education, careers, innovation and more. Media today has a huge influence on people. Be it television, computers, video games, social networking sites, it hugely impacts all aspects of a person's life. It has revolutionized the way people view themselves, the way they see others, communicate and socialize on the web. There are countless exciting improvements in technology and social media have greatly increased communication across cultures and positively brought attention to events around the world. It also allows for self-expression and can serve as a creative outlet for individuals to express themselves, share their art work and share their voice on specific topics. So it has become a great outlet for global organization to bring awareness to the causes they support. The following review of literature also highlights its far reaching impact.

A study by Sisask and Värnik (2012) researched the role of media in suicide prevention. The study focused on possible effects of media reporting on suicidal behaviours, which might impact actual suicidality (completed suicides, attempted suicides, suicidal ideation). They found that extent of suicide portrayal in films and television can create misunderstanding and mislead people who are watching it and may lead them to take risky steps in future. In a research conducted by Collings et al. (2011)on the negative influences of media on suicidal behaviour, interviews of young people in New Zealand were conducted. The study investigated the issues related to certain types of media reports and portrayals of suicide and self-harm that might increase the risk of suicidal behaviours in vulnerable people, especially young people.

In a research conducted by Pirkis and Blood (2010),a critical review of suicide and entertainment media was done. The review of studies was based on entertainment media which included music, film, television and plays across various databases from their respective years of inception to January 2010. The articles contained elements like suicide, imitation media which included films, television, music and plays. The results of the study indicated that (a) most of the studies highlighted an evidence of a relation existing between the portrayal of suicide on television/films and suicidal behaviour in reality, thereby proving that the media may enforce an influence which is negative (b) with regard to music, an association between suicidal behaviour in reality and its depiction in songs was evidenced by two third of the studies, thus reinforcing the fact that musical genres can also have an impact (c) one study found that the fictional portrayal of suicide had no negative impact in terms of level of depression or potential to commit suicide. Henceforth, it is ascertained that imitation could be enhanced through the depiction of the act of suicide by the media. As such depictions are widespread, it often reinforces the message of suicide as a course of action, often due to the graphic footage regarding the method which appeals to the naïve audience.

Objectives: The aim of the study was to get an in-depth understanding of counselors' perspectives on media's portrayal of suicide with respect to 13 Reasons Why. A qualitative research design was adopted to gain a deeper understanding regarding this particular topic and also to explore the various perspectives of counsellors. The current study was exploratory in nature which helps in understanding the perception of the counsellors about the media's portrayal of suicide.

Methodology: Purposive sampling method was adopted and five counsellors were chosen for the study. Socio-demographic details of the participants included their age, gender, marital status and years of experience. This was explained using descriptive statistics. A semi-structured interview was scheduled and interviews were conducted after taking informed consent. The interviews were audio recorded, transcribed and thematically analysed to code domains, themes and subthemes.

Results and Discussion: The socio demographic details were descriptively analysed. Out of five participants, 1 was male and 5 were female; 3 were within the age group of 35-40 years and 2 were within the age group of 41-46 years; 1 was unmarried and 4 were married and 3 had 6-10 years of experience and 2 had 11-15 years of experience. The data was also transcribed and domains were delineated using the method of Thematic Analysis.

Table 1. Explaining the domain of Portrayal of mental illness and suicide in media

Themes	Sub-themes
Media plays a vital role	Individual perspectives
	Vulnerability
	Triggering factor
	Creating awareness
	Drives thoughts and actions
Not media, but the system	Media is just a process
Sensationalizing suicide	Portraying it as a trend

According to the participants, media's portrayal of suicide plays a vital role in understanding mental illness and suicidal behaviours. Individual's thoughts and actions are driven by the content shown in the TV series. However, individual differences exist.

According to the study by Collings et. al, (2011)forty-nine participants had been exposed to suicide and self-harm themes via music and music videos. While some felt it had nil or minimal impact, or was a "release" for distressing feelings, a small number recognized some music as "trigger songs", which led them to self-harm. This shows that individuals interpret sensitive content in various ways. Since today's generation has access to everything online and offline (television), they are prone to getting influenced by the content portrayed.

Table 2. Explaining the domain of Family dynamics and parenting

Themes	Sub-themes
Parenting is an influence	Overindulgent parent Openness to talk Different roles Suicide is a taboo in parenting system
Emotional Intelligence	
Interaction among family members is an influence	Sibling interaction Family interpretation

The participants reported that parenting plays a vital role. The choice of parenting style is what influences the way an individual perceives suicide. One of the participants revealed that over-indulgent parent style leads to suffocation and intrusion into personal space of the individual since their early years. In order to free themselves from this suffocation and intrusion, certain individuals are prone to attempting suicide.

A study undertaken by University of Cincinnati (2017) indicated that the parents not engaging in behaviours evidencing their care for their children had a significant impact on the young children, especially in the age range of 12 to 17 years and it made them vulnerable to envisage, plan and attempt the act of suicide.

The results of this study further highlighted that the age group most at risk of this impact were the 12 and 13 year olds. This age group children were found to be five times more likely to have thoughts that were suicidal and seven times more likely to think of a plan for suicide and attempt it because of the cold behavior of their parents.

Table 3. Explains the domain of Role of Community

Themes	Sub-themes
Shaping of an individual	Impact on self-esteem
	Skills and competency
Individual's willingness for support	
Taboo topic to talk	
Social evils	Dowry
	Monetary failure

Sisask and Värnik (2012), said that media is a significant agent in social construction of reality, especially for vulnerable persons. Participants revealed that constant criticism about one's traits and appearance has an adverse effect on one's self concept which in turn affects their self-confidence and motivation to work towards self-growth. However, one participant reported that certain individuals use the community as a support system to shape their skills and grow. One participant said that suicide is considered a cry for help, and as such we seek to shine the light of day on the issue, reducing the stigmatic shadow that hovers over a possible path to recovery. Stack (1993), in his research, specified that the media played an imperative role in influencing suicides, especially the way media covered the incidents of suicide.

Table 4. Explains the domain of Susceptibility

Themes	Sub-themes
Personality	Isolated individuals
	Overachievers
	Extreme emotions
Age	Adolescents and teens
	Not age specific
Gender	Men after 30
	Competing not complementing
	Not gender specific
Chronic Illness	
Circumstantial	No specific criteria

The participants stated that certain personality traits such as need for over-achievement and isolation are susceptible to having suicidal ideations. It was reported that over-achievers are highly critical of themselves and strive for perfectionism and success every single time. When they fail to achieve their set goals and standards, they get very stressed and frustrated about it. A study by Collings et. al (2011) said that there was no association between age of first learning about suicidal behaviours and type of information source.

A study by Sisask and Värnik (2012), suggested that a strong modeling effect of media coverage on suicide is based on age and gender. Stack (2005),reported that copycat effect was more likely reported for celebrity suicides and female suicides.

Hagihara, Tarumi and Abe (2007), suggested that newspaper articles about suicide were a predictor of suicide for both male and female subjects. Medical illnesses and chronic illness are also a criteria for individuals to be susceptible to suicidal ideation. One of the participants reported that individuals who suffer from chronic illnesses choose to end their lives due to poor coping strategies. But, media chooses to report about only certain issues related to suicide, such as, love failure and failure in examinations. Other reasons for committing suicide was reported to be circumstantial.

Table 5. Explaining the domain of Interventions Adopted

Themes	Sub-themes
Emotional first-aid	Observing signs and signals Postponement of the event Ignore the action Listening
Cognitive Behavioural Therapy (CBT)	
Case specific	Upbringing

According to the subjects, the first step to any intervention method is to provide the client with emotional first-aid. All the participants reported that all the clients who are susceptible to suicide display certain signs and signals in different forms such are verbal or behavioral.

 The role of the parents and community is to observe and identify these signs and provide them with proper help. Once the client is with the counsellor, the role of the counsellor is not to prevent the event, but to postpone it by concentrating on the feeling and not the action. One of the subjects revealed that allowing the client to talk and not intervene in between would help them cope better.

It was also reported that Cognitive-Behavioral Therapy (CBT) is used with clients who have severe suicidal ideations. However, it was reported that the intervention plan would be made based on the case.

Adams, Overholser, and Spirito (1994), upheld that the way the family functions is very vital in the functioning of the adolescents and should be taken into consideration while they are being treated and assessed for the suicidal behviour.

Table 6. Explaining the domain of Prospective changes to be made in media's portrayal

Themes	Sub-themes
Creating Awareness	
Positive showcasing	End on a positive note Stop celebrating suicide
Cease of hyping suicide	

All the participants reported that media should act as a forum to create awareness about mental illness and suicide as this would reach out to the larger population. It was reported that shows and movies dealing with sensitive issues such as suicide must end on a positive and hopeful note such as concentrating on coping skills that could help the vulnerable individual watching. Etzersdorfer Voracek and Sonneck (2004), said that after changing the quality of media reporting the number of suicides and suicide attempts decreased.

According to a study done by Niederkrotenthaleret al. (2010) mentioned coverage on positive coping in adverse circumstances as covered in media items about suicidal ideation may have protective effect and decrease suicide rates. The participants also mentioned that media should be sensitive while reporting issues such as suicide and not celebrate or sensationalize it. Sudak and Sudak (2005), conducted a study and found that when the media dramatically or romantically portrayed the deaths due to suicide, the number increased of suicides and also this caused the people/audience to engage in self-harming actions and also to attempt suicide. Thus, the media needs to be sensitive regarding how the reporting is done on this issue so that such steps can be curtailed.

A study by Sisask and Värnik (2012), mentioned that irresponsible media reports can provoke suicidal behaviours and less about protective effect media can have adverse effects. They also said that media reports are not representative of official suicide data and tend to exaggerate sensational suicides, for example dramatic and highly lethal suicide methods, which are rare in real life. Bollen and Phillips (1982), reported that suicides increased shortly after a publicized suicide story. Sisask and Varnik (2012), reported that mass media imitation theory presumes that if modelling works in one way (copycat suicides), it can work also on the other way (positive model) and hence it is the responsibility of the media to help battle and tackle such sensitive issues.

Conclusion: According to the participants, media's portrayal of suicide plays a vital role in understanding mental illness and suicidal behaviours. Individual's thoughts and actions are driven by the content shown in the TV series. However, individual differences exist. The participants also reported that family dynamics and parenting styles also influence the way the individual interprets and understands suicide. The participants reported that the community has its own role in shaping the individual with respect to self-esteem and skill development. According to the participants, certain personality types, ages, genders and people with chronic illnesses are the most susceptible to suicidal ideations. But, it was also reported that suicide is not age or gender specific, but circumstantial. The participants reported that the first step to any treatment is to talk about it. Most participants reported that they use CBT (full form has to be mentioned, only then abbreviation can be used) in the case of severe suicidal ideations. But, every treatment adopted is case specific. According to the participants, media needs to change the way they portray sensitive topics to the public. This includes creating awareness, promoting positivity in the content related to mental illness and suicide and also not sensationalizing the event.

Chapter Twenty Four

Mindfulness and Happiness[24]

Introduction: "Mindfulness is the psychological process of bringing one's attention to the internal and external experiences occurring in the present moment, which can be developed through the practice of meditation and other training" (Kabat-Zinn, 1994). Mindfulness, described by Kabat-Zinn (2003), is 'paying attention in a particular way: on purpose, in the present moment, and non-judgmentally', which involves consciously attending to one's moment-to-moment experience (Brown & Ryan, 2003).

Happiness is a mental or emotional state of well-being defined by positive or pleasant emotions ranging from contentment to intense joy. Happy mental states may also reflect judgements by a person about their overall well-being. Happiness in this sense was used to translate the Greek eudaimonia, and is still used in virtue ethics. There has been a transition over time from emphasis on the happiness of virtue to the virtue of happiness (McMahan, Darrin, 2004). Since the turn of the millennium, the human flourishing approach, advanced particularly by Amartya Sen has attracted increasing interest in psychological, especially prominent in the work of Martin Seligman.

---

[24] **R. Vignesh** & **S.S. Srinithi,** Asst. Professor, Manonmaniam Sundaranar University

A study examined relationships between mindfulness and indices of happiness and explored a five-factor model of mindfulness. Results show that mindfulness is related to psychologically adaptive variables and that self-compassion is a crucial attitudinal factor in the mindfulness–happiness relationship (Hollis and Colosimo, 2011). In another study meditation and happiness supported the model of mindfulness and self-compassion facets as partial mediators of the meditation–happiness relationship. Findings are in line with other studies and provide evidence about the influence of mindfulness and self-compassion on happiness (Daniel et al., 2016). A quasi experimental study determines the effect of mindfulness practice on level of stress, happiness, and its usage in daily living. The level of the stress was significantly reduced after practicing mindfulness while the level of happiness was increased but not at significant level. The participants showed improvement in emotional quotient and mental health.

Objectives: The research study is to explore the relationship between mindfulness and happiness. The specific objectives are as follows:

- To examine the relationship between mindfulness and happiness of university students.

- To compare the mindfulness of university students on the basis of gender, location of residence, type of family.

Methodology: For the purpose of the present study 114 students aged between 20 and 26 (mean age = 22) from various departments of the Periyar University were used selected using convenient sampling technique. The following tools have been used to collect data. Mindfulness Attention Awareness Scale (MAAS) by Brown & Ryan (2003). The Oxford Happiness Questionnaire by Hills & Argyle (2001).

The investigator visited different department, established rapport with the participants and administered questionnaires after giving necessary instruction. Confidentiality of responses was assured. The collected data were scored as per the respective scoring keys. The collected data was tabulated and analysed. The data analysis was carried out for different levels of association and interaction. The data were analysed using SPSS 21 version. Major statistical techniques used for the analysis of data were as follows:

- Descriptive statistics were calculated for the data to identify group and total mean for each demographic variable.

- Karl Pearson coefficient correlations were also conducted to assess the relationship between variables of interest.

- 't'- test were also conducted to assess the significant difference between two groups.

Results and Discussion

Hypothesis 1: There would be significant relationship between mindfulness and happiness among university students.

Table 1: Correlation between Mindfulness and Happiness among university students

	Happiness
Mindfulness	0.425**

**Significant p<0.05

In order to test the hypothesis 1, Pearson correlation has been applied. From table 1, it can be understand that the variables mindfulness and happiness are significantly correlated with each other at 95% of confidence. It suggests that mindfulness and happiness are highly related constructs. Students high in mindfulness are likely to be in happiness. Hence, the hypothesis 1 is accepted.

Hypothesis 2: There would be significant gender difference in mindfulness.

Table 2: Gender difference in mindfulness

Variable	Male (N=41)		Female (N=73)		"t"-value
	M_1	SD_1	M_2	SD_2	
Mindfulness	56.36	14.56	60.78	11.24	1.68[NS]

Note: NS – Not Significant.

The table 2 indicates that no gender difference in mindfulness. Hence, the hypothesis 2 is not accepted.

Hypothesis 3: There would be significant difference in mindfulness based on their type of family.

Table 3: Difference in mindfulness among university students based on family Type

Variable	Nuclear (N=85)		Joint (N=29)		"t"-value
	M_1	SD_1	M_2	SD_2	
Mindfulness	59.36	12.74	58.69	12.59	0.29[NS]

From the table 3 it reveals that there is no significant difference in mindfulness between the nuclear and joint family. This indicates that the nuclear or joint family does not vary with mindfulness. Hence, the hypothesis 3 is not accepted.

Hypothesis 4:   There would be significant gender difference in happiness

Table 4: Gender difference in happiness

Variable	Male (N=41)		Female (N=73)		"t"-value
	M_1	SD_1	M_2	SD_2	
Happiness	109.44	16.42	123.40	16.25	4.37**

From table 4 it has been understood that there is a significant gender difference in happiness found at 95% of confidence. This indicates that female students are happier than male students. Hence, the hypothesis 4 is accepted.

Hypothesis 5: There would be significant difference in happiness based on their Family type.

Table 5: Difference in Happiness among university students based on Family Type

Variable	Nuclear (N=85)		Joint (N=29)		"t"-value
	M_1	SD_1	M_2	SD_2	
Happiness	119.54	17.28	114.97	18.28	1.21^{NS}

The table 5 indicates that there is no significant difference in happiness between the nuclear and joint family among university students. Hence, the hypothesis 5 is not accepted.

Conclusion: The study reveals that the variables mindfulness and happiness are significantly correlated with each other at 95% of confidence. It suggests that mindfulness and happiness are highly related constructs among university post graduates. The study indicates that the female post graduates are more mindful and female post graduates are happier than male post graduates. Students belongs to nuclear family are found to be happy.

𝔠𝔥𝔞𝔭𝔱𝔢𝔯 𝔗𝔴𝔢𝔫𝔱𝔶 𝔉𝔦𝔳𝔢

Marriage, Family, Women and Mental Health[25]

Introduction: The changes in modern marriage and family life have been defined, classified and explained in many ways. In his cyclic theory of Carle Zimmerman, traced the life cycle of family systems throughout the history of western civilization. He described a regular pattern or movement from the "trustee family" in which all individual rights are subordinated to the welfare of the family group to the "domestic family" in which family control is weakened although family remains essentially a strong unit. From the domestic family there is predictable movement to the "atomistic family" in which familism replaced by individual. The atomistic family is both the cause and effect of decay in social life (Richard, 1970). Families and other relationships sometimes buffer the mental health challenges faced by individual during their life time. However, for many people families can be a source of anxiety and stress. As an example, men and women going through marital problems are especially vulnerable to the effects of relationship conflict. They may suffer from emotional consequences such as depression, and can have a compromised immune function leading to an increased rate of physical illness (Ada and Jan, 2004). This paper looks at the issue of marriage, family, women and mental health related issues that affect our life today.

Marriage: Marriage means a lifelong emotional and legal commitment to another

---

[25] **Eashwari Vadlamudi, Ph.D.,** Asst. Professor, St. Francis College for Women, Hyderabad

147

individual. Some form of marriage has been present in all cultures and most societies have considered marriage necessary for satisfying adult life. Family or tribal relationships and economic considerations quite often take precedence over individual wishes. Some marriages result in lifelong loving relationships while others lapse into marriages of convenience and for procreation. Monogamy, the marriage of one man with one woman, is the common form of marriage in the western world. Polygyny, the union of one man and several wives, is practiced in some African tribes and Islamic cultures.

A 1980's statistical projection predicted that four out of 10 marriages of the 1970's would end in divorce. Marriage has undergone great stress and strain in the last 30 years. Traditional marriage became a subject that aroused feelings of rebellion and disdain in the late 1960's and 1970's as divorce became more common and socially acceptable and pre-marital sex became more common (Ada and Jan, 2004).

Women and Family: The functions of women in society that traditionally were home making and child rearing were expanded in the later 20th century to include increasing population in business, the military, government and other fields previously considered men's fields. The change in women's role has led in many cases to stress for women and men in their lives as competition between the sexes increases, jealousies over being the provider in the family occur and males feel an increasing loss of power and control over women in their personal or professional lives (Ada and Jan, 2004).

George R. Parkerson and colleagues at Duke university medical center reported in the Archives of family medicine (1995) that individuals who see themselves as enduring high family stress are likely to have greater health problem than those reporting low (Ada and Jan, 2004).

Family violence happens in all strata of society and there are many more cases than official records indicate because it is a subject often covered up out of fear and shame. Characteristics of persons who are victims of family violence include anxiety, powerlessness, guilt and lack of self-esteem. According to Paulette Trumm, women who are abused by their husbands or by friends not sustain injuries from physical beatings, but they also suffer from many mental and emotional scars, including post-traumatic stress disorder, depression and anxiety. In most cases women suffer from low self-esteem; the healing process takes a long time. Majority of women who seek help from family violence are between the age of 20 and 60. In 75 per cent of households in which abuse take place, the husband or boyfriend is an alcoholic or on drugs (Ada and Jan, 2004).

In 1995, more than 24,000 complaints were filed with the Crime Against Women Cell, in Delhi, relating to marital disputes ranging from cruelty to misappropriation of stridhan. The situation continues to decline further. The latest reports indicate that crime against women rate is 34.1% in Delhi and also that it has the highest dowry death rate in the country (Delhi, 1997).

 It has recently been recognized by the United Nations (1995) as a fundamental abuse of women's human rights. It lists under the category of gender based violence, abuses such as battering, sexual abuse of female children, dowry related violence, marital rape, and female genital mutilation. Female infanticide is still common in some pockets of the country. In recent years, new forms of violence have been added to the list. Most important among these are dowry deaths and female feticide (United Nations, 1995).

From a theoretical angle, Khatri (1970) maintained that the family environment of a Hindu male from childhood to adulthood developed in him trust, security, a capacity to give and receive affection and positive self-image. The male child was also likely to develop few intra and interpersonal conflicts because of his acceptance of roles assigned to him by the family and predictability of his environment; in short, child rearing practices are conducive to positive mental health. In female children, with differential treatment and open favoritism towards males, the ground is laid for the development of negative self-image, jealousy and the perception of the world as basically unfair. Khatri considered the female child to be at risk for several mental health problems (Malavika Kapur, 1940).

Families, like individuals, tend to behave the way they are expected to behave in the sub cultural group in which they exist. Especially when under stress, families often take refuge in the rituals and customs that sustained their value system in the past, even if they gave little attention to those rituals and customs in no crisis periods. This is especially true of religious ritual, but it is also true of community customs and social usage. In a family facing crisis, the conditioned expectations of the partners are often heightened. Each partner becomes even more sensitive and more critical of the role behavior of the other. When under stress, family members can become devastingly explicit in their accusations of how the other has failed to meet expectations (Richard, 1970).

Rural Vs Urban families: Mohan and Singh (1985) studied mental adjustment of rural and urban couples in relation to their personality in terms of extroversion, neuroticism, and psychotism. The analysis showed that rural couples were better adjusted than urban. Kumar and Rohtagi (1984) studied the dominance need of spouses and also attempted to identify personality factors such as intelligence and extroversion with reference to adjustment in marriage. It was found that husbands with high adjustment possessed a higher need of dominance, whereas wives with high adjustment were submissive. It was found also that couples with high adjustment were more intelligent, possessed high extroversive interest as compared to couples showing low adjustment. Kumar and Rohtagi (1985) examined the relationship of anxiety, neuroticism and security variables with adjustment in marriage and showed that anxiety affects one's adjustment in marriage.

Family life and Mental Health: Savita Malhotra and Ruchitha Shah (2015) conducted a study on women and mental health in India, an overview. Gender is a critical determinant of mental health and mental illness. The patterns of psychological distress and psychiatric disorder among women are different from those seen among men. Women have a higher mean level of internalizing disorders while men show a higher mean level of externalizing disorders. Gender differences occur particularly in the rates of common mental disorders wherein women predominate. Differences between genders have been reported in the age of onset of symptoms, clinical features, frequency of psychotic symptoms, course, social adjustment, and long-term outcome of severe mental disorders. Women who abuse alcohol or drugs are more likely to attribute their drinking to a traumatic event or a stressor and are more likely to have been sexually or physically abused than other women. Girls from nuclear families and women married at a very young age are at a higher risk for attempted suicide and self-harm. Social factors and gender specific factors determine the prevalence and course of mental disorders in female sufferers. Low attendance in hospital settings is partly explained by the lack of availability of resources for women. Around two-thirds of married women in India were victims of domestic violence. Concerted efforts at social, political, economic, and legal levels can bring change in the lives of Indian women and contribute to the improvement of the mental health of these women.

In a study by Dudhathra and Jogsan, 2012 there was a significant difference in mental health among working and nonworking women. Results indicate the non-working women have better mental health as compared working women.

India Today survey shows us that 79.3% men believe that marital rape is okay. Despite the fact that marital rape receives little public and scholarly attention, it is one of the most serious forms of violence. In a study it was indicated that women who are raped by their husbands are likely to experience assaults and often suffer from long-term physical and emotional consequences . The experience of being raped can also lead to suicidal tendencies, depression, post-traumatic stress disorder, anxiety, poor self-esteem, neurosis, chronic pain, odd sexual behaviour and substance abuse disorder (Juhi Vajpayee and Kritika Makkar 2014).

Mental health is a combination of emotional well-being (defined as the presence of positive affect and satisfaction with life and absence of negative affect), social well-being (incorporating acceptance, actualization, contribution, coherence and integration), and psychological well- being (combining self-acceptance, personal growth, purpose in life, environmental mystery, autonomy, positive relation with others) (Snyder and Lopez, 2006).

The study of insecure attachment, lost love, and failed relationships has produced significant findings that are relevant to our lives. Indeed, relationship researchers have been successful in uncovering what does not work and have attempted to teach people how to correct their relationship problems. Nevertheless, most would agree that we all struggle with identifying the right things to do in relationships. The positive psychology of close relationships include the knowledge that secure attachment and love are prerequisites for healthy relationships and incorporates a focus on appetitive processes (Snyder and Lopez, 2006).

Families meet crises more successfully and recover from them more quickly when relatives, friends, and neighbors are available to support them. In his war-separation study, Reuben Hill found that the families who were slowest to adjust to the separation were often solitary families who had moved often and to great distances from their relatives. Stating it more positively, one study concluded that, "when the doors and kitchens of the neighbors are open to almost everyone, the long-term impact of stress may be resolved. Contemporary patterns of mobile and suburban living have many advantages, including new experience, greater self-reliance, and more independence from in-laws, relatives and inquisitive neighbors. But there are disadvantages, too, and one of these is the loss of comfort and support from people who really care in time of crises (Richard, 1970).

Family theorists and marriage counselors generally agree that the family that is well organized, has defined goals, and is steadily working towards them is more likely to be successful than the family that has no purposeful direction (such goals as "good family life", a "college education for the children"). The fact that many family members no longer have some of the goal satisfactions that families used to have may be, one important reason for today's high rate of marriage difficulty. Just producing enough to keep family members alive was an important and satisfying goal for a husband in 1930s. These goals, however, derived from the necessities of living and did not have to be chosen in the same sense that family goals are chosen today.

In the present affluent society, short-range, pleasure-oriented goals are probably more easily attainable than at any time before (Richard, 1970).

1. Realize that enduring happiness doesn't come from success
2. Take control of your time
3. Act happy
4. Seek work and leisure that engage your skills
5. Follow healthy life style
6. Give your body the sleep it wants
7. Give priority to close relationships
8. Focus beyond self
9. Keep a gratitude journal
10. Nurture your spiritual self *(Snyder and Lopez, 2006)*.

Conclusion: A number of changes has been observed in the patterns of marriage and family. Family system is suffering with marital disharmony, women and elderly abuse leading to severe mental health problems. Divorce rates are the testimony for increasing husband-wife relationship conflict. Mental illness symptoms get bigger among women disrupting the family life as women is considered as backbone of the family. Understanding and practicing positive mental health is the basic necessity for the families to lead happy life.

Chapter Twenty Six

Stressors of Parents with Special Children[26]

Introduction: Stress can be defined as "any uncomfortable emotional experience accompanied by predictable biochemical, physiological and behavioural changes" (Baum, 1990). The causes of chronic stress may be a bad marriage, abusive relationships, traumatic childhood memories or taking care of a disabled child / relative (Miller, Rothstein & Smith, 1994). When parents hear that their child would no longer be developing like a typically developing child, they would definitely experience stress(Murphy, Christian, Caplin, & Young, 2011). According to Felizardo, Ribeiro and Amante (2016), the following are some of the top sources of stress as reported by parents of children with Autism spectrum disorders (ASD): Inappropriate and unpredictable behaviour of the child, education and learning, child's friendships and interactions with other children, meeting the needs of other family members, lack of and/or delay of acquiring basic developmental skills in the child, attaining the necessary support services for the child, speech and language development in the child, disruption of home life and environment, dietary restrictions on the child, understanding the child's emotional needs, finances and transport.

The review of literature showes that the experience of stress is felt differently by

---

[26] **Nausheen Hussain,** Research Scholar, Jain University
Madhurini Vallikad, Ph.D., Asst. Professor, Research Scholar, Jain University

different people even though they may be in similar situations. The parent in this case is not only a caregiver but also a therapist and a companion for the child with ASD. If the parent is stressed and suffering from emotional maladies, the parent may not be in a best position to address the concerns of the child. Understanding individual parental stressors and addressing it could lead to better child management skills in these parents. This is why it becomes important for professionals working with these children, to understand the various stressors faced by parents and help them in resolving or addressing it. Stressors in parents of children who have been given a recent of diagnosis of ASD and stressors of parents whose children are older and time has passed since the diagnosis of ASD are very different and there is a lacuna of research in this subject.

The review of existing literature indicated a lack of studies which dealt with stressors in parents whose children were recently given a diagnosis and comparing these stressors with that of parents where time has gone by after the diagnosis. Hence, the present study undertook two groups – Group A(consisting of parents whose children have been given a recent diagnosis of less than 6 months) and Group B (consisting of parents who have children in the age group of 12 to 18 years or who were in the process of being trained in vocational skills).

Objectives: This study was designed to explore the different causes of stress in parents of children with autism in the Indian context. A qualitative research was thus designed and utilized. This research design was used to develop an in-depth understanding of the phenomenon of interest. It required the researcher to establish rapport with the participants, conduct interviews, and then through theoretical reflection to address the research problem. The aim of the study was to explore the stressors in parents of children with autism spectrum disorders. To explore stressors in parents of children who have been diagnosed with ASD.

Methodology: Purposive sampling technique was used by the researcher in order to select the respondents for this study. A sample of twelve parents which included six mothers and six fathers were recruited for the study after obtaining informed consent. Six parents; of whom 3 were mothers and 3 were fathers (group A) and six parents of whom 3 were mothers and 3 were fathers (group B). The tools were administered to the participants and the interviews were audio recorded for analysis.

Socio demographic data was analysed using descriptive statistics. The interview conducted on the participants was transcribed. The data obtained in the semi structured interview was analysed using thematic analysis. Based on the objectives, the data from the semi structured interview was coded into domains, themes and sub themes. Thematic analysis was used by the researcher to review and sort the data into categories. This helped the researcher to analyse a broad areas as well as to identify patterns as well as unique experiences.

Results and Discussion: Group A consisted of six participants, in the age range of 28 to 41 years. The mean age of the participants was 33 years. Group B consisted of six participants, whose children had a diagnosis of autism spectrum disorders and were in the age group of twelve to eighteen years. The participants were in the age range of 33 to 50 years. The mean age of the participants was 44 years. In both groups, all the participants were married. One participant in each group had only one child, all the other participants had two children.

Children of the participants in group A were in the age group of 2.6 to 4.3 years, their mean age being 3.35 years. All of them were boys and the average age at diagnosis was 3 years. Children of the participants in group B were in the age group of 13 to 17 years, their mean age being 14.5 years. All of them were boys, and the average age at their diagnosis was 2.6 years.

The objective of the study based on the thematic analysis was to explore stressors in parents. On further analysis, themes and sub themes which emerged from this domain in the two groups were: a) maladaptive behaviours in the child, b) future of the child, c) therapy and therapists, d) family dynamics, e) finances and f) impact of diagnosis.

Table 1: Comparing Group A and Group B in the Domain Stressors, Theme - Maladaptive Behaviours(N=12)

Sl.No.	Theme / Sub Theme	Group A	Group B
1	Tantrums	2	1
2	Self injury		1
3	Injury to Others		1
4	Social behaviours	2	
5	Repetitive behaviours	1	
6	Obsessive behaviours	1	1
7	Unresponsiveness	2	
8	Hyperactivity	4	2
9	Lack of appropriate play	1	
10	Interest in opposite gender		2

The sub-themes that emerged were tantrums, self injury, injury to others, obsessive behavior and hyperactivity. Tantrums, obsessive behaviours and hyperactivity were seen in both groups and were seen as stressors by parents especially in social settings.

In the older age group, inappropriate behaviours towards the opposite gender were a cause of concern to parents, which led to parents isolating themselves from social settings.

Self injury and injury to others is a behaviour which is often seen in the spectrum even at a younger age. However in this study these behaviours were not reported in the group with younger children. It may be inferred that the children have not exhibited this behaviour, but it could also be speculated that at this stage parents have not reported it as they are still coming to terms with the diagnosis.

Many studies (Felizardo et al., 2016; Cerezuela et al., 2015; Hayes & Watson, 2013)have found that symptom severity of ASD to be one of the major stressors in parents. It was seen that parental stress increased as a direct consequence to severity in behavior problems displayed by the child. Increase in parental stress was attributed to difficulties arising from handling the child's behavior to changes in routines, situations and social settings. Studies by Felizardo et al., 2016, Cerezuela et al., 2015 and Goldberg, 2014 have reported increased parental stress in parents of children with ASD when compared to parents of children with other developmental disabilities. The basis was behavioral factors in child like hyperactivity and lack of social skills, lack of communication skills and their inherent lack of socialization even with their own parents.

Table 2: Comparing Group A and Group B in the Domain Stressors, Theme –Future Plans (N=12)

Sl.No.	Theme / Sub-Theme	Group A	Group B
1	Academics	2	
2	Unable to fit into conventional settings	2	
3	Living Arrangements- Sibling	2	
4	Living Arrangements- Undecided	4	1
5	Vocational Concerns		5
6	Living Arrangements- Concern		5

In Group A, most of the parents reported that they were not sure where to enroll their child for academics. This was a contrast to Group B parents whose children were already enrolled in special schools and their desire for their child to be trained in a vocation, even though they were not entirely aware of the options available to their child. In a study done in India by Desai et al., 2012, it was observed that in the early stages of diagnosis, even though parents were concerned about the child's fate and place in society, the future seemed distant and uncertain. The implications of autism in the life of the child were still hazy for many parents. In the current study it was observed that the future living arrangements of the child was a major area of concern for most of the parents in Group B. The major parental concerns as reported by Bashir, Khurshid and Qadri (2014) were: financial constraints, social stigma and concern about the child's future. Further, the study showed that more than half of the parents in the study perceived their child's disability as affecting their daily life and they had a second child just so that there could be a caretaker for the child with autism.

Table 3: Comparing Group A and Group B in the Domain Stressors, Theme – Therapies / Therapists (N=12)

Sl.No.	Theme / Sub-Theme	Group A	Group B
1	Finance	4	2
2	Problem with therapists	1	
3	Perceived lacuna	1	2
4	Involvement of parents		1
5	Satisfied with therapy		3

It was seen that all the parents in Group A felt that therapies were expensive and it was a cause of stress. Comparing this to Group B, parents there had mixed reviews about therapists. Parents in Group A felt therapists could do a better job, charge lesser and they wanted government to provide free therapy services for their children. Parents in both groups felt the need for better speech and behaviour therapists as these two were the major areas of concern in children with ASD. This is in keeping with other findings in literature, Thwala, KayiNtinda & Hlanze ,2015 in Swaziland noted that were financial constraints and long commute to reach professional services were significant stressors.

Table 4: Comparing Group A and Group B in the Domain Stressors, Theme – Reaction of family (N=12)

Sl.No.	Theme / Sub-Theme	Group A	Group B
1	Spouse	2	3
2	Sibling relationship	1	1
3	Effect on typically developing sibling	1	1
4	Stigma	1	
5	Blame	2	
6	Financial constraints	2	2
7	Lack of family support	3	2
8	Family coalitions		2

Comparing with the Group B parents, only some of the participants of Group A had full support from their families and the rest of them had partial or no support from their families. This brought out the prejudice that in the society about disability. Most of the participants in Group A did not want to share the diagnosis or its implications with their extended family. In Group A, relationship with family especially with spouse, most of the participants acknowledged that their relationships were not strained due to the presence of a special child but their partners were stressing out over the diagnosis and its implications. Comparing this to Group B parents, who had more time to acknowledge the diagnosis and its implications, most of the participants agreed that they worked in tandem with their spouses.

Table 5: Comparing Group A and Group B in the Domain Stressors, Theme –Impact of ASD.(N=12)

Sl.No.	Theme / Sub-Theme	Group A	Group B
1	Effect on health	1	
2	Effect on spouse	2	
3	Loss of work	2	
4	Effect on sibling		2
5	Loss of faith		1
6	Change in attitudes		1

It was observed that ASD had an impact on a).mental health of self, spouse, b).on typically developing sibling   c).loss of work, d).change in attitudes and e).loss of faith. The impact of ASD was seen in parents in different ways. Some parents reported it had affected their health, physically and mentally. They complained more frequently of aches and pains and fatigue brought out by the stress of parenting a child with special needs. Some parents reported how ASD has affected the other typically developing child. With the parent spending more time on the child with ASD, the other child was left to their own mechanisms. The child had to deal with his/ her own problems as well as deal with the lack of attention from parents and the ASD's child's tantrums and behaviours.

Conclusion: The current study highlights the need to educate parents about the prognosis of ASD as well as to channelize them to sources which could help them plan their child's future prospects. The needs of the typically developing sibling should not be neglected at the cost of taking care of the child with autism spectrum disorder. The findings of this study implied that helping families to understand their personal needs could go a long way in helping them deal with their child more effectively.

Pranic Healing and Quality of Life[27]

Introduction: The research focuses on women affected with endometriosis, its physiological complications like CPP and psychological conditions associated, the need and impact a complementary therapy can bring in a change physically and mentally, avoiding or reducing co morbidities which are recurrent in nature and helping them in leading a healthy life Rizk et al. (2014). The complementary therapy considered is Pranic healing therapy, focuses on the impact of this therapy, the procedure followed, and its effects documented on women who are affected with endometriosis. Documentation of the development is monitored by a decrease in the CPP, and an improvement in the QOL.

Endometrioses is a physical gynecological condition in which the endometrial lining grows out of the displaced tissues outside the uterus. And the most predominant common symptom, experienced during menstruation by most of the females is CPP (Speroff, 2005). Chronic pelvic pain (CPP) is a problem among women during their reproductive age, due to its unclear etiology, its complex natural history, and a very poor response to therapy or therapies. The CPP associated with endometriosis is considered in this research. Depression, anxiety and drug abuse is seen in patients having complex comorbidities associated with endometriosis (Asante 2011).

[27] **Vijaya Geetha Pathangae**, Research Scholar, Jain University
Smitha Baboo, Ph.D., Asst. Professor of Psychology, Jain University

Quality of life is affected for the woman who is suffering from CPP due to endometrioses, exhibiting reduced health-related QOL (HRQoL), with increased psychological distress. Some factors that affect are Depression, Acute stress, Oxidative stress, Mood disorders, Aggressiveness, Short temper, Lack of self-confidence, Anxiety, Loss of appetite, Sleep disorders, Loneliness, Frustration, Work life productivity. The effect of oxidative stress reactions causes endometriosis due to the erratic behavior of the reproductive hormones during menstruation Agarwal et al. (2012). Antecedent stressful events, with higher rates of sexual and physical abuse, these subsequently leading to posttraumatic stress disorder stated according to Lampe (2000) have been reported by such cases. And MacLean et al. (1997) has documented that transcendental meditation has an influence on hormones and stress reaction.

Objectives: To study the "Impact of Pranic Healing in CPP management and QOL among women affected with Endometriosis".

1. Is there any impact of Pranic Healing on CPP management among women affected with endometriosis?
2. Is there any impact of Pranic Healing on QOL among women affected with endometriosis?

Methodology: The sample size is 30 women. Purposive sampling method was employed on Indian population. The following tools were used. .Endometriosis health profile (EHP) and The Pranic healing protocol

Results and Discussion: The test of normality was done using the Kolmogorov-Smirnov and Shapiro-Wilk test. The Kolmogorov-Smirnov test (Chakravart, Laha, and Roy 1967) was utilized to decide the specific distribution of the sample and Shapiro-Wilk test was used to check the p value. Wilcoxon signed rank test, was used to check the t value.

Table 1 There is a significant difference between the pre-test and the post-test in CPP management in the experimental group.

Experimental group	Direction	N	Mean Rank	W
CPP	Negative	15.00	8.00	3.42**
	Positive	0.00	0.00	
	Ties	0.00		

Note: Negative: post-test<pretest; Positive: Post-test>pretest; Ties: post-test=pretest; **p <.01, *p <.05

The results show that there is a significant difference in the perception of CPP, by the intervention of Pranic healing protocol and Meditation of Twin Hearts for a period of two weeks, by increasing the self-efficacy among the participants. Hence an improvement is seen in the CPP management. Pranic Healing intervention which is another form of mindfulness meditation has created a similar difference in the area of CPP.

Table 2 There is a significant difference between the pre-test and post-test in the QOL in the experimental group.

Experimental group	Direction	N	Mean Rank	W
Control and powerlessness[#]	Negative	14.00	7.50	3.30**
	Positive	0.00	0.00	
	Ties	1.00		
Emotional wellbeing[#]	Negative	15.00	8.00	3.41**
	Positive	0.00	0.00	
	Ties	0.00		
Social support[#]	Negative	13.00	7.00	3.21**
	Positive	0.00	0.00	
	Ties	2.00		
Self image[#]	Negative	15.00	8.00	3.45**
	Positive	0.00	0.00	
	Ties	0.00		
QOL[#]	Negative	15.00	8.00	3.41**
	Positive	0.00	0.00	
	Ties	0.00		

Note: Negative: post-test<pretest; Positive: Post-test>pretest; Ties: post-test=pretest; **p <.01, *p <.05; # Higher the score, lesser is the QOL and its dimensions

In the QOL among women affected with endometriosis under control and powerlessness, which measures ones' ability to be able to overcome the pain, ones' frustration, and inability to forget the pain, a sense of un-wellness and to do a minimalistic work or be productive were seen. Ability to overcome pain increased, frustration was reduced and felt relaxed, in some cases they forgot the pain and felt refreshed, with increased determination post the healing session along with the meditation, seen in the experimental group post-test. As there was no intervention given in the control group, hence post-test results show that there is no significant difference in the CPP, as higher the scores the greater the CPP and lesser the CPP management.

Table 3 There is no significant difference between the pre-test and the post-test in the QOL in the control group.

Control group	Direction	N	Mean Rank	W
Control and powerlessness - Control and powerlessness	Negative	1.00	4.00	0.37
	Positive	3.00	2.00	
	Ties	11.00		
Emotional wellbeing - Emotional wellbeing	Negative	4.00	4.00	1.19
	Positive	2.00	2.50	
	Ties	9.00		
Social support - Social support	Negative	3.00	2.50	0.65
	Positive	3.00	4.50	
	Ties	9.00		
Self image - Self image	Negative	2.00	2.00	0.58
	Positive	1.00	2.00	
	Ties	12.00		
QOL – QOL	Negative	3.00	6.50	0.36
	Positive	6.00	4.25	
	Ties	6.00		

Note: Negative: post-test<pretest; Positive: Post-test>pretest; Ties: post-test=pretest; Not Significant; # Higher the score, lesser is the QOL and its dimensions

The post-test scores on the QOL under dimensions control and powerlessness, under emotional wellbeing, there was no intervention given hence there is no significant change in the QOL. But under social support there is a slight difference noticed, because of the intervention by the researcher in merely just explaining the nature of the ailment, its consequences and complications when not being treated on time to the affected women, has raised a need for counsellors who can extend support to such people. Under self-image there was no difference noted.

Table 4 There is a significant difference in the post-test between the experimental group and the control group in CPP management

CPP	Post test	Mean Rank	U	Z
	Experimental group	11.60	54.00	2.43*
	Control group	19.40		

Note: *p < .05

The post-test scores in CPP management in the experimental on the perception of pain levels has decreased in the experimental group, thus showing an increase in CPP management, by the intervention of Pranic healing protocol and Meditation of Twin Hearts, as higher the mean scores the greater CPP and lesser in CPP management. Improvements in ones' physical movement like standing, sitting, walking, improvement in reduction of loss of appetite, over-coming the inability to sleep due to pain, and increased self-efficacy, and being productive as a few women were doing part time jobs were documented, thus the improvement was seen in the CPP management.

Table 5 There is a significant difference in the post-test between the experimental and the control group in the QOL

QOL	Post test	Mean Rank	U	Z
Control and powerlessness	Experimental group	11.73	56.00	2.35*
	Control group	19.27		
Emotional wellbeing	Experimental group	9.20	18.00	3.98**
	Control group	21.80		
Social support	Experimental group	9.87	28.00	3.53**
	Control group	21.13		
Self-image	Experimental group	10.27	34.00	3.29**
	Control group	20.73		
QOL	Experimental group	9.60	24.00	3.68**
	Control group	21.40		

Note: **$p < .01$; *$p < .05$; Higher the score, lesser is the QOL and its dimensions

The post-test between the experimental group and the control group in the QOL and its dimensions, show that the QOL is less when compared to the control group showing that the intervention of Pranic healing protocol and Meditation of Twin Hearts have improved the QOL in the experimental group as higher the mean score the lesser the QOL.

Conclusion: In the QOL among women affected with endometriosis under control and powerlessness, which measures ones' ability to be able to overcome the pain, ones' frustration, and inability to forget the pain, a sense of un-wellness and to do a minimalistic work or be productive were seen. Ability to overcome pain increased, frustration was reduced and felt relaxed, in some cases they forgot the pain and felt refreshed, with increased determination post the healing session along with the meditation, seen in the experimental group post-test. Hence the intervention of Pranic healing with the meditation on Twin Hearts has shown a significant difference in the

QOL and its dimensions as higher the scores the lesser the QOL. Hence by putting together all the dimensions in this hypothesis the intervention of Pranic healing protocol and Meditation of Twin Hearts has improved the QOL in the experimental group post-test. Considering the Pranic healing protocol and Meditation of Twin Hearts a variant of mindfulness meditation this therapy has shown a significant difference in the experimental group.

Chapter Twenty Eight

Mental Health, Resilience and Depression among Patients[28]

Introduction: Mental Health is defined as a state of well-being in which every individual realizes his or her own potential, can cope with the normal stresses of life, can work productively and fruitfully, and is able to make a contribution to her or his community (WHO). The concepts of mental illness still are treated as stigma and mental health problems threats or stress to family or relationships. Blocks of resilience in bystanders of depression patients is a secure base of good self-esteem and a sense of self-efficacy. The brain child of Resilience originally emerged from a Latin word "Resalire" which means the ability to bounce back or spring back It has been differently used to depict a substance of elastic qualities (Joseph, 1994).It's a broad concept like an umbrella which focus on many concept regarding the positive patterns of adaptation in the face of adversity. (Masten, A. S., and Obradovic, J. 2006).The notion of resilience first came into existence in 1970 from the studies conducted in the field of psychopathology and traumatic stress .Resilience is the quality in which even when knocked down by physiological and psychological problems once ability to bounce back to normal state. Psychologists have identified

---

[28] **A.V. Alka Amala Rega, Arathy Krishna K, Mehra Fathima,** Student, Little Flower Institute of Social Sciences and Health, Calicut
Angel Sebastian, Asst. Professor, Little Flower Institute of Social Sciences and Health

some of the factors that make someone resilient, among them a positive attitude, optimism, the ability to regulate emotions, and the ability to see failure as a form of helpful feedback. Even after misfortune, resilient people are blessed with such an outlook.

Resilience in bystanders is a dynamic process that lasts a life time, immunize mental health against adversities like depression, be it patient, family member or caregiver. By 2020, depression will be the second leading cause of disability (WHO,2001) and by 2030 it is expected to be the largest contributor, to disease burden (WHO,2008) , 350 million people globally are affected by depression,(WHO-2001) and this alarming figure is a wake- up call for us to address , this global non- communicable disease, which can affect anyone.

A psychobiological construct for psychiatric disorders, study aimed that resilience is a psychobiological construct for mental disorder. The concept of resilience and its correlation with mental disorders is expected to provide information about validity of resilience, whether it is modifiable or non-modifiable .

Srivastava. K (2011), Positive Mental health and its relationship with resilience, study aimed protection facilitates resilience to desires, minimizes and delays the emergence of disabilities, and promotes the positive mental health approaches and development is heavily aligned with global mental health perspective from positive psychology.

Objectives: Purpose of study is mainly an endeavor to explore the role of bystander's and there self-efficacy and contribution in the area of developing resilience for themselves indirectly contributing to holistic wellbeing of patients suffering from depression also to focus on mental health and Resilience among the bystanders of depressive patients.

- To understand and examine mental health and resilience in bystanders, of patients suffering from depression.

- To validate the resilience of female and male adult participants.

- To validate the mental health of female and male adult participants.

- To find out whether depression is more prevalent among women than men, their mental health conflict could predict behavior problems in bystanders

Methodology: Present research in an explanatory study with cross sectional design and observational study. The study consisted of 120 participants out of which 20 were nullified, the remaining included 50 female and 50 male bystanders of patients suffering from depression in the age range of 20 and 60. The participants were chosen from different locations in Kerala, They covered lower middle to high socio – economic status from different race, without having any psychological problems. Mental Health Scale by Gireesan and Sananda Raj, (1988). The scale consists of 72 items consisted of 6 sub variables, namely, attitude towards self, self actualization, integration, autonomy, perception of reality and environmental mastery. Bharathiyar University resilience scale (BURS) by Annalakshmi in 2009 consists of 30 Likert type items.

Location of the target was randomly varied from 10 different mental hospitals across three districts of Kerala, Calicut, Trichur, and Malappuram. Data was collected with prior permission of the concerned authority of hospitals and had discussion about the purpose of study, its relevance nature and application of study. The data was collected with the informed consent of the participant involved. Confidentiality was maintained. The participants were given a briefing, on the subject of study and any queries they had were duly cleared by researcher before beginning with the test. Only necessary demographics were obtained from the participants so that identities were kept hidden. The participants were assured that data would be used for research purpose only. The participant experienced a sense of relaxation after opening up at the same time gained further insight relating the variables, indirectly promoted our scope of study as well.

Results and Discussion: Enhancing bystanders mental health, social and family support emerged through out the study .*Analysis strategy*-Initially independent sample 't' test and Karl Pearson correlation coefficient is used for analysis. Gender difference was assessed through using 't' test and correlation was measured through using Karl Pearson correlation method to explore relation between key variables like mental health and resilience.

Table No. 1: Mean, SD and t value of mental health with respect to gender

Variable	Group	N	Mean	SD	t value
Mental	Male	50	232.68	29.687	-3.471*
Health	Female	50	250.94	22.412	

p<0.05

Showing the gender difference on all key variables. Results revealed that the mean score of male on Mental health is 232.68 (SD, 29.687) and mean score of female is

250.94 (SD, 22.412). Obtained 't' value is -3.471* which was found significant (p>0.05). It was predicted that Resiliency in female bystanders is high compared to male bystanders of patients suffering from depression.

Table No 2: Mean, SD and t value of resilience with respect to gender

Variable	Group	N	Mean	SD	t value
Resilience	Male	50	99.58	22.240	1.147
	Female	50	95.02	17.207	

p>0.05

Showing the gender difference on all key variables. Results revealed that the mean score of male on resilience is 99.58 (SD, 22.240) and mean score of female is 95.02 (SD, 17.207). Obtained 't' value is 1.147 which found significant (p>0.05). Means second hypothesis was not accepted in present study. This result contradicts with previous research of Sarwar, M. et al. (2010) found that males have more resilience than females in Pakistan. Ziaian, et al. (2012) found surprisingly females tended to have higher resilience. From this it is seen that the results regarding resilience and gender difference quite vary among previous researches.

Table No.1 shows comparison of the score of mental health and its various dimensions between female and male participants .The mean score of mental health for the group of female participants is 250.94with 22.412 SD and for the group of male participants the mean score is 232.68 With29.687SD. The 't' value for the difference between these two (female and male participants) is-3.471.This't' value is significant at 0.05 level of significance, t = -3.471, p< 0.05. It means these two groups are significantly different to each other or there is

gender difference exists regarding mental health. In other words, female participants have significantly better mental health than male participants. Thus Hypotheses 1 is accepted. Thus, we can conclude that the female participants are superior to the male participants in respect to mental health.

Table No. 2 shows comparison of the score of resilience and its various dimensions between female and male participants .the mean score of resilience for the group of female students is 95.02 with 17.207 SD and for the group of male participants the mean score is 99.58 with 22.240 SD . The 't' value for the difference between these two (female and male participants) is 1.147.This 't' value is significant at 0.05 level of significance, t = 1.147, p >0.05. It means these two groups are significantly not different to each other or their gender difference does not exists regarding resilience. In other words, female participants and male participants have equal resilience. Thus hypotheses 2 is rejected

There is correlation between resilience and mental health, a positive correlation is found between both the variables. The mean score of resilience is 97.3(SD, 19.723) and mean score of Mental health is 241.81 (SD, 26.049). Results revealed that there is significant difference between resilience and Mental health ($r = .378$, $p>0.01$).

Conclusion: The present study is delimited to a sample of 120 only out of which 20 are nullified. Samples were taken only from three districts of Kerala. A significant positive correlation was found between mental health and Resilience of bystanders of depression patients, which means if one increases the other also increases. The mental health of females was found to be more superior than the mental health of male bystanders on the other hand there was no significant difference found regarding the resiliency of men and female bystanders rather found to be same . Depression was more prevalent among women than men stated that mental health conflict could predict behavior problems in bystanders but it was not so as they did not show any behavioral problem due to their high mental health as compared to men and coping skill and resiliency at par with men participants. Larger set of samples from other state may be taken considering some more set of variables. The sample of present study was taken from ten psychiatric hospital of Kerala state, same study can be undertaken from other psychiatric hospitals of different states as well.

Chapter Twenty Nine

Occupational Stress and Wellbeing of Women[29]

Introduction: Stress is the general term applied to the pressures people face in life. The presence of stress at work is almost inevitable in many jobs. Stress has commonly been defined as an environmental (workplace) Stimulus, sometimes conceived as a force applied to a person, or as a person Psychological or physiological response to such stimuli or as the process in which these two events occur. The definition of role indicates that there are inherent problems in the Performance of a role and, therefore, stress is inevitable. The term psychological well being (PWB) appears very simple and transparent but connotes a wide range of meanings usually associated with wellness. Psychological well being deals with satisfaction, self esteem, positive affect, daily activities, life satisfaction, suicidal ideas, personal control, tension, wellness, general efficacy for a healthy PWB. If one of the factors is affected, also there are possibilities of lowering of PWB.

Review of literature shows substantial work has been done in the past on this subject. From the year 1999 onwards, there has been a growing research on these topics. In these areas, the research is focused upon the study of occupational stress and psychological well being. Fielden,-Sandra-L; Davidson,-Marilyn-J (2001) Stress and

---

[29] **Shambhavi, G.** Asst. Professor of Psychology, Jain University

the woman manager, Explores the major sources of stress, both organizational and extra-organizational, encountered by women managers, and the factors that influence the responses of women managers to those stressors. The study also considers the potential impact of such stress on the behaviour and mental and physical well being of women managers, by evaluating the risks facing female managers as a result of their position within the workplace.

Objectives: The aim of the study was to compare Occupational stress and psychological wellbeing of women

1. To study the Occupational Stress among Executives and Non Executives.

2. To determine the Psychological wellbeing among Executives and Non Executives.

3. To examine the role of organizational position on the occupational stress and psychological wellbeing among women and men employees.

4. To study the relationship between Occupational Stress and Psychological Wellbeing.

Methodology: The present study aims to study the level of Occupational Stress and Psychological wellbeing among men and women employees. The sample was collected from public sector on a sample of 240 Men and Women employees, inclusive of both executives and non-executives. The subjects were given Social demographic data sheet followed with occupational stress index, psychological wellbeing questionnaire and were asked to mark the responses. Assessment tools: Occupational stress index, by A.K.Shrivastav & A.P Singh (1981) & Psychological wellbeing questionnaire, by Bhogle &Prakash (1995)

Results and Discussion: The data obtained was statistically analyzed to determine the significant difference using 't'-test between Executives and Non-Executives, men and women and Married and Single employees. Pearson's correlation 'r' was used to check the relationship between the sub-scales of Occupational stress and psychological wellbeing and also the total stress and psychological wellbeing.

Table showing the 't' value of Executives and Non Executives on Psychological Wellbeing.

PWB	Executives (N=120)	Non Executives (N=120)
Mean	19.71	20.16
SD	2.70	2.48
't' Value	2.49**	

Table showing the 't' value of single and married employees on psychological wellbeing.

PWB	single (N=120)	Married (N=120)
Mean	20.33	19.73
SD	2.90	2.35
't' Value	1.77	

Table showing the 't' value of single and married employees on Occupational Stress Index

		Single		Married		t' Value
Sl.No	Variables	Mean	S.D	Mean	S.D	
1	Role Overload	16.05	4.45	18.11	4.09	3.7*
2	Role Ambiguity	9.47	2.8	10.58	3.05	2.93*
3	Role Conflict	13.09	2.45	14	2.63	2.78*
4	Group and Political Pressure	10.21	2.86	11.02	3.11	2.10**
5	Responsibility for staff	9.55	2.1	9.42	2.06	0.47
6	Under Participation	10.91	2.21	11.21	2.63	0.94
7	Powerlessness	8.66	2.15	8.61	2.24	0.16
8	Poor Peer Relation	12.33	2.26	11.66	2.08	2.42**
9	Intrinsic Impoverishment	9.51	2.2	10.9	2.75	4.37*
10	Low Status	7.23	2.43	7.93	2.55	2.17**
11	Strenuous Working Condition	10.09	3.21	11.1	3.01	2.52**
12	Unprofitability	5.91	1.88	6.27	1.69	1.5
13	Total	123.09	16.05	130.86	17.65	3.59**

The objectives of the present study were to study the level of Occupational Stress and Psychological wellbeing between Executive and Non-Executive, married and single employees and men and the relationship between Occupational Stress and Psychological wellbeing with one another. It was hypothesized that there is no difference in the stress levels of Executive and Non-Executive, it was hypothesized that there is no difference in the Psychological wellbeing of Executive and Non-Executive, it was hypothesized that there is no difference in the stress level between single and married employees, it was hypothesized that there is no difference in Psychological wellbeing among single and married employees, it was hypothesized that there is no difference in the stress among Men and Women employees, it was hypothesized that there is no significant relationship between Occupational stress and psychological well being, and to study the relationship between occupational stress and psychological well being.

The organization as a whole is well defined with good Information system and follows a clear cut mode of communication at all levels. The structure of the organization is well defined and the management follows a good and adaptable mode of instructions regarding the guidelines which the employees has to follow in their work pattern, payment, promotions, welfare schemes, medical benefits, retirement benefits, Provident fund schemes and designations, which helps the employees to get along with the work in a very comfortable way and not face any dilemma at the work place.

To summarize the results shows that the observations done on the group as a whole have average stress level and has a medium level of psychological well being. The present study reveals that on psychological wellbeing there is a difference between Executives and Non-Executives. This study shows that both single and married men and women employees have shown differences in stress level. There is a difference in the gender groups in stress level according to the study.

Conclusion: The present study reveals that on psychological wellbeing there is a difference between executives and Non-Executives. There is no difference in stress level amongst executives and non-executives. There is a significant difference in the psychological wellbeing between men and women employees. According to the present study, some of the sub-scales of Occupational stress index are positively correlated with psychological wellbeing.

Chapter Thirty

Organizational Cynicism, Work-Life Balance and Well-Being[30]

Introduction: Anderson and Bateman (1997) define Organizational Cynicism as "an attitude characterized by frustration, hopelessness and disappointment, as well as derision toward and distrust of the organization". Dean et al., (1998) defines Organizational Cynicism as a negative attitude toward one's employing organization and has theorized three dimensions for it which is Beliefs, Affect, Behaviour. According to Byrne (2005), when they experience least conflict between work and non-work roles, they feel that their work and life are balanced. Greenhaus & Beutell (1985) defines Work-Life Conflict as a type of inter-role conflict which arises when responsibilities from the work and family spheres are not attuned and have a negative impact on both the work and family life. Frone, Russell and Cooper (1992) have identified two types of work-family conflict that are work-interfering-with family and family-interfering-with-work.

Carol Ryff's defines Psychological Well-being as being multi-dimensional and not simply about happiness or positive emotions. She purports that a good life is balanced and whole, engaging each of the different aspects of well-being, instead of being

[30] **Baisnavi Pradhan**, Research Scholar, Jain University
Smitha Baboo, Ph.D., Department of Psychology, Jain University

narrowly focused. Carol Ryff (as cited in Living Meaning, n.d.) identifies six categories of Psychological well-being. They are: Self-acceptance, Personal growth, Purpose in Life, Positive Relations with Others, Environmental Mastery, Autonomy

In the Indian scenario, though women are now largely supported to go to work, they are still expected to fulfil their traditional roles that of a home-maker and the primary care taker of the family. The progression of a woman from being just the home-maker to a career driven mother has increased the challenges for the woman who must juggle between child-care, family and work.

The challenges for a working mother increases when the person has to maintain the efficiency at the work place too. Furthermore, once she becomes a mother, the role is under scrutiny due to the new status. In a study by Cuddy, Fiske and Glick (2004), it was found out that people reported having less interest in hiring, promoting, and educating working mothers as compared to working fathers and childless employees. Budig and England (2001) have found that mothers are indeed discriminated when it came to pay and promotion as compared to women who did not have children. Vitelli (2014) states that regardless of the growing number of working mothers in the workforce, they still face incredible challenges including the limited availability of day-care as well as frequent discrimination by employers

Studies support the notion that workplace incivility and discrimination against working mothers more often than not can increases cynicism towards the organization. A study by Nazir & Ahmed (2016) and Ayyub, Awan & Bilaly (2013) both found a positive correlation between workplace incivility and Organizational Cynicism. In the study by Galletta, Portoghese, Ciuffi, Sancassiani, D'Aloja and Campagna (2016), it was found that if Organizational empowerment was low, the positive association between exhaustion and cynicism is significantly strong.

The challenges that working mothers face, especially when it is their first time as a mother, can have serious consequences on their mental and physical health. A survey conducted by Hudsonberg (as cited in P.E Express, 2015) found that the demands at work, taking care of the children and the family are resulting in more working mothers towards the edge of a nervous breakdown. The mothers reported that they suffered at least one of the health problems that ranged from headaches, anxiety, insomnia, chronic fatigue and depression. Studies have also found that many working mothers feel stressed and incompetent, when they feel the pressure to balance work and family life.

Miner, Pesonen, Smittick, Seigel and Clark (2014) found that in a work place, mothers with 3 children were treated more uncivilly than women with fewer children.

Brandes et. al, (2008) found that when faced with job insecurity cynics reported higher levels of work effort in comparison to non-cynics. Naus (2007) found a strong negative relationship between cynicism and organization-based self-esteem. Johnson and Kelly (2003) found that affective cynicism fully mediated the relationship between psychological contract breach and emotional exhaustion, suggesting that cynical attitudes have negative consequences for the attitude holder.

Losoncz and Bortolotto (2009) found that those who experienced a strong tension between work and family responsibilities indicated reduced physical and mental health and low satisfaction with family life and parenthood. Kossek, and Ozeki (1998) that a consistent negative relationship exists among all forms of w-f conflict and job–life satisfaction. A survey by Frone, Russell and Barnes (1996) found that both types of work–family conflict were significantly and positively related to depression, poor physical health, and heavy alcohol use.

Meier, Musick, Flood and Dunifon (2017) found that compared to non-working mothers, working mothers experience lower happiness and higher stress and fatigue in parenting. Hyeyoung (2009) found that unemployed women who either never married or childless married women reported lower levels of psychological well-being compared to employed mothers. Ozer (1995) found that greater childcare responsibility is associated with lower well-being and greater psychological distress.

Objectives: Not much research has been conducted to find out the effects cynicism and dissatisfaction and work-family conflict, could have on the mental and psychological health and well-being of these mothers, particularly in the Indian context, where family and role structures in urban settings have evolved tremendously over the past few years. Therefore, this study focuses in examining the effect of Organizational Cynicism and Work-Life balance on the Psychological well-being of first time mothers in IT & ITES sector in Bangalore. The motive of this study is focused on:

1. To examine the correlation between Organizational Cynicism and Psychological Well-being.
2. To examine the correlation between Work-life Conflict and Psychological Well-being.
3. To examine the correlation between Organizational Cynicism and Work-life Conflict.

Methodology: The research design was a quantitative study and used correlational research. Purposive and Snowball sampling method was employed. Samples selected were first time mothers from IT and ITES sector. Sample size of 50. Techniques of assessment used were: Organizational Cynicism scale by Dean, Brandes and Dharwakar (1998); Work-life Balance Questionnaire developed by Fisher Mcauley (2002); Psychological Well-being Scale, developed by Mehrotra, Tripathi and Banu (2013).

Results and discussion: The correlation between Affective dimension of Organizational Cynicism and Sense of engagement and growth dimension of Psychological Well-being is .455, which is significant at 0.01 level. Also, the correlation between Behavioural dimension of Organizational Cynicism and Sense of engagement and growth dimension of Psychological Well-being is .325, which is significant at 0.05 level. The results indicate a significant positive correlation, therefore the Null Hypothesis is rejected.

The results purports that when cynical feelings and behaviour of mother increases the sense of engagement and growth increases too. To explain the result, few past studies have been referenced. Studies like that of Brandes et. al, (2008) have found that when employees are insecure of their jobs, they report higher levels of work effort as compared to non-cynics. Crittenden (as cited by Gillett, 2016) writes that when a person develops a skill to comfort a troublesome toddler and manage the difficult challenges of a tumultuous household, he/she becomes readily equipped to handle crises, the demands of the managers and survive the most devious office scheming. Downey (2016) found that when new mothers joined work after having a baby they became more appreciative of the fulfillment they derived from work. They are more focused to get promotions and higher pay as well as more likely to switch jobs for higher title or more pay as found in a survey from Accenture (Santos, 2017).

The correlation between Work interferes with personal life dimension of Work-life Conflict and Sense of engagement and growth dimension of Psychological Well-being is -.325, which is significant at 0.05level. The result shows a significant negative correlation, therefore, the Null Hypothesis is rejected. The result signifies that when there is an increase in the interference of work on personal life, sense of engagement and growth decreases. Opie and Henn (2013) stated that working mothers faced challenges when it comes to balancing work and family life and the conflict in turn is negatively related to work engagement. Cooper (as cited in Deery, Jago & Stewart, 2008) found that presenteeism in organizations meant putting in more hours or appearing to be working long hours. This expectation of presenteeism and lack of flexibility were the major reasons that discouraged women from exploring career advancements opportunities (Doherty, 2004). Cinamon and Rich (2010) found that when work-family conflict occurs, employees experience burn out which leads to decrease in work engagement.

The correlation between the Affective dimension of Organizational Cynicism and Personal life interferes with work dimension of Work-life Conflict is .311, which is significant at 0.01 level. The correlation between the Behavioural dimension of Organizational Cynicism and Personal life interferes with work dimension of Work-life Conflict is .326, which is significant at 0.05 level.Results indicate a significant positive correlation, therefore, the Null Hypothesis, is rejected.

When cynicism towards an organization increases, work-life conflict increases too or vice versa. Balogun (2014)found that work-life conflict and job stress had a significant effect on job burnout. Mitra (2015) also concluded in her study that excessive work load, low job security, lack of motivation from the supervisors led to increase in stress in employees. When mothers have lower perceived Organizational support they face emotional exhaustion and cynicism. Increase in cynicism resulting in the increase in Work-life Conflict could also be explained with the help of Brandes et. al, (2008) study who found that when faced with job insecurity, cynics reported higher levels of work effort in comparison to non-cynics. Thus, leading to more time and energy spent at work and eventually finding it difficult to have energy for non-work activities.

Conclusion: From the study we can conclude that Cynicism towards the organization and Work-life Conflict does have a detrimental effect on the Psychological Well-being of first time mothers working in corporate sectors. It is therefore very important that companies recognize this issue as an urgent and serious one. Building of day care facilities in the campus, flexible work hours, required paid offs, child support regulations, therapy and counselling sessions and classes on better parenthood are few of the ways in which organizations can extend their support towards these new mothers. This will help them in reducing their challenges and will increase their efficiency not only at work but also as a mother. In turn, the cynicism and insecurities of the mothers will reduce, their commitment will increase and their morale will get boosted. Most importantly, it will ensure the good health of both the mother and the child.

Chapter Thirty One

Social Support, Psychological Wellbeing and Resilience among patients[31]

Introduction: An all-purpose term for varied disorders that affect kidney structures and functions is called chronic kidney disease (CKD) (Levey & Coresh, 2012). It includes conditions that damage the kidneys and decrease their ability to keep one healthy. The kidney disease improving global outcomes (KDIGO, 2013) after careful evaluation, classification, and stratification following a decade of focused research and clinical practice in CKD, it has updated the document aiming to provide required guidance for the treatment as well as the management for CKD patients in 2012. "CKD is defined as abnormalities of kidney structure or function, present for 43 months, with implications for health and CKD is classified based on cause, Glomerular filtration rate (GFR) category, and albuminuria category (CGA) (KDIGO, 2013)." According to the KDIGO guidelines, an individual is diagnosed based on wide range of tests and assessments but the basic test a doctor needs to do, is find out GFR of the person through urine test. Based on the test results and using KDIGO guidelines Stage 5 CKD also known as end stage renal disease (ESRD) is diagnosed when GFR is below 15, which means kidney failure. Patients with ESRD have to go under dialysis till they get donor for renal transplantation (KDIGO, 2013).

[31] **Kiran S. Sawekar**, Research Scholar, Jain University
Guneet Inder Jit Kaur, Ph.D., Asst. Professor, Department of Psychology, Jain University

CKD is a significant disease globally and in India at an estimation of 1.00,000 new patients are diagnosed with ERSD who also apply for renal transplantation programs every year (Jha et al., 2013). Till a patient receives renal transplantation dialysis helps the person by accomplishing the functions of failed kidneys by regulating the balance of fluids within the body. Nephrologist and the patient together decide on which type of dialysis suits patient's living condition. A dialyzer is used to filter body wastes and that gets rid of excess fluid from the blood, this method of dialysis is known as hemodialysis (HD). Where as in peritoneal dialysis (PD) a solution called dialysate will take away wastes and excess fluid from the body using the lining of the abdominal cavity called peritoneal membrane (Turner, 2015).

Psychosocial support is understood as also in terms of an approach to help the victims of chronic illness and to build their resilience. It provides a directive for ensuring that the life continues normally, enabling the individual to participate in perceiving social support to prevent and avoid unnecessary complications and stressors. Research examining psychosocial factors in renal populations is relatively new and has focused mostly on patients with end stage kidney dialysis (ESKD) (Woodward, 2015; Cummings & Kropf, 2013). There can be interventions planned to improve social support which uses psychosocial approach (Ahn et al, 2015).

Subjective well-being means that the people evaluate their lives by themselves but optimal human functioning is understood to signify psychological well-being. (Ryan & Deci, 2000, 2001). There are two methods to understand psychological wellbeing. The first is to differentiate positive and negative effects. Optimal psychological wellbeing and happiness are equilibrium between the two. The second approach emphasizes on life-satisfaction as the indicator of psychological wellbeing (Ryff & Keyes, 1995). One of the results of an earlier study has suggested that the perceived family support helps patients suffering from ESRD to have better psychological wellbeing (Christensen, Turner, Slaughter & Holman, 1989).

Druss and Douglas (1988) described "resilient individuals as having high self-efficacy, self-esteem and a repertoire for problem-solving skills and satisfying interpersonal relationship." That would mean the resilient individuals are known to solve problems better than an average individual, have better perception of one and are content with their relationships. Resilience can be found in each individual with varying range and in a study it was found that resilience may influence the outcome in terms of health and process in treatment of an illness. It was found that by developing preventive interventions which can allow protective factors such as resilience, an increase in the better outcome in health can occur (Cal, Sá, Glustak, & Santiago, 2015).

Earlier studies have indicated that patients with a high gastro intestinal symptoms profile have had impaired psychological general wellbeing, highlighting the contribution of physical factors in the psychological wellbeing of chronic kidney patients (Strid et al., 2002). The conclusion, drawn from one of the research proved that a multi-method assessment of children's adjustment through different informants yields a comprehensive view of child psychopathology in CKD, which indicated to research in the field of psychosocial support, leading to early identification of maladjustment (Amr et al., 2008). A study concluded saying that resilience level didn't change amongst kids with CKD and their healthy peers which gave rise to new research possibilities (Riaño-Galán et al., 2009). One of the studies concluded that the current end-of-life clinical practices did not meet the psychological needs of patients with advanced CKD (Davison, 2010). The research data indicated that some of the selective serotonin reuptake inhibitor agents and time-limited, manual, structured psychotherapies can be safe and effective for treating depression in this population and improve overall wellbeing thus implying that an alternative treatment can be structured, which is cost effective (Zalai, Szeifert, & Novak, 2012). In brief, most of the studies under review of literature showed that resilience, psychological wellbeing and perceived social support has been significantly associated with CKD and had a positive outlook (Ma et al., 2013; Knowles, Swan, Salzberg, Castle, & Langham, 2014; Hanson et al., 2015; Bennett, Weinberg, Bridgman, & Cummins, 2015; Moreira, Soares, Teixeira, e Silva, & Kummer 2015;).

Objectives: The reviews stated above suggest patients with CKD tend to have many stressors such financial problems, work-life balance, strained interpersonal/ social relationships and so on, thereby having a negative impact on their psychological wellbeing. Hence, this study attempts to understand the relationship between perceived social support, psychological wellbeing and resilience in order to provide a framework for psycho-education and psychological intervention. The present study has tried to understand the current trend in the research by going through literature available and due to paucity of literature in perceived social support, resilience and psychological wellbeing, yet it has observed the importance of the underlying variables amongst chronic kidney patient.

1. To study the relationship of perceived social support with resilience amongst patients undergoing dialysis.
2. To study the relationship of perceived social support with psychological wellbeing amongst patients undergoing dialysis.
3. To study the relationship of resilience with psychological wellbeing amongst patients undergoing dialysis.

Methodology: The Primary aim of this study was to study the relationship of perceived social support, resilience and psychological wellbeing amongst patients undergoing dialysis. Furthermore, to generate a basis for understanding the relationship of perceived social support, resilience and psychological wellbeing amongst patients undergoing dialysis.

A correlational research design was followed. This study included approaching the dialysis centers to identify and select the CKD patients who were undergoing dialysis. With the consent of the concerned hospital authority and respective patients who fitted the present research sample criteria, they were conservatively briefed about the research objective. The subjects were then administered and assessed for their perceived social support, resilience and psychological well-being respectively. The ethical considerations of informed consent and confidentiality were adhered to and care was taken that the patient didn't face further discomfort.

Due to rarity of the sample, purposive sampling method was used. CKD patients undergoing hemodialysis in Bengaluru were selected. The total number of sample consisted of 56 patients but due to the exclusion criteria, one sample with Parkinson disease was excluded making the final sample size as 55 patients. The following tests were used:

1. Multidimensional Scale of Perceived Social Support (MSPSS) (Zimet, Dahlem, Zimet & Farley, 1988
2. The Flourishing Scale (FS) (Diener, & Biswas-Diener, 2009)
3. The 14 item Resilience Scale (RS-14) (Wagnild & Young, 2009)

Descriptive Statistics were used and Shapiro Wilk test of normality was used to ascertain the assumption of normality of the sample. Further on, non-parametric statistical tool (Spearman's rank correlation coefficient) was used because the sample was not normally distributed.

Results and Discussions: The results of the Shapiro-Wilk test of normality for the three psychological factors, Indicated that the data is not normally distributed hence, Spearman's rank correlation coefficient is used. It can be observed that there is a significant positive correlation between perceived social support and resilience amongst patients undergoing dialysis ($r=0.47$, $p<0.01$). The results imply that an increase in perceived social support and availing the support in terms of economic, information and other means of support will also tend to see an increase in the level of resilience shown by the patient in the face of adverse circumstances theorized by CKD.

Massey et al. (2015) had found that intervention such as early education of kidney transplantation is beneficial in stopping them from cancelling transplantation. In that way, highlighting the imperative role of perceived social support because the study highlights social support where information is means of support and receiving it might have made the individuals perceive it as a protective factor similarly like resilience.

In another study, Waqas et al. (2016) conducted a study on burn injury patients and investigated the role of social support as well as resilience. They concluded by saying that burn injury patients were perceiving very low social support from the society in which they lived, that may have had an adverse impact on their health. The present investigation consisted of sample of patients undergoing dialysis where the symptoms are hidden if not for a trained eye to identify but the patients with burn injury may not have an option to hide their condition which may have caused them to develop some of the extrinsic factors that may have influenced the result. Pre and post treatment of patients with burn injuries may have derived different results. That being said, it is crucial to understand that the resilience was same as healthy counterpart which may have helped them to deal with their condition.

Table 1 Correlation coefficient value (Spearman's rho) between perceived social support and psychological wellbeing amongst patients undergoing dialysis

Variables	Correlation Coefficient
Perceived Social Support and Psychological Wellbeing	0.51**

*N=55**. Correlation is significant at 0.01 level (2-tailed)*

It can be observed from the table 2 that there is a significant positive correlation between perceived social support and psychological wellbeing amongst patients undergoing dialysis (r=0.51, p<0.01). The data shown in table 3 may imply that when a life threatening illness has been diagnosed and patients are getting treatment, if they receive/perceive social support that will positively improve their psychological wellbeing by making them feel less lonely and get over some of the associated psychological stressor that comes with chronic illness such as depression and anxiety (Sanathan et al., 2014; Jana et al., 2014)

Amr et al. (2009) conducted a research investigating the adjustment made by children suffering from CKD. It concluded by providing an inference that a multi-screening method of children who have been diagnosed with CKD will provide enough information about their psychological wellbeing and stressors by which they could be given psychosocial interventions and help them to overcome some of the stressors identified like maladjustment, in the screening process. This multi screening is possible if they receive more social support by which they may have to communicate more hence, providing the setup for screening without them being on guard and an early identification is possible. Thus, providing a basis of understanding that, there were indication of relationship between social support and psychological adjustment that can also be understood as one of the psychological factor of psychological wellbeing (Ryff & Keyes, 1995).

Table 2 There is no significant relationship between resilience and psychological wellbeing amongst patients undergoing dialysis.

Variables	Correlation Coefficient
Resilience with Psychological wellbeing	0.62**
N=55	
**. Correlation is significant at 0.01 level (2-tailed)*	

The results shown in the table 2 indicates that there is a significant positive correlation between resilience and psychological wellbeing amongst patients undergoing dialysis (r=0.62, p<0.01). This means that the distress caused during the treatment may be reduced if the individual has high level of resilience. Min, et al, (2013) conducted a study and concluded that the cancer patients become better in coping with emotional distress by increased level of resilience alone. Thus, they further added that the interventions that use psychosocial approach to develop resilience would be beneficial to patients with cancer.

Moreira, Soares, Teixeira, e Silva, and Kummer (2015) conducted the study and found no difference found between control group and CKD patients in terms of resilience; however they mentioned that the CKD patients scored higher with respect to psychological stressors which may be the cause for referral to mental health professionals. Hence, understanding the relationship between resilience and psychological wellbeing becomes crucial in order to provide better information for mental health professionals.

It can be observed that there is a significantly positive correlation between friends (r=0.55, p<0.01); significant other (r=0.49, p<0.01) and family (r=0.38, p<0.01) with psychological wellbeing. This highlights the role of the sub dimensions of perceived social support in fostering and maintaining of psychological wellbeing of a patient put under the naturally strenuous conditions of dialysis. It can be observed further from the table that there is positive correlation between friends (r=0.48); significant other (r=0.42) and family (r=0.39) with resilience, and which is significant at 0.01 level. Interestingly, as compared to the other sub dimensions friends have been shown to have a little higher correlational value with both psychological wellbeing and resilience, in the present sample.

Conclusion: The disproval of the first null hypothesis concludes that the patients who are well supported by their friends, families, and significant others have a higher resilience tendency. The disproval of the second null hypothesis would mean that the patients undergoing dialysis have a strong social support system that could positively influence their psychological wellbeing and help them in dealing with psychological stressors.

The third null hypothesis was also disproven which can be interpreted that the patients under dialysis would become more resilient if they have better psychological wellbeing or if they are having higher level of psychological wellbeing then it has a positive effect on their resilience level. That could give them a better stance at fighting their illness and coping with the treatment. The results shed light on positive psychological factors which make the patients much more resilient and psychologically able to deal with chronic illness such as CKD. The importance of social support and how it can make patients fight and manage their illness can be used to create a family therapeutic model which may serve well in hospital setup. Psychoeducation can be given to the caregivers to make informed decisions and let them know how their support may provide a higher survival chance for their family member.

This study can be further extended to qualitative research design which will give much more clarity. It can be replicated on different cities where there is more concentration of dialysis centers, which will broaden the understanding of different demographic areas and its patients under dialysis. A comparative study can be done by using a cross sectional design between CKD patients and Post kidney transplantation patients.

Chapter Thirty Two

Organizational Support, Self-Leadership and Innovative Work Behaviour[32]

Introduction: Innovative behaviour of employees is a key aspect of organizational effectiveness, which includes creation, introduction and application of new ideas within a group or organization, in order to benefit performance (Sanders, Moorkamp, Torka, Groeneveld & Groeneveld, 2010). Organizations consider innovation as competitive edge and aid to success (Arora & Kamalanabhan, 2013). Numerous factors are found to be associated with the Innovative Work Behaviour (IWB) of the employees. These factors include supervisor support and coworker support (Arora & Kamalanabhan, 2013), leader role expectations (Scott & Bruce, 1994), job demands and rewards received at work (Janssen, 2000) and leadership and organizational climate (Noor & Dzulkifli, 2013) etc. Among these, organizational climate and self leadership were identified as the most important factors that contribute to IWB (Tastan, 2013).

Employees are in an organizations form global beliefs concerning the extent to which the organization values their contributions and cares about their well-being (Eisenberger, Huntington, Hutchison & Sowa, 1986). Feeling of having good organiational support will develop an affective attachment in employees to the

---

[32] **C. Gnanaprakash**, **Ph.D.,** Asst. Professor, Jain University
K.R. Santhosh, **Ph.D.**, Asst. Professor, Christ University, Bangalore

organization. Apart from Perceived Organizational Support (POS), affective attachement with the organization will enhance the job involvement (Tastan, 2013). Affectively attached employees will have an expectancy that greater effort toward meeting organizational goals will be rewarded (Eisenberger, Huntington, Hutchison & Sowa, 1986). Results of the inquiry done by Janssen (2000), in a sample of 170 non-management employees from a Dutch industrial organization in the food sector revealed a positive relationship between organizational goals and IWB when employees perceived effort-reward fairness rather than under-reward unfairness

To develop POS in the employees, organization has to actively encourage the innovation through the provision of recourses and empowerment (Denti, 2013). Individual innovation shall be predicted by the inclination in taking a proactive attitude, to the profession, and by the resilience of the employees. Creative self efficacy in the employees has a mediating role in this relationship. Good leaders are able to stimulate idea generation and increase the possibility for the successful completion of the innovation projects (Denti, 2013). Study by Tastan (2013) in a sample of 400 employees of 40 small and medium sized enterprises from Ismir-turkey showed that participative work environment, socio-political support, access to recourses and access to information as the dimensions of organizational climate that have a direct and positive relationship with the IWB. The study also showed a direct positive relationship between self leadership skills and IWB.

Innovation requires self navigation competencies (Curral & Marques-Quinteiro, 2009). Self-Leadership Skills (SLS) is a self navigation competency in the employees which could be enhanced by a supportive organizational climate, will inturn influence the innovative work behaviour (Noor & Dzulkifli, 2013). As per the findings of Carmeli and Meitarand Weisberg (2006), using structured survey in a sample of employees and supervisors (N = 175) working in six organizations in Israel, SLS has a positive relationship with both self and supervisor ratings of innovative behaviours. The findings also showed that income and job tenure are significantly related to innovative behaviors at work.

Investigation done by Curral & Marques-Quinteiro (2009), in a sample of 108 employees working in development and implementation of technological solutions, indicated a positive relationship between role innovation for learning, goal orientation and intrinsic motivation. As per the findings, SLS fully mediated the relationship between learning, goal orientation and role innovation and partially mediated the relationship between intrinsic motivation and role innovation. Hence, enhancing self-navigation competences of the employees can enhance their innovative behaviour too (Curral & Marques-Quinteiro, 2009).

Organizations that are seeking ways in which to foster IWB in their employees need to recognize the importance of building up self-leaders who can successfully meet the required expectations and standards of innovative behaviour. Knowledge workers, the mainstays of any organization were strong in bringing innovative results (De Jong & Den Hartog, 2008). A few studies in literature designate the factors that influence IWB among the Knowledge Workers from Science & Technology and Humanities research organizations.

Objectives: The present study is an attempt to find if POS and SLS among the researchers in Science & Technology and Humanities research organizations can be the predictors of IWB.

H_1: Innovative Work Behaviour among the Knowledge Workers has a significant relationship with Perceived Organizational Support and Self-Leadership Skills.

H_2: Male Knowledge Workers differ significantly from female Knowledge Workers in Perceived Organizational Support, Self-Leadership Skills and Innovative Work Behaviour.

H_3: Knowledge Workers differ in Perceived Organizational Support, Self-Leadership Skills and Innovative Work Behaviour with respect to their discipline

Methodology: Sixty Knowledge Workers selected through purposive sampling method from Humanities and Science research institutions in Bangalore, India. Measures: *Innovative Work Behaviour Scale* (Janssen, 2000) was used to measure innovative work behaviour. The scale has nine items (7 point Likert scale) spreading along 3 dimensions –Idea Generation, Idea Promotion and Idea Realization. Cronbach's α of the scale in the present sample is .91. *Self-Leadership Skills Measure* (Hougton & Neck, 2002) was used. The measure consists of 35 items (5-point Likert scale), spread across 3 core strategies – Behaviour Analysis & Volition, Task Motivation and Constructive Cognition. Cronbach's α of the measure in the present sample is .92.

Adapted version of *Perceived Organizational Support Questionnaire* (Jokela, 2012) a 10 item (5 point likert scale) was used. The questionnaire has Cronbach's α of the measure in the present sample is .73.

Results and Discussion: Table 1 and table 2 summarize the sample characteristics of the present investigation. Table 1 is the summary of the distribution of the subjects in the sample with respect to the sex differences.

Table 1: Distribution of the respondents in the sample with respect to sex

Sex	Frequency	Percent
Male	38	63.3
Female	22	36.7
Total	60	100.0

Among the total of the 60 respondents in the sample 38 (63.3%) are males and 22 (36.7%) are females.

Table 2: Distribution of the subjects in the sample with respect to the discipline

Discipline	Frequency	Percent
Humanities	29	48.3
Science	31	51.7
Total	60	100.0

Of the total 60 participants, 29 (48.3%) were from Humanities discipline and 31 (51.7%) were from Science discipline. Of the total 60 participants, 26 Humanities and 29 Science discipline researchers were chosen their job as self-choice, and 3 Humanities and 2 Science discipline researchers were chosen their job as Forced / by chance.

To find out if IWB has a significant relationship with POS and SLS, correlation test was used and results of the analysis are summarized in table 3.

Table 3: Distribution of the subjects in the sample with respect to their job choice

Discipline	Self-choice	Forced / by chance
Humanities	26	3
Science	29	2

The result evidently shows that POS has significantly correlated with IWB and its dimensions. The POS measure was significantly and positively related to the General IWB ($r = 0.50$, $p<0.01$), as well as its dimensions Idea Generation ($r = 0.90$, $p<0.01$), Idea Promotion ($r = 0.97$, $p<0.01$) and Idea Realization ($r = 0.96$, $p<0.01$). General SLS was significantly and positively related to its dimensions Behaviour Analysis & Volition ($r = 0.51$, $p<0.01$), Task Motivation ($r = 0.92$, $p<0.01$) and Constructive Cognition ($r = 0.64$, $p<0.01$). Task Motivation was significantly and positively related to Behaviour Analysis & Volition ($r = 0.41$, $p<0.01$) and Constructive Cognition ($r = 0.44$, $p<0.01$). IWB was positively and significantly related to SLS ($r = 0.30$, $p<0.05$) and SLS also was related to positively and significantly to one of the IWB dimensions Idea Generation ($r = 0.43$, $p<0.01$). Hence, hypothesis 1 is accepted.

To find out the difference between males and females Knowledge Workers on POS, SLS and IWB, student's t-test was done. Results of the statistical analysis are summarized in table 5.

Table 4: Difference in Perceived Organizational Support, Self-Leadership Skillsand Innovative Work Behaviour with respect to sex

Variables	Sex	N	Mean	S.D.	"t"
POS	Male	38	28.63	3.49	2.45[*]
	Female	22	26.86	2.10	
BA&V	Male	38	12.79	1.45	1.71
	Female	22	12.18	1.05	
TM	Male	38	11.50	2.05	0.90
	Female	22	12.05	2.59	
CC	Male	38	11.87	1.65	0.15
	Female	22	11.95	1.86	
SLS	Male	38	36.16	3.64	0.02
	Female	22	36.18	4.32	
IG	Male	38	17.42	2.29	6.88[**]
	Female	22	13.81	1.74	
IP	Male	38	17.42	3.53	6.18[**]
	Female	22	10.91	4.15	
IR	Male	38	17.21	2.90	5.50[**]
	Female	22	12.05	3.81	
IWB	Male	38	52.05	8.30	6.72[**]
	Female	22	36.77	8.61	

$**p < 0.01$, $*p < 0.05$

POS = Perceived Organizational Support, BA = Behaviour Analysis, TM = Task Motivation, CC = Constructive Cognition, SLS = Self Leadership Skills, IG = Idea Generation, IP = Idea Promotion, IR = Idea Realization, IWB = Innovative Work Behaviour.

The obtained t-value value comparing male and female mean scores of Researchers towards POS (t = 2.45, p<.05), is significant. And overall measure of IWB (t = 6.72, p<.01) and the IWB dimensions Idea Generation (t-test = 6.88, p<.01), Idea Promotion (t = 6.18, p<.01) and Idea Realization (t = 5.50, p<.01) also highly significant. Hence, the hypotheses 2.1 and 2.3 were accepted. Therefore, considering the mean values it can be concluded that the male researchers get high score and significantly differ on POS, IWB and its dimensions than female.

The computed t-value comparing male and female mean scores of the researchers towards overall General SLS (t = 0.02) and its dimensions Behaviour Analysis & Volition (t = 1.71), Task Motivation (t = 0.90) and Constructive Cognition (t = 0.15) were not statistically significant. Hence, hypothesis 2.2 was rejected. Therefore, considering the mean values it can be concluded that the male and female researchers of this study were not differ on IWB and its dimensions.

To find the difference between Humanities and Science discipline Knowledge Workers on POS, SLS and IWB, student's t-test was done and results of the statistical analysis are summarized in table 5

Table 5: Difference in Perceived Organizational Support, Self-Leadership Skills and Innovative Work Behaviour with respect to discipline

Variables	Discipline	N	Mean	S.D.	"t"
POS	Humanities	29	27.86	2.97	0.29
	Science	31	28.10	3.36	
BA&V	Humanities	29	12.07	1.33	2.94**
	Science	31	13.03	1.20	
TM	Humanities	29	10.90	2.08	2.82**
	Science	31	12.45	2.19	
CC	Humanities	29	11.55	1.57	1.55
	Science	31	12.23	1.80	
SLS	Humanities	29	34.52	3.53	3.49**
	Science	31	37.71	3.56	
IG	Humanities	29	15.90	2.90	0.55
	Science	31	16.29	2.58	
IP	Humanities	29	14.93	4.57	0.16
	Science	31	15.13	5.25	
IR	Humanities	29	14.79	4.15	0.96
	Science	31	15.81	4.04	
IWB	Humanities	29	45.62	11.12	0.55
	Science	31	47.23	11.33	

**$P < 0.01$, *$P < 0.05$ POS = Perceived Organizational Support, BA = Behaviour Analysis, TM = Task Motivation, CC = Constructive Cognition, SLS = Self Leadership Skills, IG = Idea Generation, IP = Idea Promotion, IR = Idea Realization, IWB = Innovative Work Behaviour.

The obtained t-value value comparing Humanities and Science mean scores of Researchers towards POS (t = 0.29), overall measure of IWB (t = 0.55) and the IWB dimensions Idea Generation (t = 0.55), Idea Promotion (t = 0.16) and Idea Realization (t = 0.96); and SLS dimensions Constructive Cognition (t = 1.55) did not significantly differ. Hence, the hypotheses 3.1 and 3.3 were rejected. Therefore, considering the mean values it can be concluded that the Humanities and Science researchers' perception does not differ towards above mentioned variables.

The present study attempted to understand the relationship of POS and SLS on IWB of Knowledge Workers in both Humanities and Science Research Centers. It is always considered perception of organizational support provides researchers to foster their IWB by tangible (remuneration, job security, medical benefits) (Carmeli & Meitarand Weisberg, 2006) and intangible (recognition, freedom, autonomy etc.,) (Janssen, 2000; Tastan, 2013) ways. Idea Generation, Promotion and Realization can happen only by having supporting organizations because, innovation is all about taking risk in providing product, process and service to the society. When an individual fails in terms ideas and implementation, the concern organization should take the responsibility and the same time, encouraging organization only can up bring researchers to take risks so that innovation takes place.

Hence, organizations need to invest personal care and financial contribution in developing IWB to improve the overall functioning of the organization. Positive significant relationship between POS and overall IWB and its dimensions clearly indicates, the organizations are providing support the researchers' not only to generate ideas but, opportunities to promote and see the effectiveness in their respective domains. POS can influence only innovative work behavior (Denti, 2013) because; the organizations are surviving based on their innovation in the market and eventually managements focusing and fostering employees' innovative behaviour.

Unlike POS, SLS is a personal attitude of individuals and when innovation is contributed to the organization, it was not necessary to relate with POS for the researchers. One of the SLS dimensions Behaviour Analysis & Volition and general IWB as highly related variables prove self-effort to predict the future of the domain, self-motivation and ability to use the will power brings innovative work behaviour (Curral & Marques-Quinteiro, 2009). Both Task motivation and Constructive cognition are the interrelated variables, it verifies that SLS can be strengthened by complimenting motivation and cognitive process.

Especially in Indian culture, women are expected perform family based rituals very often, it might lead to seek some flexibility from the organization. Female perceives that they have a crucial role in their family life and along with professional life, hence when it comes to following complete practices of the organization, it is perceived as less-supportive organizations when compare to male. This is completely explained from the results of innovative work behaviour and its dimensions male differ than female. It was clearly accepted by studying the relationship between POS and IWB. When there is a weak perception over organizational support, automatically individuals have the tendency to limit their idea generation and realization.

Conclusion: According to the study, in both the Humanities and Science disciplines many researchers joined in their job as personal choice, it evidently says individuals in the organizations are more willing to contribute in terms of IWB (Denti, 2013), even if the organizational support vary, due to their personal attachment to their profession, researchers overall POS is comfortable. Hence, there is no difference in POS, IWB and its dimensions, and the dimensions of SLS Behaviour Analysis &Volition and Constructive Cognition. Both the Humanities and Science Researchers are almost the same in perceiving their organizational support, overall IWB, Generate ideas, promote ideas and realizing ideas. In addition to that they are same in Behaviour Analysis & Volition and cognitive approaches in dealing with their profession except Task Motivation and overall SLS. Any social research is very challenging to conduct because; it deals with many people and other aspects. When there is failure or more difficult, the researchers feel that is their weakness, gradually their motivation gets low. Actually, dealing with people is challenging and obviously that's not researchers mistake if they do not get it completed, most of the times external factors are influencing not to complete the humanities researches and the result difficult events minimizes individuals' SLS and Task Motivation. It was found that POS and SLS among the Knowledge Workers in Science & Technology and Humanities research organizations were the predictors of IWB.

Chapter Thirty Three

Cultural Variations, Values and Skills Among Two Continents[33]

Introduction: Culture plays a big role in defining values, concepts, and worldview. What is accepted in one culture may not be accepted as a value in another culture. Understanding this simple, yet complex concept needs cultural competency. Therefore, today educational psychologists, organisational pundits, and management gurus often place Cultural Competency popularly referred as CQ above IQ or EQ (Janetius & Mini, 2015). It is a popular saying among HR and Personnel Services Specialists today: IQ can fetch you a job, EQ may help you in promotions and it is CQ that will give you job satisfaction and success. In view of highlighting the need for cultural competency in organisational behaviour and human resource management, this study explores the essential skills and characteristics of a quality teacher in two different cultures.

Success in education depends on several factors such as institutional physical and personnel environment, student's personality attributes and attitudes, interaction and interpersonal relationship with teachers and peers and many more. It is a known fact that a skilled teacher is essential for optimal learning. Research findings in the

[33] **Janetius, S.T.Ph.D.,** Professor of Psychology, Jain University
Mini, T.C. (Former Faculty Gondar College of Medical Sciences, Ethiopia)
Principal, Kanoria PG Mahila Mahavidyalaya, Jaipur
Bekele, Workie, A. Assistant Professor of Internationalization of Higher Education, Ethiopian Ministry of Education & University of Gondar

Western countries identify positive classroom environment as an influential factor in the academic outcome (Ferguson, 1998; Hanushek, Kain, & Rivkin, 1999). Optimal learning generally takes place in a positive classroom. A positive classroom is that in which a teacher becomes facilitator by helping students to access information, encourage creative ideas and help to solve problems, thus pave the way for authentic learning in a multidimensional way (Janetius & Mulat, 2006; Janetius, Bekele & Mini, 2008). To lead a positive classroom, acquiring specific skills through adequate training, years of experience, appropriate education leading to academic proficiency and competency are essential for a teacher. Therefore, quality teachers with enough skills and orientation, well-bred personal attributes, and good characteristics to create a caring and conscientious classroom relationship are very essential. These, in turn, produce better academic outcome, reflected in students' interest in the course being taught, increased knowledge in the field of study, higher grades and ultimately better outcome based education for better job opportunity.

The current situation in many classroom environments and teacher-student interactions are seen in the form of an authoritarian teacher who claims exclusive authority over knowledge and who makes students drifters looking for grades. Therefore, quality teachers and positive classroom conducive to bring the desired outcome are very essential for learning. This situation further demands, proper preparation of teachers through adequate training (Janetius & Mulat, 2006) well-defined positive interpersonal relationship with students (Boynton & Boynton, 2005; Glasser, 1993), years of experience (Hanushek, 1986), adequate and proper education and degree (Ferguson, 1998; Greenwald, Hedges & Laine, 1996; Goldhaber & Brewer, 1997; Hanushek, 1986; Hanushek, Kain, & Rivkin, 1999) academic proficiency and competency in the subject being taught (Strauss & Vogt, 2001; Greenwald et al. 1996; Goldhaber & Brewer, 1997; Monk & King-Rice, 1994). If these qualities are perceived by the students in a teacher, consequential education and success can be expected.

Objectives: This study utilises data from two studies conducted by the authors at two different places, with students of different cultural orientation (Ethiopia and India) to evaluate similarities and differences in their perception of highly valued skills of quality teachers in colleges. The study is aimed at helping educationalists to prepare quality teachers through pertinent pedagogical training and renewal programs so that identified characteristics could be highlighted. The study results will help college teaching faculty to have self-awareness about the attitude and expectations of college students so that positive classroom can be created to provide quality education in the institutes of higher education.

Methodology: The African study was conducted at the University of Gondar, among students belonging to different colleges, faculties and departments, who were from different regions of Ethiopia. The Indian Study was conducted among college students in Tamil Nadu and Kerala, two southern states of India.

Data was collected from a total of 819 students (roughly 10% of the population) were selected by using simple random sampling technique.

Table1: Subjects of Ethiopian study

	Faculty	Sample size
1.	Social Sciences	157
2	Management & Economics	209
3	Vet. Medicine	26
4	Applied Sciences	158
5	Medical & Health	269
	Total	819

The Indian Study was conducted among college students in Tamil Nadu and Kerala. A total of 628 students were studied.

Table 2: Subjects of Indian study

	Department	Sample size
1	BBM	123
2	B Com	64
3	B Sc - CS	173
4	B CA	125
5	Maths	69
6	B Com - CA	74
	Total	628

Both the studies used 25 items self-administered questionnaire prepared by the authors, identifying quality teacher, positive classroom and academic success variables from local as well as foreign research literature. The questionnaire basically had five major quality teacher characteristics, each having three sub items. In addition, it had questions on academic outcome with four variables. The questionnaire was first pilot tested with 50 participants from the University of Gondar and the internal consistency of the questionnaire was established by the statistical package for social sciences (SPSS) for windows as Alpha = 0.761. The inter-item correlations mean = 0.817, a good positive correlation which indicates that the items are related and are not measuring the same thing. Since internal consistency and inter-item correlation mean were high, no items were changed after the pilot study.

Data analysis was done utilising appropriate multivariate techniques. The most significant variables explaining the presence or absence of characteristics is studied using Logistic Regression analysis. The academic outcome was considered as the dependent variable and Logistic Regression was performed to know how the set of independent variables are influencing the dependent variables collectively and separately.

Results and Discussion: The study results identify Education, Academics or knowledge, Work experience, Positive relationship with students and Personal attributes as the characteristics of a quality teacher. 93.4% of the students consider Education as the top characteristic of a quality teacher followed by Academics that is knowledge and intellectual/academic capacity (89.4%), Teaching and Work experience (87.4%), Positive relationship with the students (85.2%) and Personal characteristics, attributes, personality (80%).

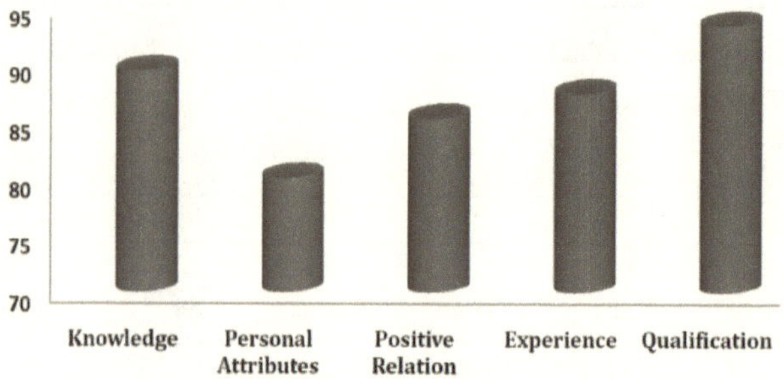

Graph 1: Skills preferred by Ethiopian students

Education or qualification of a teacher is explained significantly by the teacher's higher education in a foreign country. Knowledge is understood as intellectual curiosity and the competency in the subject matter. Work experience is explained by many years of teaching experience and teacher's experience in different fields. A positive relationship with students is explained by care and respect for students. These variables have a positive correlation with the academic achievement of the students. The Personal attributes of the teacher (self-discipline, role model, nonbiased behaviour) has been spotted low compared to other variables that contribute to the quality teacher characteristics.

When analysed further, it was identified that positive relationship with students, personal characteristics, attributes, personality and knowledge and intellectual/academic capacity of the teacher significantly explain the academic outcome as a single variable. Similarly, positive relationship with students significantly explains the interest in the subject being taught; positive relationship with students and education explains the increased knowledge in the subject being taught; positive relationship, personal characteristics and work experience explain success in life.

Indian Study Results: The study in India shows that the students perceive Knowledge and Intellectual capacity (96.39%) as the top characteristic of a quality teacher followed by Personal character and attributes (self-discipline, role model, nonbiased behaviour) 89.45%, Positive friendly behaviour in and out of classroom (86.53%) and, Teaching and Work experience (63.59%). The qualification of the teacher (which college or place of study and, higher or lower degree a teacher has gained) has been spotted very low (34.17%) and does not contribute much to the quality teacher characteristics.

The first and top most characteristic of a quality teacher identified by the students was Knowledge understood as intellectual curiosity to know many things and learn new things, up-to-date knowledge of subject matter as well as lessons being taught and explain lessons with practical application and current events.

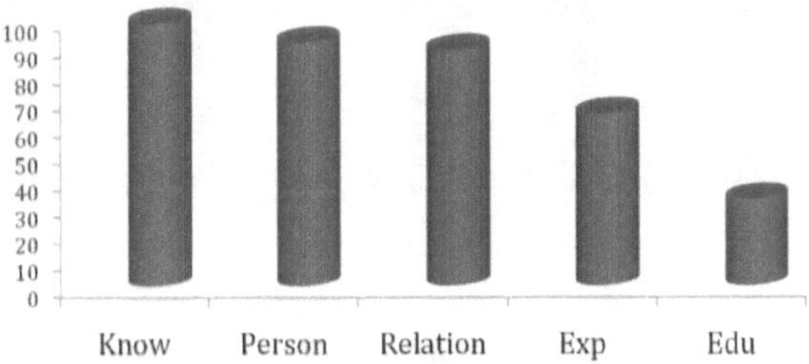

Graph 2: Skills preferred by Indian students

The second was personal attributes of the teacher identified as self-discipline and character, equal treatment and unbiased dealing with students and, exemplary behaviour as a role model. This was followed by positive relationship with the students which are reflected in caring, respect and acceptance of the students and regular encouragement to students. However, the students are apprehensive of the teacher if s/he ignores the mistakes of the students and do not correct them. Although students do not like to be punished for their mistakes, still feel that it is the duty of the teacher to correct them. The students do not give high significance to teaching and work experience of the teacher as a defining factor of a quality teacher. The students do not perceive many years of teaching experience or teaching experience at different colleges as a significant characteristic of a quality teacher; however, experience in different fields, like teaching and industry gain some amount of significance to the students in identifying a quality teacher.

This study contradicts a common belief in India that many years of experience or a degree from a reputed institution as a defining factor of a quality teacher, often considered in recruitments. The students consider this as a non-significant factor as against the knowledge and intellectual capacity of the teacher. The students also identify positive classroom and personal attributes of the teacher as top qualities. The demographic variables like sex of the students, their status (whether they work or study), parental education have no significant impact on their perception of quality teacher.

Cultural Comparison: This multi-disciplinary cultural study on quality teacher characteristics brings out some similarities and differences in valuing different skills among different cultures.

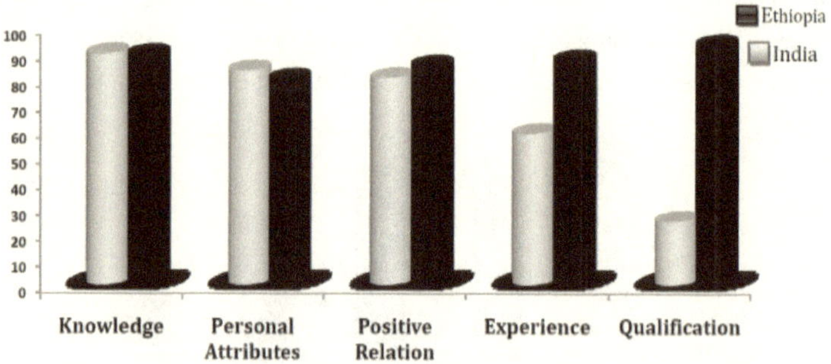

Graph 3: Preferences of Ethiopian & Indian students

Both the Indian and Ethiopian students expect the teachers to be knowledgeable. For the Ethiopian students, the place of study and the highest degree of the teacher are very important to accept a quality teacher. And they value these very much and consider them as the top characteristics of a quality teacher. Indian students don't evaluate a teacher by the degree, qualification and the place of study rather by the knowledge and intellectual curiosity the teacher has. Ethiopian students expect their faculty to maintain a high positive relationship with them whereas Indian students don't expect that much of positive relationship as Ethiopian students do.

As far as personal characteristics are concerned, the Indian students expect that their teacher has outstanding moral values and personal integrity. However, the Ethiopian students do not consider the personal life and other personal attributes of a teacher as an integral part of a quality teacher. The traditional Indian saying, '*Matha Pitha Guru Deivam*' plays a significant influence in the Indian psyche than the African understanding of a teacher.

Table 3: Differences in preferences

Qualities	Ethiopian students	Indian students
Knowledge	Important	Important
Personal Attributes	Not important	Important
Positive Relation	Important	Not important
Work Experience *(many colleges)*	Positive	Negative
Qualification *(where)*	Significant	Not Significant

If a teacher has worked in many colleges, the Ethiopian students think that the person has more knowledge and understanding, s/he is respected and valued high among Ethiopian students whereas Indian students think that the teacher is a poor performer and therefore changes many colleges or workplaces. If a teacher has foreign education, the Ethiopian students value that qualification very highly, whereas in the Indian context, the students see whether the faculty is a good performer in the classroom rather than where s/he got the degree.

Conclusion: Culture is the key player in defining values, concepts and worldview. Due to globalisation, multinational companies are spreading its wings at every nook and corner of the globe, the society is becoming more of a global village every day and, cultural competency becomes a must for success. This study identified the cultural similarities and differences in identifying values and skills in teaching profession from two different continents, India and Africa. What the students consider a value to label a teacher as a quality person in one culture differs from another culture. This study strengthens the view further that multicultural competency is a must for every employee today because of the cultural diversity we see in workplaces everywhere.

The findings will help teachers to know how the students perceive an excellent teacher so that they can improve their classroom approach for better academic outcome. The identified factors could be incorporated and reiterated for a superior pedagogical training and improved didactic modules for finer preparation of teachers in the country. The findings could also be used in recruitment of faculty so that the perceived characteristics can be given priority in selection. It can also enlighten employees who look for jobs aboard and other cultures, to understand and appreciate the uniqueness of people at different places and perform well.

Ideational Fluency, Cognitive-Emotional Regulation and Occupational Self-Efficacy[34]

Introduction: Quality of life of the people can be enhanced through research, as this domain has a crucial and unique ability to deliver facts through empirical study which gives the exact status of the society, which makes way for innovations and development in our society. Research establishes a forum for intellectual and technological advancement to improve the quality of humans in every sphere of life (Barak, 2002; Gnanaprakash, 2012). Research & development have been given immense importance and hence the population of research scientists has also considerably increased to over seven million people in science and technology alone (UNESCO, 2010). On researcher lies a massive responsibility to protect and defend, people and the society against threats and barriers which is unfavorable for the country's progress. They ensure safety looking in-depth into facts, highlighting the scope and limitations, making necessary improvement in planning and execution, patenting, developing new models, innovations for development, coding and regulating laws for the higher good and for the benefit of all. Society's status and its directions are guided by research which indeed helps to bridge a gap as it aids to the domain. To execute and accomplish research successfully researchers' knowledge, creativity, cognitive process, emotional stability and confidence become crucial as it is a comprehensive process.

[34] **Ankitha, U.**, Research Scholar, Jain University
Gnanaprakash, C. Ph.D., Asst. Professor of Psychology, Jain University

Any discovery or innovation is an intense and in-depth procedure which involves a package of psychological phenomena's occurring during the execution of research, which most researchers face but in varying intensities. Barriers to research could be due to being unable to complete tasks on time, unforeseen risks, health issues, financial aid, political interference, unfavorable work environment, personal or psychological issues. This in turn could hinder the process of the research activities which needs to be catered to. Hence, it becomes important to understand and study the psychological process in respect to ideational fluency, cognitive emotional regulation strategies and organizational self-efficacy of research scientists to help develop more effective and productive frame of mind to execute research successfully, by channelizing efforts and knowledge of scientists to its full potential.

Ideational fluency leads any researcher to provide a tactic, to overcome an existing problem or update society to reach the upscale standard by unconventional ideas in a rational and coherent manner. Amabile (1983) recognized that every individual is inherited with expertise, creative thinking skills and motivation. These components become very important to make quick wise decisions, cater to unforeseen risks, problem solving, make new innovations, improvise the plan and for execution of the research (Vidal, 2009; Miller, 1997).

Fluency in thought process is crucial in research as many collective ideas reflect on a new finding which could have a potential value to the community in large or as small as to find alternative way to execute research activity in the best possible way. Ideational fluency motivates researcher and reduces burden of the complex thinking process as it acts as a pathway to liberate human energy. On the other hand Amabile (1998) concluded that barriers to creativity include judgmental thinking, oppression and hierarchy, habits and routines, various perceptual, emotional and cultural blocks.

Cognitive emotional regulation refers to the cognitive process accompanied with emotions influencing the product of the thought process which could be negative or positive. Regulation of these cognitive and emotional thoughts will have a great effect on the functioning of the individual (Ochsner & Gross, 2008; Gross, 1998) in understanding oneself and the world around (Thomson, 1991). In connection with cognitive emotional regulations mental locks were generally influenced by perceptual, cultural, emotional, environmental and intellectual factors (Adams, 1986).

A positive approach enhances the functioning of individuals as they have optimistic outlook about self and others are prepared to accept the critical and positive situations and deal with it dynamically. With negative or pessimistic thought process, everything seems just wrong and not recoverable. Cognitions and emotions can be trained or a conscious effort can be made to help oneself to think more positively and optimistically to incur benefits. Cognitions and emotions are interlinked and they play hand in hand, thus it becomes important to manage them.

Cognitive process provides different thoughts occurring in the brain and emotions needs to be regulated right, to make work easy and execute research smoothly, without which it would lead to frustration, lack of interest, unhappy with the work progress, drop in efficiency which would lead to bias or might not be able to provide accurate results and thus might affect the research outcomes and can create damage in satisfaction level, interest and self-efficacy to involve in future research process.

Self-efficacy among scientists would help them to believe in one's ability to succeed (Lunenburg, 2011). One's sense of self-efficacy plays a major role in how one approaches goals, tasks, and challenges in their work environment. Self-efficacy is the belief in one's capabilities to organize and execute the course of action required to produce given attainments (Bandura, 1997). It helps researchers to understand themselves, take an account of their ability, skills and potential to take up challenges, work out alternative methods, undergo stress, face risks, have the right frame of mind to stay composed irrespective of the situations and to deal with it appropriately in order to accomplish the tasks (Khan et al., 2002; Bandura, 1986).

Self-efficacy in the research environment motivates not only self but also reflection cognitive process and emotional regulations. It helps individual to be flexible to adapt to different circumstances, cater to the fundamental wellbeing of research scientists, to build a successful career and keeps them intrinsically motivated to accomplish goals. Occupational self-efficacy tries to overcome the problem of constancy of general self-efficacy and the problem of having to assess different kinds of task specific self-efficacy (Birgit & Thomas, 2009). A high sense of organizational self-efficacy aids in devoting more time to plan, organize and execute tasks at work (Hsiao, 2011). Congenial creativity process, cognitive, emotional regulation strategies and self-efficacy would be great potential sources (Janssen, 2000) which does not only confine to enhancing the knowledge of the society but takes responsibility to escalate the societal eminence and country's progress assuring safety and its progress.

Objectives:

1. To find the relationship among Ideational Fluency, Cognitive-emotional regulation strategies and Occupational self-efficacy among scientists.
2. To find the difference among ideational fluency, cognitive-emotional regulation strategies and occupational self-efficacy among scientists.

Methodology: The sample consists of 74 (36 humanities and 38 science) scientists from different research institutions selected through purposive sampling method. To verify the key objectives ideational fluency measure, cognitive-emotional regulation strategies questionnaire and occupational self-efficacy scale were administered. After explaining the purpose of the present research to the sample, questionnaires were administered on 74 scientists from different research institutions, through purposive sampling method. The questionnaires were administered only after receiving an informed consent. Socio demographic details and responses to questionnaires were collected from the scientists. After obtaining the data, statistical tools were used to analyse the data.

Results and Discussion: The table below shows the composition of the total sample participated in the study. There are 36 participants from the humanities and 38 participants from the science discipline, which accounts to 48.64 percent and 51.35 percent respectively.

The table 1 presents the distribution of the respondents in the sample with respect to research scientists in the discipline of humanities and science from different research institutions.

Sample Characteristics		Frequency	Percent
Discipline	Humanities	36	48.64
	Science	38	51.35

The table 2 presents the difference in ideational fluency among researchers from different research institutions with respect to their broad discipline.

	Discipline	N	Mean	S.D	't'
Ideational	Humanities	36	8.97	2.98	2.96 **
Fluency	Science	38	7.03	2.68	

**P < 0.01

The above table presents that there is a statistically significant difference between research scientists of humanities and science disciplines with respect to ideational fluency. It is seen that researchers of humanities have higher innovative work behaviour than the researchers of the science discipline. This could be due to phenomenological work behaviour of the research scientists in the humanities domain, as they interact more with human participants for their research study which could have habituated them to think, perceive and interpret responses to allow fluency in their thought process. This diversity in thinking could have brought researchers to look for answers or solutions in every possible dimension.

In the science domain the protocol to execute research is mainly a systematic mode of work behaviour, where research scientists are generally bound to experimentation, trying different combinations to derive at a new conclusion which is a nature of laboratory setting or with natural environment. Science domain is more systematic and scientific and unlike humanities looks for one product rather than alternative solutions. This difference in the nature of work, could have by default caused, difference in ideational fluency between these two research domains. Sternberg (1999) found through his research that creativity is influenced by environment, personality, learning and cognition.

The table 3 presents the difference in CERQ and its dimensions among researchers from different research institutions with respect to their broad discipline.

Dimensions	Discipline	Mean	S. D.	't'
Self – blame	Humanities	10.14	2.392	.442
	Science	9.92	1.822	
Acceptance	Humanities	10.36	1.944	1.176
	Science	9.84	1.853	
Rumination	Humanities	10.81	2.388	1.814
	Science	9.92	1.776	
Positive Refocus	Humanities	11.22	2.439	-.088
	Science	11.26	1.483	
Focus on planning	Humanities	11.83	2.490	2.669**
	Science	10.55	1.554	
Positive reappraisal	Humanities	14.53	2.823	5.425**
	Science	11.55	1.811	
Putting into perspective	Humanities	13.69	2.974	4.334**
	Science	11.34	1.494	
Catastrophe	Humanities	10.81	2.516	.888
	Science	10.39	1.306	
Other blame	Humanities	8.17	2.602	3.437**
	Science	9.97	1.881	
CERQ	Humanities	99.75	7.145	3.051**
	Science	95.08	6.002	

$**P < 0.01$, $*P < 0.05$

The above table shows that there is a significant difference in CERQ and its dimensions among researchers with respect to their broad disciplines. Humanities researchers have higher scores than the science domain in respect to focus on planning, positive reappraisal and putting into perspective which are the positive indicators to the category of Adaptive strategies. Humanities dealing with huge sample size for their research study, uncertainties, social environment which is dynamic that demands more focus on planning. This calls for a need for positive reappraisal which caters to adapt, think about the further steps with presence of mind and evaluating the best possible alternative to execute research by putting into perspective the higher priorities into action. Science domain has a high score on others blame which is the indicator for Non-adaptive strategies. This could be due to the limitations of being flexible in conducting research which could be traced out to inappropriate work environment or condition, time limitations, monetary support, supply of materials on time etc. Self – blame, acceptance, rumination, positive refocus and catastrophe shows no significant difference among both research domains. Hence CERQ shows significant difference among humanities and science researchers in the cognitive emotional regulation strategies used in their occupation, which could be due to individual differences, the nature of work, work setting or due to personality traits they inherit.

The table 4 presents the difference in OSE and its dimensions among researchers with respect to the their broad discipline

Dimensions	Domain	Mean	S. D.	't'
Confidence	Humanities	15.36	2.045	-.635
	Science	15.66	1.977	
Command	Humanities	12.06	1.145	-.192
	Science	12.11	1.085	
Adaptability	Humanities	12.36	1.268	-1.732
	Science	12.92	1.496	
Personal Effectiveness	Humanities	16.69	1.849	1.135
	Science	16.24	1.618	
Positive Attitude	Humanities	11.89	1.909	-.802
	Science	12.21	1.527	
Individuality	Humanities	7.39	1.695	-.824
	Science	7.68	1.378	
OSE	Humanities	75.75	7.919	-.708
	Science	76.82	4.701	

The above table shows that there is no significant difference among confidence, command, adaptability, positive attitude, personal effectiveness and individuality among researchers of both humanities and science in occupational self - efficacy. This could be simply due to individual differences, different personality traits, different strengths or it could mean that each step of research domain could have its own risks, demands and challenges that a researcher needs to adapt to successfully execute it.

Table 5 presents the relationship between ideational fluency and dimensions of CERQ among researchers with respect to the their broad discipline

Dimensions of CERQ	Ideational Fluency
Self blame	-.011
Acceptance	-.133
Rumination	-.018
Positive refocussing	-.006
Focus on planning	.174
Positive reappraisal	.234*
Putting into perspective	.094
Catastrophe	.033
Other blame	-.159
CERQ	-.015

*P < 0.05

There is a significant positive relationship between ideational fluency and positive reappraisal. This could be due to fluency of thoughts that could be contributing to positive interaction within self to reassure the confidence, which helps the researcher to challenge and to adapt to any given situation. Ideational fluency takes care of mere flow of creative ideas to a solution where as positive reappraisal thinks critically to positively look into a situation or a task and choose the most optimistic and viable approach to arrive at an end product. Ideational fluency and Cognitive emotional regulation strategies does not have significant relationship as emotions and fluency in thought process could be perceived as two different entities by the researchers, where personal feeling should not have an influence in work process as duties, responsibility in research has a higher value to the society in large and hence not to compromise in the quality of the research process.

Table 6 presents the relationship between ideational fluency and dimensions of occupational self- efficacy among research scientists

Dimensions of Occupational Self Efficacy	**Ideational Fluency**
Confidence	-.002
Command	-.016
Adaptability	-.019
Personal Effectiveness	-.043
Positive Attitude	.166
Individuality	-.219
OSE	-.027

In this above table there is no significant relationship among the dimensions of ideational fluency and occupational self - efficacy. This could be due to ideational fluency being an intrinsic motivator and occupational self - efficacy being both extrinsic and intrinsic factor which is not influenced by one another, where the product of creative fluent thought is considered an idea, be it negative or positive. It is considered as contribution to the research work rather than making judgments. Therefore the ideas put together would be further altered to arrive at a solution.

The results show that individuality and focus on planning, positive reappraisal with confidence and individuality, other blame and command have positive significant relationship with one another. This could be due to individuals who work in their own unique way is independent which makes them more focused on planning their work. These individuals are generally intrinsically motivated. Confidence and individuality have a relationship as positive reappraisal is influenced by one another as there is an assurance and reliance which is positively influencing researcher's behaviour to execute research work. Command and other blame has a significant positive relationship as researchers have to look at the overall tasks involved in research and sometimes have to make their own decisions to execute research activity, in this process limitations could have been the work environment, monitory help and supply of materials.

1. There is a significant difference between research scientists of humanities and science disciplines in respect to ideational fluency.
2. There is a significant difference among research scientists of humanities and science in CERQ, with respect to the dimensions of other blame, focus on planning, positive reappraisal and putting into perspective.
3. There is no significant relationship among ideational fluency, cognitive emotional regulation strategy and occupational self – efficacy.

Conclusion: It is clearly evident that research is a unique domain where research scientists work differently from one another and in their own unique way to derive into conclusions. Individual differences and uniqueness in their approach and thought process itself could be aiding to success in this domain of research. Despite all these variations this domain has proved itself over and again through constant contribution to its society and its progress which in itself is the biggest achievement.

Chapter Thirty Five

Role Conflict, Suppressive Thoughts and Pro-Social Behaviour[35]

Introduction: Industrial revolution was the major turning point that industrial empire ever witnessed .The rise of the industrial empire lies in the foot of industrial revolution. Industrial revolution came up with remarkable transformations in the industrial world .The industrial revolution of the mid-1760s to 1840s contributed to a major shift from hand production method to the development of sophisticated machinery and promoted factory development .The new industrial innovations gradually but steadily enriched the era with a higher standard of living and almost influenced every aspect of daily life in some way .In particular the average income and life style of the populations began to exhibit unprecedented sustained growth . Such unhindered growth gifted the population with immense job opportunities in these industrial setups .The two distinctive wide classes of such opportunities had been the blue collared jobs and white collared jobs .The terms Blue collars and white collars are occupational classifications that distinguish workers who performs manual labor and who performs professional jobs. Another aspect which distinguishes the

[35] **Ariya Ajikumar, Ajmala Thasneem, R.M, Suhaina,** Student, Department of Psychology, LISSAH, Calicut
Sheron K.P.R ., Asst. Professor, LISSAH, Calicut

blue collar and white collar employs are their earnings and educational level. From the early decades of history the white collar personnel are well paid because of the educational level required for the occupation were as blue collars are daily or hourly paid. Past the industrial revolution the vast class difference among the white collared and the blue collared stretched in more tension.

Even though industrial advancement flourished economic development and replenished numerous opportunities, it also seeded foils in the organizational setups. The consistent progress of industries present more and more challenges to the employees. Figuring out a new work culture ,adjusting with coworkers ,building trust , dedication and so on put a great dare before the employees .To meet the progressive requirements of the work place the workers have to incredibly put forth mental and physical tactics . Unfortunately such tactics and effort in work demand their personal and social interests. No doubt an organizational setup invites whole lot of psychological and health concerns. Work load, stress, anxiety, psychological support, employee morale, are few nomenclatures of such psychological concerns. One among the major causes of such psychological concerns is the inefficiency in managing the work demands along with self, personal life and social life. A working individual is sure to experience at least a few psychological concerns or issues in his self, work life, personal life or in social life. This is because one enacts multiple roles in various occasions of life that may be personal, social, work related or in managing self.

At times a role conflict arises when situations falls such that individuals become incapable to choose among the available, alternative courses of job. Role conflicts are generated when role expectations are understood but due to some reason or the other they cannot be complied with. A commonly noted predominant Role conflict among the blue collared and white collared workers is that between work and family. This is because persons occupy multiple and divergent roles simultaneously in the work and family. While peeping into the work of a white collar employee we can understand a fluctuation of behavior in work place that is, the employee has to act the role of a subordinate of a bureaucrat along with the role of a superior officer. Whereas in blue collars the stunted growth of the profession does not lead them any job increment.

Role conflict can also be due to disagreements in individual perspectives, environmental stress, lack of trust and acceptance either in work place or within the family. Every person holding a particular position regardless of blue collar or white collar is expected to behave in a particular manner known as role expectation from that person. When the role expectations are not met properly, it may negatively result in the role. This role conflict brings tension and it leads to psychological imbalance in the person. This makes an adverse effect in the every aspect of everyday life. It is seen that Role conflict has considerable influence on thoughts, behavior, performance and job satisfaction of employees. Presence of role conflict complicates the job in many ways. This may overlap with his personal life or social life. Conflict in role could make employees least disclosing henceforth suppressing the thoughts. Often, suppressive thought occurs when a person consciously attempts to stop thinking about a particular thought. Resisting of some thought may be done intentionally to avoid certain behavior or a thought. In regards with employees suppressive thoughts may be the results of role bias, issues in work place, incapability to meet family and personal needs and dissatisfaction in social life. The existence of such thoughts may lead to several psychological disturbances. Studies have reported that thought suppression have behavioral consequences (Mc Rae et al 1994).

Role conflict and related suppressive thoughts influence the display of social behavior. Social behavior like 'pro social behavior' is a broad range of actions intended to benefit one or more people other than oneself. A main reason for people to engage in pro social behavior is need of reciprocal social acceptance, egoistic reasons that is improving one's self image, reciprocal benefits. Evidently the internally withheld suppressive thoughts along with the bias in role influence the wide range of pro social behavior, fore the reciprocal benefits and social acceptance comes into prominence what so ever the psychological condition of the employee may be. The degree of exhibition of pro social behavior may be depending on various individual effectively monitoring their role conflict and resulting suppressive thoughts.

The categorization of blue collar job and white collar indifferently widened causing ill psychological influence on the employee of both categories. In majority of the occasions the job demands effective engagements in the work place. In the race of industrial competition the psychological wellbeing of the workers are unseen. But irrationally this influences the peaceful life of employees. The significance of the study lies in analyzing these psychological issues in terms of three aspects namely role conflict, suppressive thoughts and pro social behavior among blue collared and white collared employees. The acknowledgement of the relationship among these three characteristics could help improve the psychological wellbeing and human excellence in an organization. The knowledge of these may effectively enhance the working condition in an organization matching parallel with self-interest, social and personal life.

Sadia Najmi , Daniel M, W.Matthew, K.Nock (august 2007), carried out a "study on Thought suppression and self-injurious thoughts and behaviors". This study proposes and tests a theoretical model suggesting the propensity to suppress unwanted thoughts is associated with presence and frequency of self-injurious thoughts and behaviors

(SITB). Results of this cross-sectional study of adolescents (N=87) revealed that the self-reported propensity to suppress unwanted thoughts is associated with the presence and frequency of non-suicidal self-injury (NSSI).

 John R. Rizzo, Robert J. House and Sidney I. Lirtzman (Jun., 1970), studied on "Role Conflict and Ambiguity in Complex Organizations". The literature indicates that dysfunctional individual and organizational consequences result from existence of role conflict and role ambiguity in complex organizations. Derived measures of role conflict and ambiguity tend to correlate in two samples in expected directions.

Susan E Jackson, Randall S Schuler (August 1985) conducted "a meta-analysis and conceptual critique of research on role ambiguity and role conflict in work settings". This study analyses 29 correlates of role ambiguity and role conflict. Meta-analysis procedures were used to measure strength and consistency of the relationship found between each of the 29 correlates and role ambiguity and role conflict.

By O'Reilly, Charles A., Chatman, Jennifer (Aug 1986) conducted "a study on Organizational commitment and psychological attachment: The effects of compliance, identification, and internalization on pro social behavior". Conducted a study on 82 non-faculty university employees (mean age 31–40 years) and 162 graduating business students to investigate relation among dimensions of commitment and extra role activities. The results indicate the importance of dimensions of commitment using notions of psychological attachment and the various forms such attachment can take.

Arthur P. Brief and Stephan J. Motowidlo conducted "the study of pro social Organizational Behavior" in which the construct of pro social organizational behavior was defined and 13 specific forms were described. They vary, whether they are functional or dysfunctional for organizational effectiveness, prescribed or not prescribed as part of one's organizational role, and directed toward an individual or organizational target.

The above studies extremely relate with the current study. The variables considered in the above review tie up with the variables of current studies that is ,role conflict, suppressive thoughts and pro social behavior .Role ambiguity, organizational commitment, psychological attachment essentially correlate with the variables of current study.

Objectives:

1. To study the significant relationship among role conflict, suppressive thoughts and pro social behavior in employees.

2. To study the significant difference of role conflict, suppressive thought, pro social behavior between blue collars and white collars.

Methodology: In the study a total of 60 participants were randomly selected as the sample in which 30 were white collar employees and 30 were blue collar employees from various parts of Calicut district, Kerala. The tools used in the present study are: Pro social tendencies measure (Carlo and Randall 2002) consists of 23 questions in which 9 are negative. White Bear Suppression Inventory (Wegner and Zanakos 1994) is a 15 -item questionnaire that is designed to measure thought suppression. Role Conflict Scale (Carlson 2000) is developed to measure role conflict among four roles. The four roles are Professional, Spouse, Parent and Self. It consists of 34 questions.

The required data were collected from blue collars and white collars from different areas of Calicut district, Kerala. They were briefed about the study and their consent for the studies was requested. The questionnaires were administered carefully among the selected samples .They were promised confidentiality for the information gathered from them. The statistical techniques selected were based on objectives and hypothesis formulated. The statistical techniques used are presented below: Karl Pearson's Product Moment correlation: Correlation is a statistical measurement of the relationship between two variables. Possible correlations range from +1 to -1. Independent t test. The t-test is a statistical test that is used to determine if there is a significant difference between the mean or average scores of two groups.

Result and Discussion: By analyzing the correlation table, it can be seen that the coefficient of correlation of the variable role conflict and suppressive thought is 0.245, role conflict and pro social behavior is -0.076 and suppressive thought and pro social behavior is 0.88 and are not significant indicating there is no significant relation between the variables role conflict, suppressive thought and pro social behavior among employees. The relationship is not significant because the display of pro social behavior is greatly influenced by cultural and social factors.

Table1: correlation table of role conflict, suppressive thoughts and pro social behavior in employees

Variables	Role conflict	Suppressive thought
Suppressive thought	0.245	-
Pro social behavior	-0.076	0.88

The nature of the profession, educational qualification, social acceptance, financial income does not affect their social commitment. Since the effect was not significant the relationship was analyzed among blue collars and white collars separately.

Therefore research hypothesis was rejected and null hypothesis was accepted.

Table 2: correlation table for role conflict, suppressive thought and pro social behavior in white collars employee

Variables	Role conflict	Suppressive thought
SUPRESSIVE THOUGHT	0.370*	-
PRO SOCIAL BEHAVIOR	0.049	0.076

*0.05 level of significant

From the table, there is a significant positive correlation between role conflict and suppressive thought in white collar employees, which is 0.370. When role conflict increases tendencies of suppression of thoughts also increases. A conflict in the role negatively results in suppression of thoughts. Therefore research hypothesis was accepted and null hypothesis was rejected.

Table3: Correlation table of role conflict, suppressive thought and pro social behavior in blue collar

Variables	Role conflict	Suppressive thought
SUPPRESSIVE THOUGHT	-0.092	-
PROSOCIAL BEHAVIOR	0.137	0.014

In accordance with the correlation table , no significant relation among role conflict, suppressive thought and pro social behavior in blue collars was observed .The coefficient of correlation between suppressive thought and role conflict is -0.092,between pro social and role conflict is 0.137 and between pro social and suppressive thought is 0.014. Therefore research hypothesis was rejected and null hypothesis was accepted

Table 4: mean, standard deviation, t value of role conflict between blue and white collar.

VARIABLE	GROUP	N	MEAN	S.D	t	P value
ROLE CONFLICT	BLUE COLLAR	30	62.13	15.856	2.575*	0.013
	WHITE COLLAR	30	79.90	35.470		

*0.05 level of significance

By analyzing the table 4, it can be concluded that there is significant difference in the role conflict of blue and white collar employees. The difference is clearly visible in the mean score values of white collar 79.90 and blue collar 62.13. The variation in the score gives the interpretation that white collar employees experience high role conflict when compared to blue collars. The probable reason behind this is that white collars being under the administration of the higher authority, follows a very complex job structure. Therefore research hypothesis was accepted, null hypothesis was rejected.

Table 5:   mean, standard deviation, t value of suppressive thoughts between blue collar and white collar

VARIABLE	GROUP	N	MEAN	S.D	T	P - Value
SUPPRESSIVE THOUGHT	WHITE COLLAR	30	50.37	14.257	0.580	0.564
	BLUE COLLAR	30	48.47	11.416		

By analyzing the table, mean score values of suppressive thoughts in white collar are 50.37 and blue collar 48.47. There is a slight difference in the suppressive thought of white collar when compared to blue collar. In correspondence with the table 3 (Correlation table of role conflict, suppressive thought and pro social behavior in blue collars.) the slight increase in suppressive thought in white collars is the outcome of high role conflict experienced by the white collars. The incompatibility in the work culture and personal, social interest sum to create suppressive thoughts more in white collars than blue collars. Therefore research hypothesis was rejected, null hypothesis was accepted.

Table 6: Mean, standard deviation, t value of pro social behavior between white collar and blue collar

VARIABLES	GROUPS	N	MEAN	S.D	T	P- Value
PRO SOCIAL BEHAVIOR	WHITE COLLAR	30	78.90	15.032	0.235	0.815
	BLUE COLLAR	30	78.19	8.042		

By analyzing the table, mean score of pro social behavior between white collars and blue collars no significant difference can be seen. The pro social attitude of a person is not altered by job nature. Secondly the pro social attitude of a person is the product of cultural and social factors and hence not altered by any psychological concern or environmental factors. The research Hypothesis   was rejected so the null hypothesis was accepted.

Conclusion: The present study focused on the relationship of the variables role conflict, suppressive thoughts and pro social behavior between blue collars and white collars. 30 blue collars and 30 white collars were selected randomly. Analysis of the study shows that white collars possess high role conflict and suppressive thought, whereas the pro social attitude remained the same in both white and blue collars, breaking a conventional norm.

Chapter Thirty Six

Adolescent Identity and Subjective Vitality[36]

Introduction: Erickson states that adolescence is the stage which has a psychosocial crisis to master between ego identity and role confusion. Adolescence is the crucial age when an individual gets over being dependent on their parents to an independent life. The problem of identity arises among them and core beliefs begin to get a new and different form that also leads to the development of the personal identity. Adolescence is a stage which is also termed as an age of 'stress and storm' which signifies the drastic changes in the individual. The growth in physical and psychological aspect of the individual and the attitude of the individual towards this change decides the further well-being of an individual. This includes how an individual experiences the quality of life, emotional reactions and judgments.

Personal identity is all about the questions an individual has on the self which arises due to the virtue possessed. Whereas a few other people say that consciousness does not have any relation with the personal identity. An individual possesses a lot of identities based upon the role. Each position has its own explanations that internalizes

[36] **Ashwini, U.R., & J. Indumathy,** Research Scholar, Madras School of Social Work
Ashwini, K.S., Avinashilingam University, Coimbatore

with the identity. A most important task of self-development during early stage of adolescence is the differentiation of multiple selves as a function of social context (e.g., self with father, mother, close friends) with awareness of the potential contradictions.

Identity may be acquired through modelling from the parents, peers and available role models around them. Children define themselves in terms of the description of their parents. If their parents see a child as worthless, they view themselves to be worthless. People who perceive themselves as likable may remember more positive than negative statements. Psychologists perceive that the formation of identity is a process of "finding oneself" by matching one's skills, potential and talents with available social roles. Thus, defining oneself within a social world is among one of difficult choice an individual finds to make. In the phase of identity struggle, when people don't find it pleasant they end up in behaviours such as drug abuse, compulsive shopper, or gambling, as a compensatory method of experiencing aliveness or staving off depression and meaninglessness in life. Identity is always in a process of evaluation and it continues to change through the lifespan. An increased awareness of an individual's identity can be a factor that increases self-esteem and reduces depression and anxiety.

Adolescence: Adolescence is generally described as a period both of suffering, passion, upheaval and rebellion against adult authority and of social change, intellectual and physical. Adolescence is a period of rapid psychological and physiological change of intensive readjustment to the school, family, and social life and of getting prepared for adult roles. The time begins with puberty and ends with the accomplishment of an adult in work role. It usually begins between 11 and 16 years in boys and between 9 and 16 years in girls. Adolescence is the 'process of growing up' or the 'period of life from puberty to maturity'. Adolescence has also been associated with the age span, varying from 10-13 as the starting age and 19-21 as the concluding age

Early Adolescence: Early adolescence is said to be the most stressful stage of all developmental transitions. It occurs within the years of age from 11 to 15, when a period of rapid and drastic biological change is experienced by the individual.

Middle Adolescence: This stage encompasses the ages from 15 to 17. The individuals at this phase of development are capable of generalizations, abstract thinking and useful introspections that are linked to the real life experience.

Late Adolescence: The ages represented in this stage are 17 years through the early 20s. The themes of body image, autonomy, achievement, intimacy, and sense of self are found to be more prominent and when integrated contributes to a whole sense of identity.

Theory of identity: Identity has been given different terms such as "sense" an "attitude." a "resolution." and few others. The most adjoining psychosocial precursor to identity in adolescence is the sense of industry attained in latency. The peculiar thing to be understood is the newly happening physical development, cognitive skills, and social expectations. These changes fetch a pathway to enable an individual from late childhood to an successful adult through the process of maturing. Young person's to son through and synthesize their childhood identifications in order to construct a viable pathway toward their adulthood. Resolution of the identity issue at adolescence guarantees only that one will be faced with subsequent identity "crises." Most empirical research into Erikson's theories stemmed around his views on adolescence and attempts to establish identity. His theoretical approach was studied and supported by James Marcia, a Canadian developmental psychologist. Marcia's work in the social psychology of development extended Erikson's. Erikson had suggested that the normative conflict occurring in adolescence is the opposition between identity and confusion (identity crisis).

Marcia elaborated on Erikson's psychosexual stages by claiming identity development in a viewpoint but the extent to which an individual has explored and committed to an identity in a variety of life domains including politics, occupation, religion, intimate relationships, friendships, and gender roles. Marcia's Theory of Identity achievement attribute two different parts that evolve adolescent identity namely a crisis and a commitment. He stated a crisis as a period of upheaval where old choices or values are re-examined. The outcome of a crisis leads to a commitment to a certain value or role. Marcia developed the four identity statuses according to dimensions of exploration and commitment:

Identity Diffusion is the stage in which the young person is not currently going through a crisis and has not made a commitment. A person has not yet made an attempt or willing to make a commitment. *Identity Foreclosure*, the stage in which the young person has made a commitment without having gone through a crisis. The individual seems to be willing in commitment to some relevant values, roles or future goals. *Identity Moratorium*, the stage in which the young person is currently in a crisis but has not made a commitment. *Identity Achievement*, this is the period where a young individual has gone through a crisis and then committed to a value or role.

Marcia distinguishes different forms of identity to substantiate that those people who form the most coherent self-concept in adolescence are those who are most able to make intimate attachments in early adulthood. This supports Eriksonian theory by suggesting that those best equipped to resolve the crisis of early adulthood are those who have most successfully resolved the crisis of adolescence.

Erikson's Ego psychology stressed the role of the ego. According to Erikson, the environment in which a child lives is crucial to providing growth, adjustment, a source of self-awareness, and identity. Role confusion is "the inability to conceive of oneself as a productive member on one's own society". This inability to conceive of oneself as a productive member is a great danger; it can occur during adolescence when looking for an occupation. When the youth is unsuccessful at this task, identity diffusion may lead to delinquency and even psychotic episodes.

Formation of identity occurs because of socialization. Erikson elaborated socialization with the theory that individuals face challenges throughout their life that develop and shape their personality indefinitely. He also mapped out these potential challenges within eight stages. These stages extended to include infancy, toddlerhood, preschool, preadolescence, adolescence, young adulthood, middle adulthood, and old age.

The term vitality has its etymological source in the idea of life and is accordingly defined as an animating force, or principle of life. According to the Oxford English Dictionary, an individual with vitality has vigor and liveliness, a general energy for life. Colloquially, vitality is typically employed to describe manifest excitement and energy and is applied to those who appear spirited, enthusiastic, and spontaneous. The conceptual tie between vitality and life is at once broad and vague. In part this is because even within theoretical biology definitions of life itself remain controversial.

Subjective vitality is highly related with the self-realization, mental health, positive emotions and greater self-motivation, and on other hand distress, negative emotions and external locus of control have a less relation with the same. Different researches represent that subjective vitality has a considerable interrelationship with mental health, life satisfaction, and optimistic performance.

The concept of subjective vitality refers to the state of feeling alive and alert–to having energy available to the self. Vitality is known as an aspect of eudemonic well-being of being active and energetic is part of which means to be psychologically well and fully functioning. Subjective vitality is a reflection of both psychological wellness and organismic and hence expected it to be influenced by both somatic and psychological factors.

Adolescence constitutes of transformation period and formation of identity. Completing this stage of adolescence could lead to a formation of an identity based upon their interest, values possessed, experiences faced at this age. Based on the level of acceptance the individual have towards the changes they have gone through their well-being is determined. Hence the changes that an individual goes through the stage of adolescence very well determine the happiness and satisfaction of life. This also proves that the identity formation has its influence on the subjective vitality and well-being of an individual. Additionally there are very few studies done recently on the identity of adolescents. The current study explores the relationship between subjective vitality and personal identity among adolescents.

Objectives: This study is focused on the following research questions.

- To assess the Personal Identity of adolescents
- To assess the Subjective Vitality of adolescents
- To find the relationship between Personal Identity and Subjective Vitality
- To find the gender differences in Personal Identity and Subjective Vitality

Methodology: There are limited reviews that study the variables of the current study. Hence the study follows the exploratory research design to get new insights about the relationship between Personal Identity and Subjective Vitality. The samples of the study were 127 adolescents whose age range from 18 – 19 years. The participants are selected from 4 different academic institutions, selected using lottery method of simple random sampling technique.

Tools: Aspects of Identity Questionnaire consists of 45 statements with 5 alternatives namely "1 = Not important to my sense of who I am; 2 = Slightly important to my sense of who I am; 3 = Somewhat important to my sense of who I am; 4 = Very important to my sense of who I am; 5 = Extremely important to my sense of who I am". The questionnaire is divided into 4 dimensions namely Personal Identity Orientation, Relational Identity Orientation, Social Identity Orientation and Collective Identity Orientation. From this the items under Personal Identity are alone chosen for the study (i.e items 2 5 8 11 14 18 21 25 27 32). The sum of these 10 items is taken as the score for personal identity. The Cronbach's Coefficient alpha is a preferred statistic used to indicate the level of internal consistency which is 0.73. The tool also has good content validity.

Ryan and Frederick (1997) developed a scale of subjective vitality that has two versions. One version is considered an individual difference. The other version of the scale assesses the state of subjective vitality rather than its enduring aspect. A scale score is formed by averaging the individual's items scores. If the item #2 is used, that item is reverse scored before it is averaged with the other items. The remaining scores are summed up for the total score on subjective vitality. The test re-test reliability of the test is 0.70 and good construct validity.

The scores of the sample were statistically analysed using parametric test in SPSS 20 version.

- Karl Pearson Product Moment Correlation – Relationship between Personal Identity and Subjective Vitality

- Independent Sample t test – Gender differences in Personal Identity and Subjective Vitality

Results and Discussion: Product moment correlation was computed to study the relationship between personal identity and Subjective vitality. Results indicate a positive correlation between personal identity and subjective vitality. The coefficient of correlation is significant at the level of 0.01. It is noted that when a person develops his or her personal identity due course in time throughout their life, they tend to improve the subjective vitality. They develop a sense of positivity, means and ways to keep them alive and true to their nature. They develop a lifestyle or a skill set for their well-being to keep them active throughout their lives. Hence it is safe to say that Personal Identity is co related to Subjective identity.

Therefore hypothesis stating that "There is a no significant relationship between Personal Identity and Subjective Vitality" is rejected

Table – 1 Mean scores and the level of significance of the variables on the basis of gender

Variables	Gender	N	Mean	SD	t value
Personal Identity	Female	64	34.89	6.935	0.106[NS]
	Male	63	35.02	6.318	
Subjective Vitality	Female	64	40.97	5.303	1.198[NS]
	Male	63	42.16	5.884	

NS - Not Significant

Independent Sample 't' test was used to compare the differences between females and males in all the variables. There is no significant gender difference among adolescents in Personal identity and Subjective vitality. It is safe to say that there is no gender biased difference when it comes to finding both these qualities. Both male and female individuals in their adolescence tend to display equal amount of the two qualities

Thus the hypothesis stating "There will be no significant gender differences in Personal identity" is accepted. "There will be no significant gender differences in Subjective Vitality" is accepted.

Conclusion: The need to have an identity for one self is equally important as any other accomplishment. During the adolescent period the search for identity is high, when an individual find a stand for oneself they are more happy and active. Individuals who face a crisis or confusion during this stage are not very stable and they are found confused about themselves, searching something. When a person is confused about them, they become very dull and fatigue which in turn affects their daily life. Thus the self – identity and vitality of a person are interdependent in nature.

Chapter Thirty Seven

Self-Compassion, Self-Esteem, Life Satisfaction and Stress[37]

Introduction: Recently, some studies have shown positive effects of self-compassion (SC) that often seem to outweigh the benefits of self-esteem (SE). These constructs appear to have unique underlying processes through which they help individuals cope with problems. It is important to understand the relationship between SC and SE and distinguish their role in influencing individual life circumstances as they are both closely discussed concepts. The problem of paucity of studies exploring these constructs together and understanding their meaning and value in the cultural context. Therefore, the concept of SC requires further investigation, particularly in relation with an analogous concept of SE.

SC involves six primary components; self-kindness versus self-judgment, common humanity versus isolation, and mindfulness versus over-identification. They are found to mutually interact and tend to overlap with each other (Neff, 2003). Showing kindness towards oneself, recognizing that mistakes and personal failures are common to humanity and being aware of one's emotional experiences and the present moment, are characteristics of self-compassion. Research on SC has examined its association

[37] **Sandhya Shivakumar,** Student, Women's Christian College, Chennai
Veena Easvaradoss, Ph.D., Head-Dept. of Psychology, Women's Christian College, Chennai

with multiple aspects of life; life satisfaction, emotional intelligence, social connectedness, learning goals, wisdom, personal initiative, curiosity, happiness, optimism, and positive affect, self-criticism, depression, anxiety, fear of failure, thought suppression, perfectionism, performance goals, and disordered eating behaviors (Neff, 2009). Therefore, high SC individuals are likely to feel more connected with others, may not feel alone in suffering, and be more accepting of difficult situations. It also appears to help the individual balance their emotional experiences as opposed to catastrophizing or ruminating on the negative experiences (Neff, 2011)

Many studies have documented a positive relationship between SC and life satisfaction (Anggraeni & Kurniawan, 2012; Bhat & Shah, 2015; Yang, Zhang & Kou, 2016). Mülazım and Eldeleklioğlu (2016) investigated the relationship between SC (subscales) and subjective happiness, and life satisfaction. They found that self-kindness, common humanity, and mindfulness were positively, self-judgment and isolation were negatively related to subjective happiness and life satisfaction. While over-identification was negatively associated with subjective happiness, there was no correlation between over-identification and life satisfaction. Further, subjective happiness and life satisfaction were predicted positively by common humanity and mindfulness, and negatively by self-judgment, isolation, and over-identification.

Studies investigating the direct relationship between perceived stress and SC have only been a few. Newsome, Waldo and Gruszka (2012) reported positive effects of SC on lowering perceived stress, based on the outcomes of a mindfulness intervention. Tholouli, Maridaki-Kassotaki, Varvogali and Chrousos (2016) found that students who had experienced a greater number of stressful events during the past year reported having higher levels of perceived stress, and that higher SC was correlated with less perceived stress. In addition, the mediating role of SC partially explained the adverse effects of the stressful events on the levels of perceived stress. Similar findings from other studies show that SC may be strongly associated with perceived stress (Unger, 2016; Arnos 2017; Homan & Sirois, 2017).

Rosenberg (1965) defined self-esteem (SE) as a favorable or unfavorable attitude towards the self. Global SE was conceptualized as an individual's negative or positive perception towards the self in totality, and was expected to be critical in influencing their overall levels of psychological well-being. It holds self-acceptance or self-respect as its primary characteristic feature. A closely related but different construct was specific SE, i.e., which relates to specific facets of one's life such as academic performance and other skill sets, as opposed to a multi-dimensional global SE (Rosenberg, Schooler, Schoenbach & Rosenberg, 1995) studies have documented a positive relationship between SE and life satisfaction, across various age groups and life circumstances (Edura, Rashid, Nordin, Omar & Ismail, 2011; Moksnes & Espnes, 2013; Fanaj & Melonashi, 2014; Lu et al., 2015) and perceived stress involving work, physical activity, general health, religion and so on (Murphy, 2009; Hubbs, Doyle, Bowden & Doyle, 2012; Lee, Joo & Choi, 2013)

SE and SC are similar constructs in that they both involve a positive perception or regard towards oneself. Research has shown an inter-correlation ranging from 0.57 to 0.59 between the two using the Rosenberg (1965) self-esteem scale and the self-compassion scale (Neff, 2003). However, the primary distinction between the two constructs seems to emerge from the self-evaluative component involved in SE but absent in SC. In other words, the non-evaluative, accepting and kind attitude towards oneself facilitates self-love whereas in SE, making a positive "judgment" about oneself is important to increase confidence or feelings of superiority (Neff, 2011). The objective of this study was, therefore, to evaluate the relationship between SC and SE, assess their impact on life satisfaction and perceived stress, and identify age or gender differences. It was hypothesized that a strong correlation would be found between SC and SE, and that SC subscales will significantly predict perceived stress and life satisfaction.

Objectives: Studies indicate that there are significant global influences of SC and SE across age groups in many cultures. While positive outcomes have been recorded for both constructs, it is unclear whether they have a similar effect on perceived stress and life satisfaction when included together. The objective of this study was therefore, to evaluate the relationship between self-compassion and self-esteem, assess their impact on life satisfaction and perceived stress, and identify age and gender differences in self-compassion. Moreover, it is also expected to contribute to addressing the gaps in the literature, since past studies have more often explored the influence of SC and SE separately.

Methodology: The study utilized an ex post facto research design. The independent variables were self-esteem and self-compassion subscales, and the dependent variables were life satisfaction and perceived stress. A sample of 126 participants were included through purposive sampling of whom 52.4% were females and 47.4% were males. 42.9% were between 18-24 years of age, 30.2% belonged to the age group between 25-30 years, and 29% were between 31-40 years of age. They primarily belonged to the following occupations: engineers, graduate and post-graduate students, professors, media professionals, insurance policy makers, managing directors and home-makers. Most participants' present place of residence was Chennai, and a very few lived in other states in South India.

Neff's Self-Compassion Scale (Neff, 2003): This is a 26 item 5 point Likert Scale. It consists of six subscales i.e., self-kindness, common humanity and mindfulness, and self-judgment, isolation and over-identification. It is known to have high internal consistency, predictive, convergent and discriminant validity. High scores indicate high self-compassion.

Cohen's Perceived Stress Scale (Cohen, 1983): This is a 10 item 5 point Likert Scale originally developed in 1983. Test-retest reliability, concurrent and predictive validity have been thoroughly established. Higher scores indicate greater levels of perceived stress. Rosenberg's Self-Esteem Scale (Rosenberg, 1965): Rosenberg Self-Esteem Scale is a 10 item 4 point Likert scale. High scores reflect a healthy or high self-esteem. High internal consistency and test-retest reliability has been established. Diener's Satisfaction with Life Scale (Diener, 1985): It is a short 5-item and 7 point Likert scale measuring global life satisfaction. High life satisfaction is indicated by greater scores on this scale. Robust internal consistency, test-retest reliability, construct and convergent validity have been established. Factory analysis confirmed that it was a measure of single dimension.

The original responses measuring self-esteem, satisfaction with life and perceived stress were also scored and coded manually on SPSS. For demographic variables, gender was recoded dichotomously. For age, "18-24, "25-31" and "31-40" years were recoded as 0,1 and 2, respectively. Pearson product-moment correlation was used to examine the relationship between SC and SE. The subscale components of SC were entered individually in stepwise regression analysis along with SE. The influence of gender on SC was also assessed using two-way analysis of variance. SPSS Version 20 was used for the statistical analysis.

Results and Discussion

Table 1 – Demographic characteristics of the sample

Age(n=126)	**(%)**
18-24 years	42.9%
25-30 years	30.2%
31-40 years	29%
Gender	
Male	47.4%
Female	52.4%

Table 2- *Correlation coefficient showing the relationship between SC and SE*

Variable(n=126)	1	2
1.Self-esteem		-.446**
2. Self-compassion	-.446**	

**p<0.01 significant at the 0.01 level (two-tailed)

A significant negative relationship exists between SE and SC (Table 2) for adults in this sample.

Table 3 - Summary of the step-wise regression analysis for SC subscales and SE predicting satisfaction with life

Variable(n=126)	β	t	r	r^2	Adjusted r^2
Step 1			.494[a]	.244	.238
Self-esteem	.494	6.322***			
Step 2			.529[b]	.280	.268
Self-esteem	.349	3.631***			
Isolation	-.238	-2.476*			

*p < .05, **p < .01, ***p< .001

In stage one, hierarchical regression analysis (Table 3) showed that SE was a significant positive predictor of life satisfaction and accounted for 23% of the variation in life satisfaction F(39.96) p<0.001. In stage two, the isolation subscale negatively predicted life satisfaction and explained an additional 26% of the variation along with SE. The relationship between isolation and life satisfaction was significant at the 0.05 level.

At stage one, stepwise regression model (Table 4) revealed that SE significantly predicted perceived stress negatively F (46.77) (p<0.001) and accounted for 26% of the variance. In stage two, SE and over-identification subscale together explained an additional 33% of the variation in perceived stress, F (32.44) p<0.001. In stage three, adding mindfulness explained an additional 35% of the variance along with SE and over-identification, F (23.48) p<0.001.

Table 4 – Summary of step-wise regression analysis for SE and SC subscales as predictors of perceived stress

Variable(n=126)	β	t	R	R^2	Adjusted R^2
Step 1			.523[a]	.274	.268
Self-esteem	-.523	-6.839***			
Step 2			.588[b]	.345	.335
Self-esteem	-.374	-4.484***			
Over-identification	.306	3.665***			
Step 3			.605[c]	.366	.351
Self-esteem	-.336	-3.962***			
Over-identification	.241	2.722**			
Mindfulness	-.170	-1.997*			

*p < .05, **p < .01, ***p< .001

This study clearly established a negative relationship between SC and SE, a finding which is inconsistent with past literature. This negative relationship could be because; individuals with a high self-esteem may also have expectations of meeting high overall standards to feel good about themselves. This can often lead to self-criticism and feelings of worthlessness when the standards are unmet, resulting in lower self-compassion. It may also be relevant to examine the developmental tasks associated with the participants' age in the study. When the skills and abilities necessary to complete specific developmental tasks are inadequate or lacking it can cause high levels of psychological distress (Schulenberg, Bryant, & O'Malley, 2004). Therefore, it is possible that they are pushed towards target goals, driven to seek opportunities, achieve goals, and strive to succeed in work and relationships. Consequently, less value is asserted to compassionate attitudes, until later adulthood or old age.

This study also showed that increased SE predicted an increase in life satisfaction, which is consistent with past literature (Moksnes & Espnes, 2013; Khatib, 2012). Isolation, was the only subscale predicting life satisfaction negatively. Though very few studies have examined SC subscale relationships, Mülazım & Eldeleklioğlu (2016) found similar results in their study. However, past evidences have shown a robust positive relationship between life satisfaction and SC total score. (Yang, Zhang & Kou, 2016; Bhat & Shah, 2015; Anggraeni & Kurniawan, 2012).

In addition, SE was the strongest predictor throughout, although mindfulness and over-identification also significantly predicted perceived stress. All the other predictor variables, i.e., self-judgment, self-kindness, common humanity, and isolation were non-significant. Mindfulness shared a negative relationship with perceived stress, indicating that increased mindfulness was associated with a decrease in perceived stress, whereas a positive relationship with over-identification indicating that, increased over-identification can increase perceived stress. One of the few studies involving SC subscales showed a similar relationship with stress. It was found that self-judgment-self-kindness subscales and over-identification-mindfulness subscales were predictive of managing life stressors (Hall, Row, Wuensch & Godley, 2013). Therefore, these findings reestablish the use of compassion-based interventions to improve psychological well-being of individuals (Kirby, Tellegen & Steindl, 2017). Lastly, gender and age did not interact to produce any significant effects on an individual's SC. Some studies have however found otherwise (Yarnell et al., 2015; De Souza & Hutz, 2016).

Conclusion: Self-compassion and self-esteem have both been significant contributors to our understanding of mental health, and may have unique processes by which they influence an individual's satisfaction with life and perceived stress. A great deal of empirical research in the Indian context is required to obtain clarity regarding their underlying dynamics and to understand their cultural relevance. Replication and large scale studies in future may facilitate further exploration and clarify the role of self-compassion and self-esteem in influencing psychological outcomes.

Chapter Thirty Eight

Coronary Heart Disease and Its Indicators[38]

Introduction: Scientifically, health means a highly complex and dynamic product of interaction of variables viz. genes, eco-social environment and individual health behavior. Thus, health is central to human happiness, well-being and wellness as it is multidimensional issue which sustains to the totality of human existence (Mohan, 2016). World Health Organization (WHO, 1996) defines health as "a complete state of physical, mental and social well-being, and not merely the absence of disease or infirmity." William Harvey termed the heart as "the sovereign of the body"; today man knows the heart as a technical motor piece and a timeless metaphor. It is protected in a bone structured chest cavity. The heart links body to the spirit, further heart is attached to a seat of mind with different chores of feelings and emotions. (Hooli, Gavimath & Ravishankera, 2012).

Globalization and modernization has brought a change in the face of death. From the communicable diseases it has been shifted to lifestyle and non-communicable diseases (NCDs). NCDs are defined as diseases of long duration, and are generally slow in progression. The global burden of NCDs is increasing and is a major barrier to development and achievement of Millennium Development Goals (Beaglehole et al., 2011). Gupta (2011) opined that there are country-specific differences in cardiovascular mortality in the world. The report shows that there are substantial country-level variations. The highest age-adjusted mortality is observed in countries

---

[38] **Sukhmani Singh, Ph.D.,** Asst. Professor, Chandigarh University, Gharuan

of Central Asia, East and Central Europe, some countries in Africa and the lowest rates are observed in West European and North American countries.

According to World Health Organization (2014) statistics coronary heart disease in India reached 1,215,414 or 13.70% of total deaths. On the basis of the death rate India ranks 39 in the world. One of the reasons could also be increase in life expectancy (Memarian, Azaraeen & Koupaei, 2015). Presently, NCDs, including heart diseases are collectively responsible for almost 70% of all deaths worldwide. In low - and middle-income countries, 82% of the 16 million people died prematurely due to smoking, being overweight, having high blood pressure and/or high cholesterol, heavy drinking and physical inactivity. They died even before reaching 70 years of age (WHO, 2017).

Coronary heart disease is the umbrella term for various syndromes of heart ischemia that are caused by atherosclerotic obstruction of the coronary arteries. This damage ranges from gradual narrowing of the coronary arteries mainly due to the bulging patches of plaque that lead to the sudden obstruction of a coronary artery by a blood clot (Katz & Ness, 2015). Epidemiological studies beginning in the 1950's have identified several traditional risk factors such as – Age, Diabetes, Overweight and Obesity, are associated with cardiovascular diseases (Mohan, Mahajan & Sehgal, 2006). The interplay of biological and psychological factors in the development of cardiovascular disorders has long been suspected (Suresh & Yeedulapally, 2016).

Objectives: As the face of the disease has transformed over the time and coronary heart disease has become the most potent and lethal threat to the health. The objectives of the present study are:

1. To understand the indicators of coronary heart disease.
2. To delve deep and understand the various types of indicators of coronary heart disease.
3. To understand the existence of gender differences with respect to coronary heart disease.

Health Psychology: The main theme of this research is related to Health Psychology with special concern to Coronary Heart Disease, which ranks as one of the major killers and posits a danger to the health of the mankind. .

Changing Indicators For Coronary Heart Disease – On the basis of review of literature there are various behavioral and psychosocial risk factors the adversely affect the human heart. Behavioral Risk Factors:

Diet Patterns - In India due to change in lifestyle, wealth, and the availability of

"Western style" foods, there is a considerable body of evidence regarding the nutritional background of atherosclerosis in general and coronary heart disease in particular. High dietary intakes of saturated fat, trans-fat, cholesterol and salt whereas low intake of fruits, vegetables and fish are linked to cardiovascular risk (WHO, 2010). Approximately 1.7 million (2.8%) of deaths worldwide are attributable to low fruit and vegetable consumption. (Kotseva, Wood & Backer, 2010).

Physical Inactivity – Generally people who are physically inactive have a 20% to 30% increased risk of all-cause mortality compared to those who engage in at least 30 minutes of moderate intensity physical activity most days of the week. It was estimated that in study done in eleven cities across India showed that 38.8% of men and 46.1% of women were physically inactive (Gupta et al., 2012).

Tobacco Use and Smoking - Smoking is estimated to cause nearly 10% of coronary heart disease. In the Inter Heart Study, the population attributed risk due to smoking for myocardial Infarction was 35.7% (Goenka, Prabhakaran, Ajay & Reddy, 2009). Nearly six million people die from tobacco use and exposure to second hand smoke each year, accounting for 6% of all female and 12% of all male deaths in the world.

Alcohol Use - Although alcohol when use judiciously is beneficial for health but excessive alcohol intake has been associated with increasing prevalence of coronary heart disease and is one of the leading causes of death in India. On an average, adult per capita consumption of alcohol in India was estimated to be 32.1% in males and 10.6% in females. In general, prevalence of heavy episodic drinking was found higher in males and abstention was higher in females (WHO, 2014).

Psychosocial Risk Factors: Didactically, psychosocial risk factors for the initiation and progression of cardiovascular diseases (Table 1).

SOCIAL ENVIRONMENT	PERSONALITY	NEGATIVE AFFECT
Low socioeconomic status	Anger-proneness	Depression
Life events, including adverse childhood experiences	Hostility	Anxiety and Anger
Family stress	Type A and Type D Personality	Exhaustion
Job stress	Neuroticism	Hopelessness
Low social support	Over commitment to work	Bereavement

Source: *Von Kanel, R. (2012). Psychosocial stress and cardiovascular risk - current opinion. Swiss Med Wkly, 142, w13502.*

Type A Behavior: Sir William Osler (1960), often called the father of British

Medicine wrote, "It is many time much more important to know what patient has the disease than what kind of disease the patient has." Generally, specific personality types influence individual's reaction towards other people, problems and stress. In the 1950s cardiologists Meyer Friedman and Ray H. Rosenman created the concept of the Type "A" personality, linking it to heart attacks. Type "A" personality is associated with relatively stable behavior characterized by competitiveness, the desire to achieve, aggression, haste, impatience, explosive way of speaking, facial muscle tension and excess liability (Morys, Bellwon, Jeżewska, Adamczyk & Gruchała, 2015). People with Type A personality are more vulnerable to heart disease than Type B personality persons, because they have a substantially greater sympathetic nervous system response to stressful or demanding circumstances that produce more wear and tear on the cardiovascular system (Rohit, Rajendrasinh & Atul, 2016).

Stress: The relationship between stress and illness is complex. The susceptibility to stress varies from person to person. Events must interact with a wide variety of background factors to manifest as an illness. Among the various factors that influenced the susceptibility to stress are genetic vulnerability, coping style, type of personality and social support. When individuals are confronted with a problem, they assess the seriousness of the problem and determine whether or not they have the resources necessary to cope with problem. Thus, it is our way of reacting to the situations that makes a difference in our susceptibility to illness and our overall well-being (Salleh, 2009).

Gohel et al. (2014) opined that male and female subjects with CHD were found to have high level of psychosocial stress as compared to healthy controls. Mainly 72.31% of CHD patients as compared to 10% of healthy individuals were found to have high or very high level of psychosocial stress.

Lifestyle: The term style of life was used by psychiatrist Alfred Adler as one of several constructs describing the dynamics of the personality. Life Style/Health Habits generally means a pattern of individual practices and personal behavioral choices that are related to elevated or reduced health risk. Lifestyle of populations across the world have changed dramatically in the 20th century which is brought about by a number of developments in science and technology that now affects every facet of human existence. Most human societies have moved from standard healthy diets and active lives to fast foods and sedentary habits, resulted in epidemic of cardiovascular disease (Prabhakaran & Yusuf, 2010).

Menotti, Puddu, Maiani and Catasta (2015) opined that some lifestyle behaviours are considered as possible determinants and causes not only of CHD but also for cancer, all-cause mortality and indirect expectancy of life. This applies at least to cigarette smoking, physical activity and dietary habits. Investigations on these habits started several decades ago and findings were documented in different ways. Many reports dealt with single behaviour, i.e., cigarette smoking, physical activity and dietary habits, some with multiple lifestyle behaviour contributed in the increasing prevalence of CHD.

Anger and Hostility: Buddhism actually refers anger as one of the Three Poisons of the Mind, along greed and foolishness. Hostility is typically described as a negative attitude or cognitive trait directed toward others, Anger is an emotional state that consists of feelings that vary in intensity from mild irritation or annoyance to intense fury (Chida & Steptoe, 2009).

Hostility is a tendency to view the world in a negative, cynical fashion. It is primarily a cognitive construct involving negative attitude toward others, consisting of enmity, denigration, and ill will (Smith, Glazer, Ruiz & Gallo, 2004). As disease-prone personality traits, hostility and anger have been associated with the wide range of undesired health outcomes. Hostility, feeling of anger (anger in) and expression of anger (anger out) have both similar and specific health effects (Assari, 2016).

Perfectionism: Shafran, Cooper and Fairburn (2002) developed a competing model of "clinical perfectionism." According to their model, perfectionism is a unidimensional construct which increases risk for psychopathology. Fry and Debats (2009) found that earlier mortality was more common among perfectionists. They examined 450 adults aged 65 years and older and were followed up for 6.5 years. Ultimately, they found that those with high perfectionist tendencies were 51 percent more likely to die earlier than those with lower perfectionist scores. This was mainly due to high levels of stress and anxiety among these people that also lead to the emergence of chronic diseases among them namely CHD. Thus perfectionism is considered as an important psychosocial risk factor. Although being perfectionist sounds like an admirable trait, but it is often a cause of heart diseases (Mohan & Kaur, 2015).

Lack of Social Support: Social support is regarded as resources provided by others, as coping assistance, or as an exchange of resources (Endler & Parker, 1990). Several types of social support have been investigated, such as instrumental support, tangible support, informational support, and emotional support among others. Social support exert beneficial effects on various health outcomes (Schroder, Schwarzer & Endler, 1997). Also higher level of social support have been linked with a number of health benefits, including protection against cardiovascular morbidity and mortality. Having someone around to talk out and share feelings, protects them from the physical damage caused due to stress. Thus social support has a very strong and significant impact on patients with cardiovascular diseases and how they are able to deal with their illness. On the contrary, lack of social support has adverse effects on the health of CHD patient (Taylor, Gooding, Wood & Tarrier, 2011).

Gender Differences in Coronary Heart Disease: Present day, it is considered as a myth that coronary heart disease (CHD) is less common and less severe in women. According to Tan, Gast and van der Schouw (2010) there is substantial variation in the rates of age-standardized CHD incidence and mortality across nations. Countries with high rates of CHD among men also have high rates for women. Since women are more likely to develop CHD a decade later than men, they usually have more adverse outcomes than men do. 87% of women were surveyed who failed to cite heart disease as a major threat to their health. These misperceptions may lead women to underestimate their risk for CHD, resulting in a delay in seeking medical care, thus increasing their morbidity and mortality rates. Women are twice as likely to die of a first myocardial infarction (MI), and have a less favorable long-term survival as compared with men. There are certain risk factors like menopause that pertain only to women which may have increased their predisposition for developing coronary heart disease. Additionally, risk factors like smoking, hypertriglyceridemia and low high-density lipoprotein cholesterol levels have greater impact in women than in men.

Sahu, Epari, Patnaik, Lenka and Soodireddy (2015) found that prevalence of risk factors of CHD among males in decreasing order were high LDL (54.4%), low HDL (49.7%), high triglyceride (44.2%), central obesity and BMI $\geq$23 (43.5%). However, in females they were: central obesity (59.6%) followed by sedentary life style (51.7%), high LDL (49.3%) and high BMI (40.9%). It was evident that prevalence of central obesity and sedentary life style was significantly higher among females, while high TG and LDL was significantly more among males. Lack of physical exercise as risk factor was known to only 22% of individuals. Although awareness about risk factors of CHD was encouraging, high prevalence of risk factors indicates lack of healthful practices among male and female CHD patients. Thus, the rapid transition in life style owing to urbanization resulted in increased incidence of reversible cardiovascular risk factors in females also (Vamadevan & Prabhakaran, 2010).

Dehghani and Dafei (2016) found that a positive history of CHD was obtained from 12% of men and 18.9% of women, i.e. 15.3% in the entire sample. Thus, the incidence and prevalence of CHD in women has exceeded that of men over the past four decades (Davis, Gorog, Rihal, Prasad & Srinivasan, 2017).

Conclusion: On the basis of review, it is suggested that in order to overcome this life threatening disease, there is the need for interventions to address heart health taking into account both the individual and the environment. Counseling and education can be provided to raise awareness regarding the modifiable factors in CHD like training in effectiveness, modifying lifestyle and cultivating positive emotions. These can help patients gain control of their health and accompanying lifestyle. Henceforth, awareness is required among the general population about these risk factors which can be dealt by following healthy diet, doing exercise and refraining from indulging in detrimental health habits, namely, use of alcohol and drugs. The science of health psychology *has also advanced the concept of promoting excellence in human health, which requires a "community-based, multilevel, interdisciplinary approach." There is a need of Government and scientific community to work hand in hand and make integrative policies to promote excellence in health (Sehgal, 2016). Thus, improving the human resource capacity for the prevention and control of CHD is a national priority. This calls for tracking down and monitoring CHD along with efficient intervention policies that aim at prevention, control and treatment of CHD in all the sections of the populations.

Chapter Thirty Nine

Smoking and Perceived Social Support Among Young Adults[39]

Introduction: Burning of substance and inhaling the resultant smoke is primarily the definition of smoking. The resulting smoke is also breathed in to be absorbed into the blood-stream and tasted. Smoking is primarily used as a recreation. In certain cases, like cigarettes smoking substances are mixed with aerosol particles and gasses and include alkaloid nicotine. Over the last few decades, smoking has become public health epidemic, with over 80% of regular adult smokers beginning tobacco use before age of 18. Smoking is often viewed as a learned behaviour that evolves through several stages, including preparation, initiation, experimentation, regular smoking and nicotine addiction.

A multitude of factors can influence smoking among young adults and their subsequent success in quitting. These include: sex, age and developmental stage,

[39] **Niki Das, Reshma Antony, Spoorti Chimmalgi,** Student, Jain Univesity

socioeconomic status; sexual orientation, education level; cultural background; ethnicity; external support of cessation; time availability; knowledge; sense of control; and behavioural skills, media, marketing, and the modelling of cigarette products through popular roles. So, these factors can also act as motivators if taken in positive way and the smokers have perceived social support. The single most important change that smokers can take to enhance the length and quality of their lives is to stop smoking i.e. smoking cessation.

Motivation is a process of including, inspiring and energizing people to work willingly with zeal, initiative, confidence, satisfaction and an integrated manner to achieve desired goals (Kelley, J., 2013). It is a moral boosting activity. It is commonly accepted that a man cannot be pulled from the front or pushed from behind. He can only be moved from within and it is an ongoing process (Mahesh & Kasturi, 2006). Motivation for an activity starts with the need which may be the perceived as the deficiency in an individual (Zkjadoon, 2015). Following are the basic phases of the process of motivation proposed by Zkjadoon: Need identification, exploring ways to fulfil the need, selecting goals, performance, rewards/punishments as consequences of performance, reassessment of deficiencies of need.

There are two types – Intrinsic and Extrinsic proposed by Ryan and Deci (2000). Extrinsic Motivation is geared towards external rewards and reinforcement. It is a construct that pertains whenever an activity is done order to attain some separable outcomes. Factors that promote extrinsic motivation are peer and group, consequences and punishment, praise and recognition. Intrinsic Motivation is defined as performance of an activity for its inherent satisfaction rather than for some separable consequence. It is geared towards internal rewards and reinforcement. Factors that promote intrinsic motivation are: challenge (personally meaningful goals), curiosity, control, fantasy, competition, cooperation and recognition

Social support is defined as 'any behaviour by others that are presumed by either the giver or receiver to facilitate a positive and desired behaviour change' (Lion Shabab, 2012). Social support also includes any type of communication that helps individuals feel more certain about a situation and therefore feel as if they have control over the situation. The various types of social support are put forth by (Lion Shabab, 2012) are: emotional support, esteem support, network support, information support and tangible support

Model proposed by Westmaas and Bauer looks at attempts of majority smoker to quit smoking on their own, but in any given year, only 5% or less are successful. To improve cessation rates, tapping social networks for social support during quitting has been recommended or tested in some interventions. The model also describes social support constructs that are believed to be important in determining how socially supportive strategies help smokers quit, regardless of whether the support is provided from health professionals or peers. Social support plays a role in smoking cessations in the following ways:

1. Abstinence-specific emotional support: providing a smoker the opportunity to vent emotions about the difficulty of abstaining
2. General -Emotional support: Provide a calm and secure interpersonal environment that helps make the difficult task of quitting more achievable
3. General instrumental support: helping a partner with daily chores that might have the effect of reducing feelings of stress or involving the partner in activities that distract him or her from withdrawal symptoms

The model was based on survey of interventions as well as review of literature in the United States of America in the last decade. This study aims to examine the perception of social support and level of motivation among young adult smokers of metropolitan India and attempt to inculcate a similar model to support cessation of smoking.

Lieberman, Solomon and Ginzberg (2004) found that perceived social support and self-esteem were negatively correlated with suicidal ideation in young male soldiers. Perceived social support was also found to be correlated negatively with mental distress and positively with perceived health and perceived functioning. Bovier, Chamot and Perneger (2004) studied the mental health among young adults and found that social support played a role in strengthening internal resources, such as self-esteem and mastery while diminishing perceived stress.

Patten and Brockman (2008) found that lower level of perceived social support are associated with increased symptoms of stress and depression which lead people to engage in high risk behaviours like smoking. Therefore, there is substantial evidence that social support plays a very important role in physical and psychological health. Its influence on physical health may be evident in the changes in health-related behaviours such as decreased use of alcohol or cigarette smoking, improved exercise routines and diet, etc. (Cohen & Syme, 1985; Krantz, Grunberg & Baum, 1985).

Motivation to quit smoking may be driven by both extrinsic and intrinsic factors. Holterman, et al. (2010) studied the motivation to quit smoking in parents of children with asthma and found that it was higher in parents who believed that their child's asthma was not under control. Turner and Mermelstein (2004) found that the most reported extrinsic and intrinsic motivating factors to quit smoking was financial and health-related concerns, respectively. A study by Butler, et al. (2011) found that relatives of lung cancer patients had increased motivation to quit smoking due to their relative's disease. Personality factors also may influence the motivation to quit smoking, as shown by a study by Bishry, et al. (2012) that found a positive correlation between novelty seeking, persistence, cooperativeness, and the motivation to quit smoking. Khati, et al. (2015) analysed the factors influencing successful cessation of smoking habits in young adults and found that work and family environment, co-occurring substance use and psychological difficulties, like hyperactivity or inattention, were the most prominent. A similar study by Marcus et al. (2007) on young adult smokers concluded the significance of positive relationships with parents in the successful cessation of smoking.

Social support being a key factor in motivating positive changes in health-related behaviours, smoking cessation interventions often incorporate social support for better outcomes. Pirie, et al. (1997) conducted a community-based smoking cessation contest with and without social support and found better rates of smoking cessation in the former group. In a study by Wagner, Burg and Sirois (2004), that examined the role of perceived social support in smoking cessation using the Transtheoretical Model constructs, social support was positively associated with behavioural and experiential processes of change. Perceived social support from friends and family was found to increase the use of processes of change that lead to smoking cessation in adult smokers.

Carlson, et al. (2002) found evidence for improvement in 3 month smoking cessation rates after the addition of a support person group to a behavioural program. An interesting finding by Ramo, Liu and Prochaska (2015) was that nearly one in three young adult smokers would want to get help in quitting smoking using Facebook, citing social support and convenience as the main reasons for favouring the social network. However, according to some studies (Lichtenstein, Glasgow & Abrams, 1986; May, et al., 2006; Park, Schultz & Campbell, 2015) social support was not found to produce significantly better smoking cessation rates when compared to cognitive-behavioural programs.

Objectives: The above studies evoked the researcher to find the relationship between motivation to quit smoking and perceived social support in an Indian setting, as very few studies in India have focused and assessed social support in relation to the motivation to quit smoking. The existing studies on social support give mixed findings, which further necessitate a study of its influence in motivating smoking cessation. India has the second largest number of smokers in the world (Mishra, et al., 2015) and focused research in this area is necessary for any positive change to occur in this scenario.

Null hypotheses were set because there has been a lack of studies that demonstrate a relationship between both the variables within a study, especially in the urban Indian setting.

1. There is no significant difference between intrinsic and extrinsic motivation to quit smoking.
2. There is no significant difference in perceived social support between intrinsic and extrinsic motivation to quit smoking.
3. There is no significant relationship between motivation to quit smoking and perceived social support among young adult smokers.

Methodology: This study is non-directional and correlational. The sample of the study consisted of 30 individuals, in the age group of 20 and 29. The group belonged to urban metropolitan setting. The following questionnaires were used. Fagerstorm Test for cigarette dependence, Multidimensional Scale of Perceived Social Support, The Reason for Quitting Questionnaire.

The study was conducted on young adult smokers. The questionnaires are electronically administered to all the participants. First the consent form was presented, and only if the individual agreed to be a part of the study did s/he move ahead to the questionnaire. The researcher ensures the confidentiality of the results. The estimated time required to complete the three questionnaires along with a smoking behaviour questionnaire was around 15 minutes.It is the manner of quantitatively explaining the main features of the collected data. This provides a description of the sample as well as the data obtained. Pearson Product Moment Correlation and Paired Sample t-test were used.

Results and Discussion: In the present study motivation to quit smoking and perceived social support among young adult smokers was studied. Descriptive analysis of motivation to quit smoking in its dimensions of intrinsic motivation is mean of 4.1067 and SD of 1.84558 and extrinsic motivation is mean of 2.5333 and SD of 2.10178. Perceived social support in its dimensions of family is mean of 4.6917 and SD of 1.72042, friends is mean of 4.7250 and SD of 1.90207 and significant others is mean of 4.0083 and SD of 1.70886.

To analyze if motivation to quit smoking differ a paired sample t-test is used. Table 1 summarizes the result of paired sample t-test.

Table 1: Showing score of intrinsic and extrinsic motivation to quit smoking

Variables	Mean	SD	df	Std. Error Mean	p
Intrinsic Motivation	4.1067	1.84558	29	0.33696	.000**
Extrinsic Motivation	2.5333	2.10178		0.38373	

**p<0.01

Table 1: shows the score of the sample in paired sample t-test. The mean score of the present sample in intrinsic motivation is 4.1067, S.D is 1.84558 and standard error mean is 0.33696. In extrinsic motivation, the mean score of the present sample is 2.5333, S.D is 2.10178 and standard error mean is 0.38373. As it seen in the table the p value is .000 that is, it is significant at 0.01 levels which means there is significant difference between the two conditions, in this intrinsic motivation and extrinsic motivation.

The results imply that there is significant difference between intrinsic and extrinsic motivation to quit smoking. Since there is a difference between intrinsic and extrinsic motivation there will also be a difference between perceived social support between intrinsic and extrinsic motivations to quit smoking. To analyze if there is a relationship between motivation to quit smoking and perceived social support Pearson Product Moment Correlation is used.

Table 2: Showing relation between variables of motivation to quit smoking and perceived social support

Variables	Intrinsic Motivation	Extrinsic Motivation	Significant Others	Family	Friends
Intrinsic Motivation		.393*	.487**	.570**	.593**
Extrinsic Motivation			.128	.100	-.56
Significant Others				.613**	.809**
Family					.783**
Friends					

*p<0.05, **p<0.01

The table above presents the results obtained on running a Product Moment Correlation, to understand the relationship between dimensions of Motivation to Quit Smoking and Perceived Social Support.

The correlational value obtained for intrinsic and extrinsic motivation is .393 significant at 0.05 level. This means intrinsic motivation can lead to increase in extrinsic motivation among them. This can happen due to various reasons such as internalization and also other various reasons which are interrelated such as health concern and better appearance.

The correlational value obtained for intrinsic motivation and significant others, family and friends are .487, .570 and .593 respectively significant at 0.01 level, which means that increased perceived social support from significant others, family and friends could result to increased intrinsic motivation to quit smoking.

The correlational value obtained is -0.56 between perceived social support from friends and extrinsic motivation. Though the value is not significant it shows a negative relationship between the two variables. This means change in one variable will not have a change in the other variable in the given sample.

Conclusion: This study primarily validates the underlying mechanisms between social support constructs and smoking cessation. The results derived, specifically indicate that:

1. There is a significant difference between intrinsic and extrinsic motivation to quit smoking.
2. The perceived social support differ between intrinsic and extrinsic motivation to quit smoking.
3. There is a significant relationship between motivation to quit smoking and perceived support.

Although the ability of smokers to quit is undoubtedly influenced to some degree by community-level or population-level factors (e.g., smoking restrictions, advertising, culture), many smokers have been helped in quitting by receiving social support from family, friends and significant others. The roles that social support constructs may play in facilitating cessation were presented, including a stress-buffering perspective (Abstinence-specific emotional support).

Models aimed at cessation of smoking can include providing various forms of social support such as friends, family and significant others by amalgamating them with traditional models of psychotherapeutic interventions like group behavioural therapy, or individual counselling. The friends, family and significant others of individuals in the process of quitting smoking can be given psycho-education to facilitate abstinence-specific emotional support, general emotional support and instrumental support.

The interventions applied in today's times can be further refined by developing tailored cessation treatments that would aim at providing optimal type, timing, and amount of social support for a particular individual.

The evolving world of psychotherapeutic interventions has started to heavily rely on modern technology to further enhance the efficacy of cessation support provided by professionals. Social support for health behaviour change is being provided by Internet and electronic technologies such as text messaging, E-mail, video-conferencing and social networking. Electronic technologies can also assist therapists and professionals to monitor the progress made by the client. Advances in the world of technology ensure that treatment reaches a larger range of population.

References

Adams, D. M., Overholser, J. C., & Spirito, A. (1994). Stressful life events associated with adolescent suicide attempts. The Canadian Journal of Psychiatry, 39(1), 43-48.

Adams, J.L. (1986). Conceptual blockbusting. Addison-Wesley, Reading, MA.

Adler, A. B., Bliese, P. D., & Castro, C. A. (2011). Deployment psychology: Evidence-based strategies to promote mental health in the military. Washington, DC, US: American Psychological Association. Retrieved from http://dx.doi.org/10.1037/12300-000

AGCAS (2007) Institutional Approaches – Employability Case Studies, AGCAS, Sheffield. Retrieved on April 22, 2007, from http://www.agcas.org.uk/employability/strategic_approaches/ index.htm@se.

Ahang, A. (2014). The relationship between spiritual intelligence and anxiety mediate the religious attitude in undergraduate students of Islamic Azad University, Fars science and research branch. Indian Journal of Fundamental and Applied Life Sciences, 4, 977-989.

Ahn, K. S., Kim, B. K., Lee, I. H., Lee, J. H., Woo, J. M., & Kang, G. W. (2015). FP762 The role of social support in hemodialysis patients. Nephrology Dialysis Transplantation, 30(3), iii332-iii332.

Ahrens, S., Burt, G & Gallagher, M (1975) Broadcast Evaluation Report No. 1:M231 Analysis, Open AGCAS (2006) Careers Education Benchmark Statement, AGCAS, Sheffield.

Akin, A. (2008b). Self-compassion and achievement goals: A structural equation modeling approach. Eurasian Journal of Educational Research, 31, 1-15.

Akın, Akın, A., & Abaci, R. (2007). Self-compassion Scale: A study of validity and reliability. Hacettepe University Journal of Education, 33, 1–10.

Akin. A, (2008a). Scale of Psychological Well-being: A study of validity and reliability. Educational Science: Theory & Practice, 8(3), 721-750.

Albrecht, T.L., & Goldsmith, D. (2003). Social support , social networks, and health. In T. L. Thompson, A.M. Dorsey, K.I.Miller, & R. Parrott (Eds.), Handbook of health communication (pp. 263-284).

Amabile, T. (1983). The social Psychology of Creativity.Springer. NY

Amato, P. R (1994).Father-child relations, mother-child relations, and offspring psychological well-being in early adulthood. Journal of marriage and the family, 1031-1042

Amirian, M.E., & Pour, M.F. (2016). Simple and multivariate relationships between spiritual intelligence with general health and happiness. J Relig Health, 55, 1275–1288.

Amr, M., Bakr, A., El Gilany, A. H., Hammad, A., El-Refaey, A., & El-Mougy, A. (2009). Multi-method assessment of behavior adjustment in children with chronic kidney disease. Pediatric Nephrology, 24(2), 341-347.

Ande Welling. (2015). What Does a Dance/Movement Therapy Session Look Like? Retrieved from http://blog.adta.org/2015/03/15/what-does-a-dancemovement-therapy-session-look-like/Benefits of Dance/Movement Therapy. Retrieved on August 24, 2016, from http://www.northshoredancetherapy.com/benefitsofdancemovementtherapy.html.

Andersson, L. M., & Bateman, T. S. (1997). Cynicism in the workplace: Some causes and effects. Journal of Organizational Behaviour, 18(5), 449-469.

Ang, S. & Van Dyne, L. (2008). Handbook of Cultural   Intelligence. ME Sharpe.

Annalakshmi, N. (2007). *Resilience in relation to Extraversion-Introversion, Psychoticism, and Neuroticism*. Indian Journal of Psychometry& Education, 38, 51-55

Armsden, G. C., & Greenberg, M. T. (1987). The inventory of parent and peer attachment:Indivvidual   differences and their relationship to psychological wellbeing in adolescence. Journal of youth adolescence, 16(5), 427-454.

Arora, V, & Kamalanabhan, T. J. (2013, 2 27). Linking supervisor and coworker support to employee innovative behaviour at work: role of psychological conditions. Retrieved from Academic and Business Research Institute: http://www.aabri.com

Ashton, A. (2013). Issues in Psychology and Psychiatry Research and Practice: 2012 Edition. Atlanta, Scholarly Editions. Retrieved from https://books.google.co.in.

Assari, S. (2017). Hostility, anger, and cardiovascular mortality among Blacks and Whites. Research in Cardiovascular Medicine, 6(1).

Astrid, M., & Richardson, R. J. (1995). Models of burnout: Implications for interventions. International Journal of Stress management, 1-13.

Ayyub, S., Awan, A., & Bilal, M. (2013). Interactive effect of organizational cynicism and interpersonal mistreatment on turnover intentions. In Proceedings of International Conference on Business Management & IS, North America.

Baba, B., Patanjali (1990). Yogasūtra of Patañjali: with the commentary of Vyās, Motilal Banarsidass Publishers, New Delhi.

Baer, J., Kamarack, T., Cohen, S., &Mermelstein, R. (1986).Social Support and Smoking Cessation and Maintenance.

Baer, R. A., Smith, G. T., Hopkins, J., Krietemeyer, J., & Toney, L. (2006). Using self-report assessment methods to explore facets of mindfulness. Assessment, 13(1), 27-45.

Bahr, S.J. & Hoffmann, J.P. (2010).Parenting style, peers and adolescent heavy drinking.Journal of studies on Alcohol and Drugs, 71, 539-543.

Baker.L, J.K. McNulty Self-compassion and relationship maintenance: The moderating roles of conscientiousness and gender. Journal of Personality and Social Psychology, 100 (2011), pp. 853-873

Balogun, A. G. (2014). Job burnout among working mothers in Nigeria post-consolidation banks: Effects of work-family conflict and job stress.International Journal of Research Studies in Psychology, 5(5), 27-36.

Bandura, A. (1986). Social foundations of thought and action: A social cognitive theory. Englewood Cliffs, NJ: Prentice-Hall.

Bandura, A. (1986). Social foundations of thought and action: A social cognitive theory. Englewood Cliffs,: Prentice-Hall; NJ.

Bandura, A. (1997). Self-efficacy: The exercise of control. Freeman; New York.

Barak, M. (2002). Fostering Systematic Innovative Thinking & Problem Solving: Lessons Education can learn from Industry. International Journal of Technology & Design Education, 12: 227-247.

Barker, G. (2007).Adolescents, social support and help-seeking behavior.Geneva, Switzerland: World Health Organization.

Bartlett (2005), Internet usage among Greek university students. Demographic Associations with the phenomenon, using Greek Version of Internet Addiction Test. International Journal of Economic sciences and applied research 3(1), 49-74.

Baum, A. (1990). Stress intrusive imagery, and chronic distress. Health Psychology, 6,653-675.

Beaglehole, R., Bonita, R., Horton, R., Adams, C., Alleyne, G., Asaria, P., ... & Cecchini, M. (2011). Priority actions for the non-communicable disease crisis. The Lancet, 377(9775), 1438-1447.

Beck, A.T., Ward, C. H., Mendelson, M., Mock, J., &Erbaugh, J. (1961).An inventory for measuring depression. Archives of General Psychiatry, 4, 561-571.

Benabou, R. &Tirole, J. (2003).Intrinsic and extrinsic motivation.

Benabou, R., &Tirole, J. (2002).Self-confidence and personal motivation.Quarterly journal of economics, 117, 871-915.

Bennett, P. N., Weinberg, M. K., Bridgman, T., & Cummins, R. A. (2015). The happiness and subjective well-being of people on haemodialysis. Journal of Renal Care, 41(3), 156-161.

Bhalla, Prem, P. (2006). Hindu Rites, Rituals, Customs and Traditions: A to Z on the Hindu Way of Life, Pustak Mahal, Noida

Bhaskaram, P. (1996). Nutrition-Immunisation interactions and relevance to child health. Nutrition News, 17 (4).

Bhatt, D. J. and Gida, G. R. (1992). The Mental Hygine Inventory (M.H.I.). Construction and standardization. Unpublished M.PhilDissertation , Department of Psychology, Saurashtra University, Rajkot.

Birgit, S. & Thomas, M. (2009).The value of occupational self-efficacy in selection and development. Conference Proceedings, Brighton: British Academy of Management.

Bishry, Z., Fekry, M., Shahawy, H. E., Soltan, M., Haroun, A. &Moneim, D. A. (2012). The role of personality profile in the motivation to quit smoking. Middle East Current Psychiatry, 19.

Blacher, J. and McIntyre, L.L. (2006). Syndrome specificity and behaviour disorders in young adults with intellectual disability: Cultural differences in family impact. Journal of Intellectual Disability Research, 50,184-198.

Blass, T. (1999). Obedience to Authority: Current Perspectives on the Milgram Paradigm, Psychology Press.

Bollen, K.A., & Phillips, D.P. (1982). Imitative suicides: A national study of the effects of television news stories. American Sociological Review, 47, 802-809.

Boud, D (Ed.) (1988).Developing a Student Autonomy in Learning (2nd Ed.), London: Kogan Page.

Bovea, M D & Gallardo, A (2006) Work placements and the final year project: a joint experience in the industrial engineering degree, International Journal of Engineering Education, 22(6), 1319–1324.

Bovey, W. H., & Hede, A. (2001). Resistance to organizational change: the role of cognitive and affective processes. Leadership & Organization Development Journal, 22(8), 372-382.

Boynton, M., & Boynton, C. (2005). The Educators Guide to Preventing and Solving Discipline Problems, London: ASCD.

Brandes, P., Castro, S. L., James, M. S., Martinez, A. D., Matherly, T. A., Ferris, G. R., ...Hochwarter, W. A. (2008). The interactive effects of job insecurity and organizational cynicism on work effort following a layoff. Journal of Leadership & Organizational Studies, 14(3), 233-247.

Bräuninger, I. (2012). Dance movement therapy group intervention in stress treatment: A randomized controlled trial (RCT). The Arts in Psychotherapy, 39(5), 443–450.

Bräuninger, I. (2012). The efficacy of dance movement therapy group on improvement of quality of life: A randomized controlled trial. The Arts in Psychotherapy, 39(4), 296-303.

Bray, C.B. (2008). Military Psychology. International Encyclopaedia of the Social Sciences. . Retrieved from http://www.encyclopedia.com/social-sciences/applied-and-social-sciences-magazines/military-psychology

Briere, J. (2000). Cognitive distortion scales: Professional manual. Psychological Assessment Resources.

Brown, K. W., & Ryan, R. M. (2003). The benefits of being present: mindfulness and its role in psychological well-being. Journal of personality and social psychology, 84(4), 822-848.

Brown, K. W., & Ryan, R. M. (2003). The benefits of being present: mindful ness and its role in psychological well-being. Journal of personality and social psychology, 84(4), 822.

Brown, K. W., Ryan, R. M., & Creswell, J. D. (2007). Mindfulness: Theoretical foundations and evidence for its salutary effects. Psychological Inquiry, 18(4), 211-237.

Budig, M. J., & England, P. (2001). The wage penalty for motherhood. American Sociological Review, 66(2), 204-225.

Butler, K. M., Rayens, M. K., Zhang, M., & Hahn, E. J. (2011). Motivation to Quit Smoking among Relatives of Lung Cancer Patients. Public Health Nursing, 28(1), 43-50. doi:10.1111/j.1525-1446.2010.00916.x

Byrne, U. (2005). Work-life Balance: Why are we talking about it at all? Business Information Review, 22(1), 53-59.

Cal, S. F., Sá, L. R. D., Glustak, M. E., & Santiago, M. B. (2015). Resilience in chronic diseases: a systematic review. Cogent Psychology, 2(1), 1024928.

Campbell, A., Converse, P. E., & Rogers, W. L., (1976). The Quality of American Life: Perceptions, Evaluations, and Satisfactions. New York: Russel Sage Foundation.

Campbell-Sills, L., Cohan, S.L. & Stein, M.B. (2006). Relationship of Resilience to Personality, Coping, and Psychiatric Symptoms in Young Adults. Behavior Research and Therapy, 44, 585-599.

Caplan (1974).Socialsupport.Retrieved on January 31, 2017 from http:/www.definition of social support/social-support.

Carlson, L. E., Goodey, E., Bennett, M. H., Taenzer, P., & Koopmans, J. (2002). The addition of social support to a community-based large-group behavioral smoking cessation intervention. Addictive Behaviors, 27(4), 547-559. doi:10.1016/s0306-4603(01)00192-7

Carlson-Jones, D. (2011). Interpersonal and familial influences on the development of body image. In Body image: A handbook of science, prevention and practice (pp. 110-118). New York: Guilford Press.

Carmeli, A., Meitar, R., & Weisberg, J. (2006). Self-leadership skills and innovative behaviour at work. International Journal of Manpower, 27 (1), 75-90.

Cash, T. (2002). A "negative body image"- evaluating epedemiological evidence. In T. Cash, & T. Pruzinsky, Body image: A handbook (pp. 269-277). New York: Guilford Press.

Cassel, J. (1976). The contribution of social environment to host resistance.American Journal of Epidemiology, 104, 107-123.

Chaskalson, M. (2011). The mindful workplace: Developing resilient individuals and resonant organizations with MBSR. John Wiley & Sons.

Chen,Y.F. Deng S.S(2008), University students- Internet use and its relationships with academic performance, interpersonal relationship, Psychosocial adjustment and self-evaluation, cyber psychology& Behavior,11, 467-46.

Chida, Y., & Steptoe, A. (2009). The Association of Anger and Hostility with Future Coronary Heart Disease. A Meta-Analytic Review of Prospective Evidence. Journal of the American College of Cardiology, 53(11), 936-946. doi:10.1016/j.jacc.2008.11.044.

Chou,C, condron,L & Belland J.C.(2005). A review on research on Internet Addiction. Educational Psychology review 17(3), 363-388.

Chou.C & Hsiao; M.C (2000). Internet addiction, usage and gratification of the Taiwan's college students case. computer & Education 35,65-80.

Chou.C (2001). Internet heavy use and addiction among Taiwanese college students. An online interview study cyber psychology & Behavior 4(5), 573-585.

Christensen, A. J., Turner, C. W., Slaughter, J. R., & Holman, J. M. (1989). Perceived family support as a moderator psychological well-being in end-stage renal disease. Journal of Behavioral Medicine, 12(3), 249-265.

Cobb, S. (1976). Social support as a moderator of life stress.Psychosomatic Medicine, 38, 300-314.

Cockburn, D &Dunphy, J (2006) Working together: enhancing students' employability, Quality Assurance Agency, Gloucester. Retrieved from http://www.enhancement themes.ac.uk/documents/employability/Employability_Overview_QAA113.pdf. (accessed 22 April 2007).

Cohen, S. D., Sharma, T., Acquaviva, K., Peterson, R. A., Patel, S. S., & Kimmel, P. L. (2007). Social support and chronic kidney disease: An update. Advances in Chronic Kidney Disease, 14(4), 335-344.

Cohen, S.,Kamarck, T., Mermelstein, R. (1983). A global measure of perceived stress. Journal of Health and Social Behavior, 21(4), 385–396.

Cohn, M. A., Fredrickson, B. L., Brown, S. L., Mikels, J. A. & Conway, A. M. (2009). Happiness unpacked: Positive emotions increase life satisfaction by building resilience. Emotion, 9, 361–368.

Collings, S. C., Fortune, S., Steers, D., Currey, N., Hawton, K., Wang, J., ...Slim, B. (2011) Media influences on suicidal behaviour: An interview study of young people in New Zealand. Auckland, New Zealand

Connor, K. M., Davidson, J. R., & Lee, L. C. (2003). Spirituality, resilience, and anger in survivors of violent trauma: A community survey. Journal of traumaticstress, 16(5), 487-494.

Connor, K., & Davidson, J. (2003). Development of a new resilience scale: The Connor-Davidson Resilience Scale (CD-RISC). Depression and Anxiety, 18, 76-82.

Coomaraswamy, K. A. (2011). Hinduism and Buddhism, Golden Elixir Press.

Corporation for National & Community Service (2010). Learn and Serve America's National Service-Learning Clearinghouse. Retrieved February 3,2017, from www.servicelearning.org

Couper, J. L. (1981). Dance therapy: effects of motor performance of children with learning disabilities. Physical Therapy, 61(1), 23–26.

Coyne, J. C., & Gotlib, I. H. (1983). The role of cognition in depression: A critical appraisal. Psychological bulletin, 94(3), 472.

Creswell, J. D. (2016). Mindfulness Interventions. Annual Review of Psychology, 68.

Cuddy, A. J., Fiske, S. T., & Glick, P. (2004). When professionals become mothers, warmth doesn't cut the ice. Journal of Social Issues, 60(4), 701-718.

Cummings, S. M., & Kropf, N. P. (2013). Handbook of Psychosocial Interventions with Older Adults: Evidence-based approaches. Routledge; New York.

Curral, L., & Marques-Quinteiro, P. (2009). Self-leadership and Work Role Innovation: Testing a Mediation Model with Goal Orientation and Work Motivation. Revista de Psicología del Trabajo y de las Organizaciones, 25 (2), 165-176.

Curry et al., (1997).The Reasons For Quitting (RFQ). Retrieved on February 2, 2017 from http://09_RFQ_motivation_to_quit_smoking.pdf.

Curtis, D and McKenzie, P (2001) Employability Skills for Australian Industry: Literature Review and Framework Development. Available online at, http://www.dest.gov.au/archive/ty/publications/employability_skills/literature_research.pdf.

Cutrona and Russel, (1990).Positive Motivation |definition of positive motivation by medical dictionary. Retrieved on February 3, 2017 from http:/medical-dictionary.thedictionary.com/

Dance/Movement Therapy as an Alternative Treatment for Young Boys Diagnosed as ADHD: A Pilot Study. Retrieved March 10, 2017, from https://www.researchgate.net

Davidson, R. J., Kabat-Zinn, J., Schumacher, J., Rosenkranz, M., Muller, D., Santorelli, S. F., & Sheridan, J. F. (2003). Alterations in brain and immune function produced by mindfulness meditation. Psychosomatic medicine, 65(4), 564-570.

Davis, E., Gorog, D. A., Rihal, C., Prasad, A., & Srinivasan, M. (2017). "Mind the gap" acute coronary syndrome in women: A contemporary review of current clinical evidence. International Journal of Cardiology, 227, 840-849.

Davison, S. N. (2010). End-of-life care preferences and needs: perceptions of patients with chronic kidney disease. Clinical Journal of the American Society of Nephrology, 5(2), 195-204.

Davison, T.& McCabe, M. (2005 30-April). Men's and social, and sexual functioning women's body image and their psychological, part 1. Retrieved from http://www.healthyplace.com/sex/bodyimage/relationships-between-mens-and-womens-body-image-1/menu-id-66/

De Jong, J. P, & Den Hartog, D. N. (2008). Innovative Work Behaviour: Measurment and Validation.: Scales: Scientific Analysis of Enterpreneurship and SMEs; Netherlands.

Dean, J. W., Brandes, P., &Dharwadkar, R. (1998). Organizational cynicism. Academy of Management Review, 23(2), 341-352.

Deci, E., & Ryan, R. (1999). A Meta-Analysis Review of Experiments examining the effects of extrinsic motivation on intrinsic motivation.

Deery, M., Jago, L., & Stewart, M. (2008). Work-life balance in the tourism industry: A case study. In S. Richardson, L. Fredline,A. Patiar,& M. Ternel, (Eds.). CAUTHE 2008: Tourism and Hospitality Research, Training and Practice; "Where the 'Bloody Hell' Are We?" (pp. 1032-1044). Gold Coast, Qld.: Griffith University.

Dehghani, A., & Dafei, M. (2016). Coronary Artery Disease among Young Indians and it's Preventive Strategy. Journal of Client Care, 1(1), 24-32.

DeNov, N. (n.d.). Mind-Body Connection Awareness Workshop. Retrieved March 18, 2016, from http://nadiadenov.weebly.com.

Denti, L.(2013). Leadership and Innovation in Research and Development Teams. Gothenburg: Department of Psychology, University of Gothenburg.

Diener, E., Wirtz, D., Biswas-Diener, R., Tov, W., Kim-Prieto, C., Choi, D. W. Oishi, S. (2009). New measures of well-being. Assessing Well-Being, 247-266.

Diener, E., Wirtz, D., Tov, W., Kim-Prieto, C., Choi, D. W., Oishi, S. Biswas-Diener, R. (2010). New well-being measures: Short scales to assess flourishing and positive and negative feelings. Social Indicators Research, 97(2), 143-156.

Diller, J. V. & Moule, J. (2005). Cultural competence: A primer for educators. Cincinnati, OH: Wadsworth.

Doherty, L. (2004). Work-life balance initiatives: implications for women. Employee Relations, 26(4), 433-452.

Downey, A. (2016, April 26). Why Becoming Parents Makes People Better Employees. Fast Company. Retrieved October 08, 2017, from https://www.fastcompany.com/3059064/why-becoming-parents-makes-people-better-employees.

Druss, R.G., & Douglas, C.J. (1988). Adaptive responses to illness and disability. Healthy denial. General Hospital Psychiatry, 10, 163-168.

Dudhatra R., R. andJogsan, Y. A. (2012).Mental health and depression among working and non-working women.International Journal of Scientific and Research Publications, 2(8). Retrieved from http://www.ijsrp.org/research-paper-0812/ijsrp-p0835.pdf

Dudhatra, R. and Jogsan, Y.A. (2012). Mental Health and Depression among Working and Non-Working Women. International Journal of Scientific and Research Publications, Vol. 2, Issue 8, Retrieved from http://www.ijsrp.org/research-paper-0812/ijsrp-p0835.pdf.

Duff, A. (1839). India, and India Missions: Including Sketches of the Gigantic System of Hinduism, Both in Theory and Practice: Also Notices of Some of the Principal Agencies Employed in Conducting the Process of Indian Evangelization, & Johnstone, C. J. Oxford University, London.

Eastman, S. T., & Riggs, K. E. (1994). Televised Sports and Ritual: Fan Experiences. Sociology of Sport Journal, 11(3), 249-274.

Eisenberger, R., Huntington, R., Hutchison, S., & Sowa, D. (1986). Perceived Organizaitonal Support. Journal of Applied Psychology, 71 (3), 500-507

Elgood, H. (2000). Hinduism and the Religious Arts : Religion and the Arts, A&C Black, London.

Endler, N. S., & Parker, J. D. (1990). Multidimensional assessment of coping: A critical evaluation. Journal of Personality and Social Psychology, 58(5), 844-854.

Ernst Kossek, E., &Ozeki, C. (1998). Work–family conflict, policies, and the job–life satisfaction relationship: A review and directions for organizational behavior–human resources research. Journal of Applied Psychology, 83(2), 139.

Erwin-Grabner, T., Goodill, S. W., Hill, E. S., & Neida, K. V. (1999). Effectiveness of Dance/Movement Therapy on Reducing Test Anxiety. American Journal of Dance Therapy, 21(1), 19–34.

Etzersdorfer, E. Voracek, M. &Sonneck, G. (2004). A dose-response relationship between imitational suicides and newspaper distribution. Archives of Suicide Research, 8, 137-145.

Fagerstrom (1978). Fagerstorm test for nicotine dependence. Retrieved on February 2, 2017 from http://ndri.curtin.edu.au/btitp/documents.

Farb, N. A., Anderson, A. K., Mayberg, H., Bean, J., McKeon, D., & Segal, Z. V. (2010). Minding one's emotions: Mindfulness training alters the neural expression of sadness. Emotion, 10(1), 25.

Felizardo, S., Ribeiro, E. and Amante, M. (2016). Parental adjustment to disability, stress indicators and the influence of social support. Procedia - Social and Behavioral Sciences, 217, 830 - 837.

Ferguson, R. (1998). Can schools narrow the Black-White test score gap? In C. Jencks & M. Phillips (Eds.), The Black-White test score gap (pp. 318-374). Washington, DC: The Brookings Institution.

Forbes, P and Kubler, B (2006) Degrees of Skill, Student Employability Profiles, A Guide for Employers, The Council for Industry and Higher Education, London. Available online at, http://www.cihe-uk.com/publications.php.

Frangos, C.C & Kiohas, A. P; (2009). Internet Addiction among Greek university students. International Journal of Economic sciences and Applied Research 3(1): 49-74.

Freestone, R and Thompson, S (2006) Student experiences of work-based learning in planning education, Journal of Planning Education and Research, 26(2): 237–249.

Frone, M. R., Russell, M., & Barnes, G. M. (1996). Work–family conflict, gender, and health-related outcomes: A study of employed parents in two community samples. Journal of Occupational Health Psychology, 1(1), 57.

Frone, M. R., Russell, M., & Cooper, M. L. (1992). Antecedents and outcomes of work-family conflict: testing a model of the work-family interface. Journal of Applied Psychology, 77(1), 65.

Fry, P. S., & Debats, D. L. (2009) Perfectionism and the five-factor personality traits as predictors of mortality in older adults. Journal of Health Psychology, 14(4), 513–524.

Funk, D. C., & James, J. (2001). The Psychological Continuum Model: A Conceptual Framework for Understanding an Individual's Psychological Connection to Sport. Sport Management Review, 4(2), 119-150.

Funk, D. C., & James, J. D. (2006). Consumer loyalty: The meaning of attachment in the development of sport team allegiance. Journal of Sport Management, 20(2), 189.

Gabble, R., Babayan, A., Disante, E., & Schwartz, R. (2016). Smoking Cessation Intervations for Youths.

Gabbott PL, Warner TA, Jays PR, Salway P, & Busby SJ. (2005) Prefrontal cortex in the rat: projections to subcortical autonomic, motor, and limbic centers. J Comp Neurol. 492:145–177

GaliCinamon, R., & Rich, Y. (2010). Work family relations: Antecedents and outcomes. Journal of Career Assessment, 18(1), 59-70.

Galletta, M., Portoghese, I., Ciuffi, M., Sancassiani, F., D'Aloja, E., & Campagna, M. (2016). Working and Environmental Factors on Job Burnout: A Cross-sectional Study among Nurses. Clinical Practice& Epidemiology in Mental Health, 12, 132-141.

Gandhi, M. K. (2017). Hindu Dharma Diamond Pocket Books Pvt Ltd, New Delhi.

Ganesan, V. "Knowledge Workers: Organizational Climate for Creativity", Doctoral Thesis, Department of Psychology, Madras University, 1985.

Garnefski, N. V. Kraaij & P. Spinhoven.(2001).Negative life events, cognitive emotion regulation and emotional problems. Personality and Individual Differences, 30(8), 1311–27.

Garner, D. (1997, February). Survey Says: Body Image Poll Results. Psychology today. Retrieved from http://www.psychologytoday.com/articles/199702/survey-says-body-image-poll-results

Gau, L. S., James, J. D., & Kim, J. C. (2009). Effects of team identification on motives, behavior outcomes, and perceived service quality. Asian Journal of Management and Humanity Sciences, 4(2-3), 76-90.

Gillette, R. (2016, January 23). Parents tend to be less healthy than non-parents. Business Insider. Retrieved October 08, 2017, from http://www.businessinsider.in/9-scientific-ways-having-a-child-influences-your-success/Parents-tend-to-be-less-healthy-than-non-parents-/slideshow/50699668.cms

Gireesan, P., &Sananda Raj S. (1988). Mental Health Status Scale (M.H.S.S), Department of

Giulianotti, R. (2002). Supporters, Followers, Fans, and Flaneurs: A Taxonomy of Spectator Identities in Football. Journal of Sport and Social Issues, 26(1), 25-46.

Glasser, W. (1993). The quality school teacher. New York: Harper – Collins.

Glomb, T. M., Duffy, M. K., Bono, J. E., & Yang, T. (2012). Mindfulness at work. Research in Personnel and Human Resource Management, 30, 115–157.

Gnanaprakash, C. (2012). Perceived Organizational Climate, Supervisory Ratings and Creativity in R & D Organization. Abhigyan, 14 (4) 1-10

Goenka, S., Prabhakaran, D., Ajay, V. S., & Reddy, K. S. (2009). Preventing cardiovascular disease in India - translating evidence to action. Current Science, 97, 367-377.

Gohel, B. M., Nagar, S. S., Patel, A. B., Bhogayata, K. H., Vithalani, T. N., & Chhaya, B. M. (2014). Role of psycho-social stress as a risk factor for coronary artery disease: A case control study among the people of Rajkot District. International Journal of Integrated Medical Research, 1(1), 8-14.

Gold, Jeffrey I.,Taft, Casey T.,Keehn, Molly G.,King, Daniel W.,King, Lynda A.,Samper, Rita E. Military Psychology, Vol 19(2), 2007, 71-81

Goldberg, D. P.(1972). The detection of psychiatric illness by questionnaire, Oxford University Press: London.

Goldhaber, D., & Brewer, D. (1997). Evaluating the effect of teacher degree level on educational performance. In W. Fowler (Ed.), Developments in school finance, 1996 (pp.

197-210). Washington, DC: U.S. Department of Education, National Center for Education Statistics.

Goleman, D. (1998). Working With Emotional Intelligence. New York: Bantum Books.

Goodman, L. S., & Holroyd, J. (1993). Are dance/movement therapy trainees a distinctive group? Initial differences and effects of training. American Journal of Dance Therapy, 15(1), 35–45.

Grammas, D., & Schwartz, J. (2009). Internalization of messages from society and perfectionism as predictors of male body image. Body Image, 31-36. Grogan, S. (1999). Body image: Understanding body dissatisfaction in men, women and children. London: Routledge.

Greenwald, R., Hedges, L., & Laine, R. (1996). The effect of school resources on student achievement. Review of Educational Research, 66(3), 361-396.

Grogan, S. (1999). Understanding body dissatisfaction in men, women and children. London: Routledge.

Gross, J.J. (1998). The emerging field of emotion regulation: An integrative review. Review of General Psychology, 2, 271–299.

Grossman, D.(1995). On Killing, Boston: Little, Brown. Retrieved from http://www.bookverdict.com/details.xqy?uri=Product-11097754927526.xml

Gupta, R. (2011). Epidemiology and regional variations in cardiovascular disease and risk factors in India. Journal of Preventive Cardiology, 1, 7-15.

Gupta, R., Sharma, K. K., Gupta, A., Agrawal, A., Mohan, I., Gupta, V. P., ... & Guptha, S. (2012). Persistent high prevalence of cardiovascular risk factors in the urban middle class in India: Jaipur Heart Watch-5. Journal of the Association Physicians India, 60, 11-16.

Hagihara, A., Tarumi, K., & Abe, T. (2007). Media suicide-reports, Internet use and the occurrence of suicides between 1987 and 2005 in Japan. BMC Public Health, 7(1), 321.

Halpern, M.T., & Warner, K.E. (1993). Motivations for Smoking Cessation: A Comparison of Successful Quitters and Failures, 247-258.

Halterman, J. S., Borrelli, B., Conn, K. M., Tremblay, P., &Blaakman, S. (2009). Motivation to quit smoking among parents of urban children with asthma. Patient Education and Counseling, 79(2), 152-155. doi:10.1016/j.pec.2009.09.004

Hanson, C. S., Chadban, S. J., Chapman, J. R., Craig, J. C., Wong, G., Ralph, A. F., & Tong, A. (2015). The expectations and attitudes of patients with chronic kidney disease toward living kidney donor transplantation: A thematic synthesis of qualitative studies. Transplantation, 99(3), 540-554.

Hanushek, E. (1986). The economics of schooling: Production and efficiency in public schools. Journal of Economic Literature, 24(3), 1141-78.

Hanushek, E., Kain, J., & Rivkin, S. (1999). Do higher salaries buy better teachers? Working Paper No. 7082. Cambridge: National Bureau of Economic Research

Hargreaves, D., &Tiggemann, M. (2006). 'Body Image is for girls'. A qualitative study of boys' body image. Journal of Health Psychology, 11(4), 567-576.

Härmä, M. (2006). Workhours in relation to work stress, recovery and health. Scandinavian journal of work, environment & health, 502-514.

Harris Committee (2000) Developing Modern Higher Education Careers Services, Report of the Review, Manchester University, Department for Education and Skills. Available online at, http://www.dfes.gov.uk/hecareersservicereview/report.shtml.

Health Canada. Quit 4 Life – 12 months follow-up evaluation. Retrieved on February 2, 2017 from hhtp:/www.hc-sc.gc.ca/hc-ps/pubs/tobac/quit-cesser-anneval/index-eng.php#conclusion.

Heard, S and Hole, M (2006). Designing effective learning opportunities and promoting employment skills through a range of continuous assessments, Planet, 17: 40–41. Available online at, http://www.gees.ac.uk/planet/#P17.

Heidbreder CA, Groenewegen HJ. The medial prefrontal cortex in the rat: evidence for a dorso-ventral distinction based upon functional and anatomical   characteristics. Neuroscience Bio-behavior. Rev. 2003;27:555–579.

Herring, S., Gray, K., Taffe, J., Tonge, B., Sweeney, D., and Einfeld, S. (2006). Behaviour and emotional problems in toddlers with pervasive developmental disorders and developmental delay: Associations with parental mental health and family functioning. Journal of Intellectual Disability Research, 50, 874-882.

Higher Education Academy (2006) Student Employability Profiles: A Guide for Higher Education Practitioners, The Higher Education Academy, NewYork. Available online at, http:// www.heacademy.ac.uk/profiles.htm.

Higher Education Academy (2007) Employability and Enterprise. Available online at, http://www.heacademy.ac.uk/Employability.htm.

Hiltebeitel, A. (1991). The Cult of Draupadi, Volume 2: On Hindu Ritual and the Goddess, University of Chicago Press, Chicago and London.

Hollis-Walker, L., &Colosimo, K. (2011). Mindfulness, self-compassion, and happiness in non-meditators: A theoretical and empirical examination. Personality and Individual differences, 50(2), 222-227.

Hooli, R. S., Gavimath, C.C., & Ravishankera, B. E. (2012). Study to asses stress among cardiac surgical patients. International Journal of Pharmaceutical Applications, 3(1), 282-288.

Horn, K., Dino, G., &Mody, R. (2003). The impact of Not on Tobacco on teen smoking cessation: End-of-program evaluation results. Journal of Adolescent Research: 640-661.

Hoshmand, L. T. and Hoshmand, A. L. (2007), Support for military families and communities. J. Community Psychol. Retrieved from http://onlinelibrary.wiley.com/

Houghton, J. D., Dawley, D., & DiLiello, T. C. (2012). The abbreviated self leadership questionnaire (ASLQ): A more concise measure of self leadership. International Journal of Leadership Studies, 7 (2), 216-232.

Hsiao, H.C., Chang, J.C., Tu, Y.L, & Chen, S.C. (2011). The impact of self-efficacy on innovative work behaviour for teachers. International Journal of Social Science and Humanity, 1(1), 31-36.

Hülsheger, U. R., Alberts, H. J., Feinholdt, A., & Lang, J. W. (2013). Benefits of mindfulness at work: the role of mindfulness in emotion regulation, emotional exhaustion, and job satisfaction. Journal of Applied Psychology, 98(2), 310.

Hunt, K. A., Bristol, T., & Bashaw, E. (1999). A conceptual approach to classifying sports fans. Journal of Services Marketing, 13(6), 439-452.

Hyland, P. K., Lee, R. A., & Mills, M. J. (2015). Mindfulness at work: A new approach to improving individual and organizational performance. Industrial and Organizational Psychology, 8(4), 576-602.

Iskender, M (2009), The relationship between self-compassion, self-efficacy and control belief about learning in Turkish university students. Social Behavior and personality 37(5): 711-720.

Jackson, L. (2002). Physical Attractiveness: A Sociocultural Perspective. In T. Cash, & T. Pruzinsky (Eds.), Body image: A handbook of theory, research and clinical practice (pp. 13-21). New York: Guilford Press.

Jahoda, M. (1958). *Current concepts of positive mental health*. New York: Basic Books

Jain, N. P., Shahnawaz, M., Gupta, S., Jha, R., & Bhatta, G. (2014). Personal Effectiveness of Public Health Management Personnel in South East Asia Region: A Study. SAARC Journal of Tuberculosis, Lung Diseases and HIV/AIDS, 10(2).

Jain, R. B., Kumar, R., & Khanna, P. (2013). Assessment of self-awareness among rural adolescents: A Cross sectional study. Indian Journal of Endocrinology and Metabolism, 17, 367 – S372.

Jana, A. K., Sircar, D., Waikhom, R., Praharaj, S. K., Pandey, R., Ray Chaudhury, A., Dasgupta, S. (2014). Depression and anxiety as potential correlates of post-transplantation renal function and quality of life. Indian Journal of Nephrology, 24(5), 286-290.

Janetius, S.T. & Mini, T.C. (2015). Quo Vadis College Campus – Glimpses of Indian Higher education, Amazon CS Publication.

Janetius, S.T., Bekele, W., & Mini, T. C. (2008). Students' perception of Quality Teacher and its Implication on Academic Outcome - Paper Presented at the 18th Annual Research Conference, University of Gondar, Ethiopia, June 27-28, 2008.

Janetius. S. T. & Mulat. A. (2006). Multiple Intelligence Learner-Centered Teaching (MILCT): A new paradigm for college education in Ethiopia, Proceedings of the conference on Teacher education for Sustainable Development in Ethiopia, Debre Zeit, May 5-6, 2006.

Janssen, O. (2000). Job demands, perceptions of effort-reward fairness and innovative work behaviour. Journal of Occupational and Organizational Psychology, 73 (3), 287-302.

Jha, V. (2004). End-Stage Renal Care in Developing Countries: The India Experience. Renal Failure, 26(3), 201-208.

Jha, V. (2009). Current status of chronic kidney disease care in southeast Asia. Seminars in Nephrology, 29(5), 487-496.

Jha, V., Garcia-Garcia, G., Iseki, K., Li, Z., Naicker, S., Plattner, B., Yang, C. W. (2013). Chronic kidney disease: global dimension and perspectives. The Lancet, 382(9888), 260-272.

Johnson, B. E. R. (2014). Early Life Emotional, Physical, and Sexual Abuse and the Development of Premenstrual Syndrome: A Longitudinal Study. Journal of Women's Health, 23 (9).

Jokela, M. (2012). Relationship between perceived organizational support and willingness to pursue a career in the hospitality industry. Haaga-Helia University of Applied Sciences.

Jones, D., Vigfusdottir, T., & Lee, Y. (2004). Body image and the appearance culture among adolescent girls and boys: An examination of friend conversations, peer criticism, appearance magazines, andthe internalization of appearance ideals. Journal of Adolescent Research, 19(3), 323-339.

Jones, M. V., Coffee, P., Sheffield, D., Yanguez, M., & Barker, J. B. (2012). Just a game? Changes in English and Spanish soccer fans' emotions in the 2010 World Cup. Psychology of Sport and Exercise, 13(2), 162-169.

Joyce, P. Y., (2005). Stress-Resilience, Illness, and Coping: A Person-Focused Investigation of Young Women Athletes. Journal of Behavioural Medicine, 28(3).

Kabat-Zinn, J. (1994). Catalyzing movement towards a more contemplative/sacred-appreciating/non-dualistic society. In Meeting of the Working Group.

Kabat-Zinn, J. (2003). Mindfulness-based interventions in context: past, present, and future. Clinical psychology: Science and practice, 10(2), 144-156.

Kaplan, R. M., & Kronick, R. G. (2006). Marital status and longevity in the United States population. Journal of Epidemiology and Community Health, 60(9), 760-765.

Kasekende, Munene, Ntayi,&Ahiauzu, (2015). Motivation: definition and types. Retrieved on February 1, 2017 from http://motivation.types.of.motivation.org

Katz, M. J., & Ness, S. M. (2015). Coronary artery disease (CAD). Wild Iris Medical Education, Inc. Retrieved from https://wildirismedicaleducation.com/courses/492/CAD-CEU-Course-Wild-Iris-Medical-Education.pdf

Kearney-Cooke, A. (2002). Familial influences on body-image development. In T. Cash, & P. T (Eds.), Body image: A handbook of theory, research and clinical practice (pp. 99-107). New York: Guilford Press.

Kelley, J. (2013). Definition or meaning of motivation. Retrieved on April 27, 2017 from www.bconsi.blogspot.com/2013/06/definition

Kenny, D. A. (1993). The recovery of identity among adolescents from middle school to high school. Sociology of Education,66(1), 21-40.

Keyes, C.L.M. and Lopez, S.J. (2002). Toward a science of mental health: Positive directions in diagnosis and interventions. Oxford University Press, New York.

Khalil, R. B., Aoun-Bacha, Z., & Richa, S. (2011). Financial Motivation of Smokers to Quit Smoking. The American Journal on Addictions, 20(5), 487-487. doi:10.1111/j.1521-0391.2011.00163.x

Khan, E.B., Ramsey, L.T., Brownson, R.C., Heath, G.W., Howze, E.H., Powell, K.E., et al. (2002). The effectiveness of interventions to increase physical activity: A systematic review. American Journal of Preventive Medicine, 22, 73-107.

Khati, I., Menvielle, G., Chollet, A., Younès, N., Metadieu, B., & Melchior, M. (2015). What distinguishes successful from unsuccessful tobacco smoking cessation? Data from a study of young adults (TEMPO). Preventive Medicine Reports, 2, 679-685. doi:10.1016/j.pmedr.2015.08.006

Kidney Disease: Improving Global Outcomes (KDIGO) (2013). CKD Work Group. KDIGO 2012 Clinical Practice Guideline for the evaluation and management of chronic kidney disease. Kidney International Supplement, 3, 1-150.

Klemer, R. (1970). Marriage and Family Relationships. New York: Joanna Cottler Books.

Kneale, P E (2007) Introducing workplace PDPs, PDP-UK Newsletter, 10: 3–5. Available online at, http://www.recordingachievement.org/pdpuk/default.asp.

Knight, P T and Yorke, M (2003) Assessment, Learning and Employability, Maidenhead: Society for Research into Higher Education and Open University Press.

Knowles, S., Swan, L., Salzberg, M., Castle, D., & Langham, R. (2014). Exploring the relationships between health status, illness perceptions, coping strategies and psychological morbidity in a chronic kidney disease cohort. The American Journal of the Medical Sciences, 348(4), 271-276.

Kotseva, R., Wood, D., & De Backer, G. (2010). EUROASPIRE Study Group. EUROASPIRE III. Management of cardiovascular risk factors in asymptomatic high-risk patients in general practice: Cross-sectional survey in 12 European countries. European Journal of Cardiovascular Prevention and Rehabilitation, 17, 530-540.

Kraaij, V., Garnefski, N., & Van Gerwen, L. (2003). Cognitive coping and anxiety among people with fear of flying. In R. Bor& L. Van Gerwen (Eds.), Psychological perspectives on fear of flying (pp. 89-99). Ashgate; Burlington, VT.

Kumar, P. & Rohtagi, K. (1984). Certain personality correlates of marital adjustment. Indian Journal of Social Work, Vol.45, 325-330.

Kumar, P. & Rohtagi, K. (1985). Marital adjustment: Study of some personality correlates. Indian Journal of Clinical Psychology, Vol.12, 15-18.

Kwon, H. H., & Armstrong, K. L. (2002). Factors Influencing Impulse Buying of Sport Team Licensed Merchandise. Sport Marketing Quarterly, 11(3), 151-163.

Lakey& Cohen (2000).Social Support Theory and Measurement.

Lazarus, R. S. and Folkman, S. (1984). Stress, appraisal, and coping. Springer, New York.

Leary, M. R., Tate, E. B., Adams, C. E., Allen, A. B., & Hancock, J. (2007). Self-compassion and reactions to unpleasant self-relevant events: The implications of treating oneself kindly. Journal of Personality and Social Psychology, 92(5), 887–904.

Lecavalier, L., Leone, S. and Wiltz, J. (2006). The impact of behaviour problems on caregiver stress in young people with autism spectrum disorders. Journal of Intellectual Disability Research, 50,172-183.

Lee, A. World Politics, 2011 April, Volume 63.2. Who Becomes a Terrorist?. Retrieved from http://www.sas.rochester.edu/psc/clarke/214/Lee11.pdf

Leeuwen, L. V., Quick, S., & Daniel, K. (2002). The Sport Spectator Satisfaction Model: A Conceptual Framework for Understanding the Satisfaction of Spectators. Sport Management Review, 5(2), 99-128.

Levey, A. S., & Coresh, J. (2012). Chronic kidney disease. The Lancet, 379(9811), 165-180.

Levine, M., &Smolak, L. (2002). Body image development in adolescence. In T. Cash, & T. Pruzinsky (Eds.), Body image: A handbook of theory, research and clinical practice (pp. 74-82). New York: Guilford Press.

Levy, D. M., Wobbrock, J. O., Kaszniak, A. W., & Ostergren, M. (2012, May). The effects of mindfulness meditation training on multitasking in a high-stress information environment. In Proceedings of Graphics Interface 2012 (pp. 45-52). Canadian Information Processing Society.

Lichtenstein, E., Glasgow, R. E., & Abrams, D. B. (1986). Social support in smoking cessation: In search of effective interventions. Behavior Therapy, 17(5), 607-619. doi:10.1016/s0005-7894(86)80098-3

Lincoln, A., Swift, E. and Shorteno-Fraser, M. (2008), Psychological adjustment and treatment of children and families with parents deployed in military combat. J. Clin. Psychol., Retrieved from 10.1002/jclp.20520. Livermore, D. (2011). The cultural intelligence difference,   AMACOM.

Lu, M., Yang, G., Skora, E., Wang, G., Cai, Y., Sun, Q., & Li, W. (2015). Self-esteem, social support, and life satisfaction in Chinese parents of children with autism spectrum disorder. Research in Autism Spectrum Disorders, 17, 70–77.

Lunenburg, C.F. (2011). Self-Efficacy in the Workplace: Implications for Motivation and Performance. International Journal of Management, Business, and Administration.14 (1).

M. R. Leary & R. H. Hoyle (Eds.), Handbook of Individual Differences in Social Behavior (pp. 561-573). Guilford Press: New York.

Ma, L., Chang, H., Liu, Y., Hsieh, H., Lo, L., Lin, M., & Lu, K. (2013). The relationship between health-promoting behaviors and resilience in patients with chronic kidney disease. The Scientific World Journal, 1-7.

MacKillop, J., & Anderson, E. J. (2007). Further psychometric validation of the mindful attention awareness scale (MAAS). Journal of Psychopathology and Behavioral Assessment, 29(4), 289-293.

Maguire, M (2005). Delivering Quality: Quality Assurance and Delivery of Careers Education, Information and Guidance for Learning and Work Within Higher Education, London: Department for Education and Skills. Available online at, http://www.agcas.org.uk/quality/docs/ delivering-quality-executive-summary.pdf.

Mahajan, B. S. (1996). Microbes and disease. India: Oxford University Press.

Mahesh &Kasturi (2006). How scholars define motivation- Google sites. Retrieved on April 28, 2017 from http://sites.google.com/sites/howscholardefinempotivation.

Malavika, K. (1940). Mental Health of Indian Children. New Delhi: Sage Publications.

Malhotra, S. and Shah, R. (2015). Women and Mental Health in India: An Overview. Indian Journal of Psychiatry, Vol.57, pp. 205-211. Retrieved from https://www.ncbi.nlm.nih.gov/pmc/articles/PMC4539863.

Malinowski, P., & Lim, H. J. (2015). Mindfulness at work: Positive affect, hope, and optimism mediate the relationship between dispositional mindfulness, work engagement, and well-being. Mindfulness, 6(6), 1250-1262.

Marchant, K. H. and Medway, F. J. (1987), Adjustment and achievement associated with mobility in military families. Psychol. Schs. Retrieved from 1002/1520-6807(198707)24:3<289::AID-PITS2310240315>3.0.CO;2-A

Marcus, S. E., Pahl, K., Ning, Y., & Brook, J. S. (2007). Pathways to Smoking Cessation Among African American and Puerto Rican Young Adults. American Journal of Public Health, 97(8), 1444-1448. doi:10.2105/ajph.2006.101212

Maslach, C. (1982). Historical and conceptual development of burnout. In C. Maslach, Burnout: The Cost of Caring. 17-24.

Maslach, C., Schaufeli, W. B., & Leiter, M. P. (2001). Job burnout. Annual review of psychology, 52(1), 397-422.

Maslach,C. & Schaufeli, W. B. (1982) The Burnout Syndrome. In C. Maslach, Burnout: The Cost for caring (pp. 1-16)

Massey, E. K., Gregoor, P. J. S., Nette, R. W., van den Dorpel, M. A., van Kooij, A., Zietse, R., & Weimar, W. (2015). Early home-based group education to support informed decision-making among patients with end-stage renal disease: a multi-centre randomized controlled trial. Nephrology Dialysis Transplantation, 31(5), 823-830.

Masten, A. S., &Obradovic, J. (2006). *Competence and resilience in development. Annals of the New York Academy of Sciences*,1094,13 –27, http://dx.doi.org/ 10.1196/annals.1376.003.

Maudgalya, T., Wallace, S., Daraiseh, N., & Salem, S. (2006)Workplace stress factors and 'burnout'among information technology professionals: A systematic review. Theoretical Issues in Ergonomics Science, 7(3), 285-297.

May, S., & West, R. (1999).Do Social Support intervention aid smoking cessation? A Review, 415-421.

Maya, S., Westa, R., Hajekb, P., McEwena, A. &McRobbiec, H. (2006) Randomized controlled trial of a social support ('buddy') intervention for smoking cessation. Patient Education and Counseling, 64.

Mayer, J.D., &Salovey, P. (1997). What is emotional intelligence? In P. Salovey& D. Sluyter (Eds.), Emotional development and emotional intelligence: Implications for educators, 3-31. New York: Basic Books.

Mc Mahan, David, L. (2008). The Making of Buddhist Modernism, Oxford University Press.

Mcauley, F. (2002). Work/personal life balance: A construct development study (Doctoral dissertation, ProQuest Information & Learning).

McLeod, D., Pullon, S., & Cookson, T. (2003).Factors that influences changes in smoking behavior.New Zealand Medical Journal, 116-173.

Melnick, M. J., & Wann, D. L. (2011). An examination of Sport Fandom in Australia:

Socialization, Team Identification, and Fan Behavior. International Review for the Sociology of Sport, 46(4), 456-470.

Memarian, S., Azaraeen, S., &Koupaei, M. S. (2015). The Relationship between Stress Coping Strategies and Mental Health in Patients with Cardiovascular Disorders. Journal of Applied Environment and Biological Sciences, 5(11), 869-873.

Menotti, A., Puddu, P. E., Maiani, G., &Catasta, G. (2015). Lifestyle behaviour and lifetime incidence of heart diseases. International Journal of Cardiology, 201, 293-299.

Mermelstein, R., Cohen, S., & Lichtenstein, E. (1986). Social Support And Smoking Cessation and Maintenance. Journal of Consulting and Clinical Psychology 1986, vol. 54, No.4, 447-453.

Military psychology. (2018 January 31) Retrieved from https://en.wikipedia.org/wiki/Military_psychology.

Miller GW. (1997). E. Paul Torrence – "The Creativity Man." Ablex Publishing; NJ.

Miller, L. H., Rothstein, L. and Alma Dell, S. (1994). The stress solution: An action plan to manage the stress in your life , Pocket Books, New York, U.S.A.

Min, J. A., Yoon, S., Lee, C. U., Chae, J. H., Lee, C., Song, K. Y. & Kim, T. S. (2013). Psychological resilience contributes to low emotional distress in cancer patients. Supportive Care in Cancer, 21(9), 2469-2476.

Moallemi, S., Raghibi, M., &SalariDrgy, Z. (2009). Comparison of Spiritual intelligence and mental health in addicts and non-addicts. J of Medical Sciences of Yazd, 18(3), 235-242.

Mohan, J. (2016). Biopsychosocial Model of Health. Keynote Address at 2nd International Conference of Indian Academy of Health Psychology, Gautam Buddha University, Greater Noida, Uttar Pradesh.

Mohan, J., & Kaur, N. (2015). Resilience and Perceived Social Support in Institutionalized Adolescents. Conference Proceedings, 3rd WCE, Chandigarh.

Mohan, J., Mahajan, V., & Sehgal, M. (2006). Cardiac Psychology: An Indian Experience. In Mohan J. & Sehgal, M. (Eds.), Health Psychology (pp. 1-27), Delhi: Abhijeet Publishers.

Mohan, V. and Singh, S. (1985). Eysenck's personality dimensions as related to marital adjustments. Indian Journal of Community Guidance Service, Vol. 2, 25-33.

Moksnes, U. K., &Espnes, G. A. (2013). Self-esteem and life satisfaction in adolescents-gender and age as potential moderators. Quality of Life Research, 22(10), 2921–2928.

Monk, D., & King-Rice, J. (1994). Multi-level teacher resource effects on pupil performance in secondary mathematics and science: The role of teacher subject matter preparation. In R. Ehrenberg (Ed.), Choices and consequences: Contemporary policy issues in education (pp. 29-58). Ithaca, NY: ILR Press.

Moreira, J. M., Soares, C. M. B. M., Teixeira, A. L., e Silva, A. C. S., & Kummer, A. M. (2015). Anxiety, depression, resilience and quality of life in children and adolescents with pre-dialysis chronic kidney disease. Pediatric Nephrology, 30(12), 2153-2162.

Morgan, J. (2008). The invisible man: A self-help guide for men with eating disorders, compulsive exercising and Bigorexia. East Sussex: Routledge.

Morys, J. M., Bellwon, J., Jezewska, M., Adamczyk, K., &Gruchała, M. (2015). The evaluation of stress coping styles and type D personality in patients with coronary artery disease. Cardiology Poland, 557-566.

Murphy, N. A., Christian, C., Caplin, D. A. and Young, P. C. (2011). The health of caregiver of children with disabilities: caregiver perspectives. Child Care Health Dev. 33, 180-187.

Naderi, F., Asgari, P.Rooshani, kh, Aderyani, M. (2009). The relationship between spiritualintelligence and emotional intelligence and life satisfaction, Journal of New findings in Psychology, 127-138.

Nalwa and Anand.A (2003). Internet addiction in students; A cause of concern. Cyber psychology & Behavior. 6(6), 653-656.

Neff K. D. (2003b). The development and validation of a scale to measure self-compassion. Self and Identity, 2(3), 223−250.

Neff, K. (2003). Self-Compassion: An alternative conceptualization of a healthy attitude toward oneself. Self and Identity, 2(2), 85−101.

Neff, K. D. (2003). The development and validation of a scale to measure self-compassion. Self and Identity, 2, 223−250.

Neff, K. D. (2009). The role of self-compassion in development: A healthier way to relate to oneself. Human Development, 52(4), 211−214.

Neff, K. D. (2011). Self-compassion, self-esteem, and well-being. Social and Personality Psychology Compass, 5(1), 1−12.

Neff, K. D., Hsieh, Y., & Dejitterat, K. (2005). Self-compassion, achievement goals, and coping with academic failure. Self and Identity, 4, 263−287.

Neff, K. D., Pisitsungkagarn, K., & Hsieh, Y. P. (2008). Self-compassion and self-construal in the United States, Thailand, and Taiwan. Journal of Cross-Cultural Psychology, 39(3), 267−285.

Negrin, L. (2008). Appearance and identity: Fashioning the body in post-modernity. New York: Palgrave Macmillan.

Nelson, H., & Jones, L. (1995). Theory and practice of counseling. London: Holt & Rinehart Winston Ltd

Newsome, S., Waldo, M., &Gruszka, C. (2012). Mindfulness group work: Preventing stress and increasing self-compassion among helping professionals in training. Journal for Specialists in Group Work, 37(4), 297–311.

Niederkrotenthaler, T., Voracek, M., Herberth, A., Till, B., Strauss, M., Etzersdorfer, E., ...&Sonneck, G. (2010). Role of media reports in completed and prevented suicide: Werther v. Papageno effects. The British Journal of Psychiatry, 197(3), 234-243.

Niemiec, C P., Ryan, R. M., Patrick, H., Deci, E. L. &Williams, G. C. (2010). The energization of health-behaviour change: Examining the associations among autonomous self-regulation, subjective vitality, depressive symptoms, and tobacco abstinence. The Journal of Positive Psychology, 5(2),122- 138.

Noor, H. M., & Dzulkifli, B. (2013). Assessing leadership practices, organizational climate and its effect towards innovative work behaviour in R & D. International Journal of Social Science and Humanity, 3 (2), 129-133.

Nordqvist, C. (2018, February 13). Suicidal ideation: Symptoms, causes, prevention, and resources. Retrieved February 27, 2018, from https://www.medicalnewstoday.com/

O. Janssen, (2000) "Job demands, perceptions of effort-reward fairness and innovative work behaviour," Journal of Occupational and Organizational Psychology, vol. 73, pp. 287–302.

Ochsner, K.N., & Gross, J.J. (2008).Cognitive Emotion Regulation: Insights from Social Cognitive and Affective Neuroscience. Current Directions In Psychological Science, 17 (2), 153-158.

Ortner, C. N., Kilner, S. J., & Zelazo, P. D. (2007). Mindfulness meditation and reduced emotional interference on a cognitive task. Motivation and emotion, 31(4), 271-283.

Ozad, B.E &Kutoglu.U (2010). The use of internet in media online of education. The Turkish journal of education and Technology TOJET (92), 245- 275.

Ozcan,N.k & Buzlu. s (2005). An assistive tool in determining problamatic internet use. Validity & reliability of the online cognition scale in a sample of university students. Journal of Dependence 6 (1),19-26.

Park, E. (2004). Does Enhancing Partner Support and Interaction Improve Smoking Cessation? A Meta-Analysis. The Annals of Family Medicine, 2(2), 170-174. doi:10.1370/afm.64

Patten, C. A., Smith, C. M., Brockman, T. A., Decker, P. A., Anderson, K. J., Hughes, C. A., . . . Lichtenstein, E. (2008). Support Person Intervention to Promote Smoker Utilization of the QUITPLAN® Helpline. American Journal of Preventive Medicine, 35(6).

Payne, R., & Pheysey, D. (1971). G. G. sterns organizational climate index: A reconceptualization and application to business organizations. Organizational Behavior and Human Performance, 6(1), 77-98.

Pethe, S.,Chaudhari S.,& Dhar, U. (2005). Manual for Occupational Self-Efficacy Scale, Agra: National Psychological Corporation.

Phua, J. (2012). Use of Social Networking Sites by Sports Fans: Implications for the Creation and Maintenance of Social Capital. Journal of Sports Media, 7(1), 109-132.

Pirie, P. L., Rooney, B. L., Pechacek, T. F., Lando, H. A., & Schmid, L. A. (1996). Incorporating social support into a community-wide smoking-cessation contest. Addictive Behaviors, 22(1), 131-137. doi:10.1016/0306-4603(95)00106-9

Pirkis, J., & Blood, R. W. (2001). Suicide and the media: Part II. Portrayal in fictional media. Crisis: The Journal of Crisis Intervention and Suicide Prevention, 22(4), 155.

Prabhakaran, D., & Yusuf, S. (2010). Cardiovascular disease in India: Lessons learnt & challenges ahead. Indian Journal of MedicalResearch, 132, 529-530.

Ramo, D. E., Liu, H., & Prochaska, J. J. (2015). A Mixed-Methods Study of Young Adults Receptivity to Using Facebook for Smoking Cessation: If You Build It, Will They Come? American Journal of Health Promotion, 29(4). doi:10.4278/ajhp.130326-qual-128

Reddy, V., Rao, N. P., Sastry, J. G. &Kasinath, K. (1993). Nutrition trends in India. Hyderabad: National Institute of Nutrition.

Reid, R. L., & Yen, S. S. C. (1981). Premenstrual syndrome. American Journal of Obstetricsand Gynecology, 139(1), 85-104.

Riaño-Galán, I., Málaga, S., Rajmil, L., Ariceta, G., Navarro, M., Loris, C., & Vallo, A. (2009). Quality of life of adolescents with end-stage renal disease and kidney transplant. Pediatric Nephrology, 24(8), 1561-1568.

Richardsen, A. M., & Burke, R. J. (1995). Models of burnout: Implications for interventions. International Journal of Stress Management, 2(1), 31-43.

Rohit, R., Rajendrasinh, C., &Atul, T. (2016). Type A Personality & Coronary Artery Disease: A Case Control Study. Journal of Research in Medical and Dental Science, 4(1).

Rosenberg, M., Schooler, C., Schoenbach, C., & Rosenberg, F. (1995). Global self-esteem and specific self-esteem: different concepts, different outcomes. American Sociological Review, 60(1), 141.

Rout, U. R. (1997). Working and non-working mothers: a comparative study. Women in ManagementReview. Retrieved from http://www.emeraldinsight.com.

Rudd, N., & Lennon, S. (1994). Aesthetics of the Body and Social Identity. In M. DeLong, & F. AM (Eds.), Aesthetics of Textiles and Clothing: Advancing Multi-Disciplinary Perspectives (pp. 163-175). Monument, CO: International Textiles and Apparel Association.

Ryan, R. M., & Deci, E. L. (2000). Self-determination theory and the facilitation of intrinsic motivation, social development, and well-being. American Psychologist, 55, 68–78.

Ryan, R. M., & Deci, E. L. (2001). On happiness and human potentials: A review of research on hedonic and eudaimonic well-being. Annual Review of Psychology, 52, 141–166.

Ryan, R.M., Stiller, J., & Lynch, J.H., (1994). The social context of internalization: Parents and teacher influences on autonomy, motivation and learning.

Ryff, C. D., & Keyes, C. L. M. (1995). The structure of psychological well-being revisited. Journal of Personality and Social Psychology, 69(4), 719-727.

Ryff, C. D., & Singer, B. H. (2006).Best news yet on the six-factor model of well-being. Social Science Research, 35, 1103–1119.

Sahu, T., Epari, V., Patnaik, L., Lenka, S. S., & Kiran, A. (2015). Coronary Heart Disease Risk factors of in an urban locality of Eastern India. Journal of Cardiovascular Disease Research, 6, 78-84.

Salami, O.S. (1996) "Attitudes towards Counseling among rural college students in Nigerai". Ife PsychologIA. Reproduced by Sabinet Gateway under licence granted by the Publisher (dated 2009.)

Salleh, M. R. (2009). Life event, stress and illness. Malaysian Journal of Medical Sciences, 15(4) 9-18.

Sanathan, S. R., Menon, V. B., Alla, P., Madhuri, S., Shetty, M. S., & Ram, D. (2014). Depressive symptoms in chronic kidney disease patients on maintenance hemodialysis. World Journal of Pharmacy and Pharmaceutical Sciences, 3, 535-548.

Sanders, K., Moorkamp, M., Torka, N., Groeneveld, S., & Groeneveld, C. (2010). How to support innovative behaviour? The role of LMX and satisfaction with HR practices. Technology and Investment, 1, 59-68.

Sarason, I.G., Shrearin, N.E., Sarason, B.R., & Pierce, G.R. (1987). A brief measure of social support: practical and theoretical implications, 499-508.

Sarwar, M., &Inamullah, H., Khan, N., and Anwar, N. (2010) *Resilience And Academic*

Schaefer, Coyne, & Lazarus, (1981). Perceived social support retrieved on January 31, 2017 from www.what is perceived social support/perceived-social-support/1145/4178.

Schane, R.E., Ling, P.M., &Glantz, S.A., (2010). Health effects of light and intermittent smoking.

Schaufeli, W. B., Maslach, C., & Marek, T. (Eds.). (1993). Professional burnout: Recent developments in theory and research. Taylor & Francis.

Schaufeli, W.B., Salanova, M., Gonzalez-Roma,V., & Bakker, A.B. The measurement of engagement and burnout- a confirmative, analytical approach. Journal of Happiness studies, 3, 71-92, 2002

Schmitt, M. T., & Branscombe, N. R. (2002). The meaning and consequences of perceived discrimination in disadvantaged and privileged social groups. European review of social psychology, 12(1), 167-199.

Schooler, D., & Ward, L. (2006). Average Joes: Men's Relationships with Media, Real Bodies and Sexuality. Psychology of Men & Masculinity, 7(1), 27-41.

Schroder, K., Schwarzer, R., &Endler, N.S. (1997).Predicting cardiac patients' quality of life from the characteristics of their spouses. Journal of Health Psychology, 2(2), 231-244.

Schulenberg, J. E., Bryant, A. L., & O'Malley, P. M. (2004). Taking hold of some kind of life: How developmental tasks relate to trajectories of well-being during the transition to adulthood. Development and Psychopathology, 16(4), 1119–1140.

Schultz, Duane, P., Schultz, S.E. & Sydney, E. (1976). Theories of Personality (10thed.). Delhi: Cengage Learning India Private Limited.

Scott, S. G., & Bruce, R. A. (1994). Determinants of innovative behaviour: A path mode of individual innovation in the workplace. Academy of Management Journal, 37 (3), 580-607.

Sehgal, M. (2016). Excellence in Health: A multidimensional perspective. In J. Mohan (Ed.), Excellence: A Multidimensional Appraisal (pp 160-199). Chandigarh: Panjab University Press.

Seto, F. (2017, April 5). How Does Trend Forecasting Really Work? Retrieved from HighSnobiety: https://www.highsnobiety.com/2017/04/05/trend-forecasting-how-to/

Shafran, R., Cooper, Z., & Fairburn, C. G. (2002). Clinical perfectionism: A cognitive behavioral analysis. Behavior Research and Therapy, 40, 773–791.

Shahab, L. (2012). Smoking Cessation interventions involving significant others: the role of social support. Retrieved from www.ncsct.co.uk

Shahani-Denning, C., Dudhat, P., Tevet, R., &Andreoli, N. (2010, April). Effect of Physical Attractiveness on Selection Decisions in India and the United States. Retrieved 2011, 20-February from Find Articles: http://findarticles.com

Singh, M., Ashok, L., Binu, V., Parsekar, S., &Bhumika, T. (2015, December). Adolescents and Body Image: A cross-sectional study. Indian Journal of Pediatrics, 82(12), 1107-1111.

Sinha, P & Sayeed O.B. (1980), "Measuring Quality of Working Life: Development of an Inventory", Indian Journal of Social Work, 41: 219-26.

Sisask, M., &Värnik, A. (2012). Media roles in suicide prevention: a systematic review. International Journal of Environmental Research and Public Health, 9(1), 123-138.

Smith, T. W., Glazer, K., Ruiz, J. M., & Gallo, L. C. (2004). Hostility, anger, aggressiveness, and coronary heart disease: An interpersonal perspective on personality, emotion, and health. Journal of Personality, 72(6), 1217-1270.

Snyder and Lopez (2006). Positive psychology- the scientific and practical explorations of human.The Times of India, (1997, March 8). Delhi has the highest dowry death rate in the country, p. 17. 28.

Srivastava, S. R., Srivastava, P. S., &Ramasamy, J. (2013). Implementation of public health practices in tribal populations of India: Challenges & remedies. Health Care in Low Resource Settings, 1 (1).

Srivastava, S., & Pathak, D. (2011).Moderating Effect of Personality Variable on Stress-Effectiveness Relationship: An Empirical Study on B-School Students. Vision: The Journal of Business perspective, 15(1), 21-30.

Stack, S. (1993). The media and suicide: A nonadditive model, 1968–1980. Suicide and Life Threatening Behavior, 23, 63-66.

Stack, S. (2005). Suicide in the media: A quantitative review of studies based on nonfictional stories. Suicide and Life-Threatening Behavior, 35(2), 121-133.

Stanier, L (1997), Peer assessment and group work as vehicles for student empowerment: a module evaluation, Journal of Geography in Higher Education, 21(1): 95–98.

Sternberg RJ. (1999). Handbook of creativity. Cambridge University Press, UK.

Strauss, R., & Vogt, W. (2001). It's what you know, not how you learned to teach it: Evidence from a study of the effects of knowledge and pedagogy on student achievement. Paper presented at the annual meeting of American Educational Finance Association, Cincinnati.

Strid, H., Simrén, M., Johansson, A. C., Svedlund, J., Samuelsson, O., & Björnsson, E. S. (2002). The prevalence of gastrointestinal symptoms in patients with chronic renal failure is increased and associated with impaired psychological general well-being. Nephrology Dialysis Transplantation, 17(8), 1434-1439.

Sudak, H. S., &Sudak, D. M. (2005). The media and suicide. Academic Psychiatry, 29(5), 495-499.

Suresh, C. V., &Yeedulapally, N. R. (2016). Influence of various psychological correlates in cardiovascular disease patients. International Archives of Integrated Medicine, 3(5), 24-28.

Sutton, W. A., McDonald, M. A., Milne, G. R., & Cimperman, J. (1997). Creating and fostering fan identification in professional sports. Sport Marketing Quarterly, 6, 15-22

Tan, Y. Y., Gast, G. C. M., & van der Schouw, Y. T. (2010). Gender differences in risk factors for coronary heart disease. Maturitas, 65(2), 149-160.

Tantleff-Dunn, S., &Gokee, J. (2002). Interpersonal Influences on Body Image Development. In T. Cash, & T. Pruzinsky (Eds.), Body Image: A Handbook of Theory, Research and Clinical Practice (pp. 108-116). New York: Guilford Press.

Tashakkori, A., &Teddlie, C. (Eds.). (2003). Handbook of Mixed Methods in the Social and Behavioral Research. Thousand Oaks, California: Sage Publications.

Tastan, S. B. (2013). The Influences of Participative Organizational Climate and Self-Leadership on Innovative Behavior and the Roles of Job Involvement and Proactive Personality: A Survey in the Context of SMEs in Izmir. Procedia - Social and Behavioral Sciences, 75 (3), 407-419.

Taylor, I. M.& Lonsdale, C. (2010).Cultural differences in the relationships among autonomy support, psychological need satisfaction, subjective vitality, and effort in British and Chinese physical education. Human Kinetics Journal, 32(5), 655-673.

Taylor, P. J., Gooding, P., Wood, A. M., &Tarrier, N. (2011). The role of defeat and entrapment in depression, anxiety, and suicide. Psychology Bulletin, 137(3), 391-420.

Taylor, S.E., Sherman, D.K., H.S., Jarcho, J., Takagi, K., &Dunagan, M.S. (2004). Culture and Social support: who seeks it and why? Journal of Personality and Social Psychology, 87 , 354-362.

Tedeschi, R. G., & Calhoun, L. G. (1996). The Posttraumatic Growth Inventory: Measuring the positive legacy of trauma. Journal of traumatic stress, 9(3), 455-471.

Tedeschi, R. G., & Calhoun, L. G. (2004). " Posttraumatic growth: Conceptual foundations and empirical evidence". Psychological inquiry, 15(1), 1-18.

Theodorakis, N. D., Wann, D. L., Nassis, P., & Luellen, T. B. (2013). The relationship between sport team identification and the need to belong. International Journal of Sport Management and Marketing, 12(1-2), 25-38.

Tholouli, E., Maridaki-Kassotaki, A., Varvogli, L., &Chrousos, G. P. (2016). Compassion as a mediator between stressful events and perceived stress in Greek students. Psychiatriki, 27(2), 89–97.

Thompson, R.A. (1991). Emotional regulation and emotional Development Educational Psychology Review, 3(4), 269–307.

Tiggemann, M. (2011). Sociocultural Perspectives on Body Image. In T. Cash, & L. Smolak (Eds.), Body Image: A Handbook (2nd Ed.)(pp. 12-20). New York: Guilford Press.

Tiggemann, M., Martins, Y., &Churchett, L. (2008). Beyond Muscles: Unexplored Parts of Men's Body Image. Journal of Health Psychology, 13(8), 1163-1172.

Triplett, K. N., Tedeschi, R. G., Cann, A., Calhoun, L. G., & Reeve, C. L. (2012). Posttraumatic growth, meaning in life, and life satisfaction in response to trauma. Psychological Trauma: Theory, Research, Practice, and Policy, 4(4), 400. Advance Online Publication. Doi:10.1037/a0024204.

Trzesniewski, K. H., Donnellan, M. B., & Robins, R. W. (2003). Stability of self-esteem across the life span. Journal of Personality and Social Psychology, 84(1), 205–220.

Turner, N. (2015). Oxford Textbook of Clinical Nephrology. UK: Oxford University Press.

Udai Pareek, Surabhi Purohit. Training Instruments in HRD and OD. New Delhi: Tata McGraw-Hill; 2011

Ullah, Z., Jaan, S. and Qamar, E. U. 2012. Cognition, resistance and turnover intentions of employees. World Applied Sciences Journal, 20(11), 1443-1447

United Nations Educational, Scientific and Cultural Organization.(2010). Annual report of the Current Status of Science around the World.

United Nations. (1995). Focus on women and violence. Paper presented at the 4th World Conference on Women, Beijing, China.

Universities UK (2007) Enhancing employability, recognizing diversity: making links between higher education and the world of work. Available online at http://www.universitiesuk. ac.uk/employability/.

University of Cincinnati. (2017, December 5). Parenting behaviors linked to suicide among adolescents: Junior high school-aged children at significantly higher risk than peers when parents are not emotionally responsive. ScienceDaily. Retrieved February 27, 2018 from www.sciencedaily.com/

Vajpayee, J. and Makkar, K. (2014). Mental health of women in India. Working paper. file:///C:/Users/welcome/Downloads/MentalHealthofWomeninIndia.pdf.

Vamadevan, A. S., &Prabhakaran, D. (2010). Coronary heart disease in Indians: Implications of the INTERHEART study. Indian Journal of Medical Research, 132(5), 561.

Vidal, R.V.V. (2009). Creativity for problem solvers.AI & Society, 23: 409-432.

Vijayakumar, L. (2010). Indian research on suicide. Indian Journal of Psychiatry, 52(Suppl1), S291–S296.

Von Kanel, R. (2012). Psychosocial stress and cardiovascular risk - current opinion. Swiss Medical Weekly, 142, w13502.

Wagner, J., Burg, M., & Sirois, B. (2004). Social support and the transtheoretical model: Relationship of social support to smoking cessation stage, decisional balance, process use, and temptation. Addictive Behaviors, 29(5), 1039-1043.

Wagnild, G. M., & Collins, J. A. (2009). Assessing resilience. Journal of Psychosocial Nursing and Mental Health Services, 47(12), 28-33.

Wagnild, G. M., & Young, H. M. (1993). Development and psychometric evaluation of the Resilience Scale. Journal of nursing measurement.

Walach, H., Buchheld, N., Buttenmuller, V., Kleinknecht, N., Schmidt, S. (2006). Measuring mindfulness. The Freiburg Mindfulness Inventory (FMI). Personality and Individual Differences, 40, 1543-1555

Walton, R. E. Criteria for quality of work life. In: DAVIS, L. E. et al. Quality of working life: problems, projects and the state of the art. New York: Macmillian, p. 91-104, 1975.

Wang, X., Chen, Z., Poon, K. T., Teng, F., & Jin, S. (2017). Self-compassion decreases acceptance of own immoral behaviours. Personality and Individual Differences, 106, 329–333.

Wann, D. L. (2006). Understanding the Positive Social Psychological Benefits of Sport Team Identification: The Team Identification Social Psychological Health Model. Group Dynamics: Theory, Research, and Practice, 10(4), 272.

Wann, D. L., & Branscombe, N. R. (1992). Emotional Responses to the Sports Page. Journal of Sport and Social Issues, 16(1), 49-64.

Wann, D. L., Grieve, F. G., Zapalac, R. K., End, C., Lanter, J. R., Pease, D. G., Wallace, A. (2013). Examining the Superstitions of Sports Fans: Types of Superstitions, Perceptions of Impact, and Relationship with Team Identification. Athletic Insight, 5(1), 21-44.

Waqas, A., Naveed, S., Bhuiyan, M. M., Usman, J., Inam-ul-Haq, A., & Cheema, S. S. (2016). Social Support and Resilience among Patients with Burn Injury in Lahore, Pakistan. Cureus, 8(11), 867.

Werner, K. H., Jazaieri, H., Goldin, P. R., Ziv, M., Heimberg, R. G., & Gross, J. J. (2012). Self-compassion and social anxiety disorder. Anxiety, Stress, and Coping, 25(5), 543–558.

Westmaas, J. L., Bontemps- Jones, J., & Bauer, J. E. (2010). Social Support in smoking cessation: Reconciling theory and evidence. Nicotine and Tobacco Research, 1-13. doi:10.1093/ntr/ntq077

Whang, L.S.Lee, S & chang. G (2003). Internet over-user's psychological profiles. A behaviour sampling analysis on Internet addiction. Cyber psychology &Behavior 6(2), 143-150.

Wheeless, I.R(1976) self-disclosure and interpersonal solidarity. Measurement, validation and relationships. Human communication research, 3, 47-61.

WHO (1948). What does good health really mean? Retrieved fromhttps://www.medicalnewstoday.com/articles/150999.php.

WHO Framework Convention on Tobacco Control.Parties to WHO Framework Convention on Tobacco Control.Geneva, world Health organization; 2013.Retrieved on February 1, 2017 from Interaction.www.who.int/fctc/signatories)_analysis/en/index.html,.

WHO. (1996). Preamble to the constitution of the world health organization as adopted by the international health conference, New York.

Wolever, R. Q., Bobinet, K. J., McCabe, K., Mackenzie, E. R., Fekete, E., Kusnick, C. A., &Baime, M. (2012). Effective and viable mind-body stress reduction in the workplace: A randomized controlled trial. Journal of Occupational Health Psychology, 17(2), 246.

Woodman, A., Mawdsley, H. and Hauser-Cram, P. (2015). Parenting stress and child behavior problems within families of children with developmental disabilities: Transactional relations across 15 years, Research in Developmental Disabilities, 36, 264-276.

Woodward, K. (2015). Psychosocial Studies: An introduction. New York: Routledge.

World Health Organization (2010). Global estimate of the burden of disease from second-hand smoke, Geneva.

World Health Organization (2014). World Health Ranking. Retrieved from: http://www.worldlifeexpectancy.com/india-life-expectancy

Wykes, M., & Gunter, B. (2005). The Media and Body Image: If Looks Could Kill. New Delhi: Sage Publications

Yang, Y., Zhang, M., & Kou, Y. (2016). Self-compassion and life satisfaction: The mediating role of hope. Personality and Individual Differences, 98, 91–95.

Yarnell, L. M., Stafford, R. E., Neff, K. D., Reilly, E. D., Knox, M. C., &Mullarkey, M. (2015). Meta-analysis of gender differences in self-compassion. Self and Identity, 14(5)

Young K.S & Nabuco de Abrees,c(ed) 2011. Inernet addiction, A handbook and guide to education and treatment. Hoboken. John Wiley & sons; Inc.

Young K.S & Rogers R.C, 1998. The relationship between depression and internet addiction. Cyber psychology & Behavior, Volume 1,Mary and liebert,Inc.

Zalai, D., Szeifert, L., & Novak, M. (2012). Psychological distress and depression inpatients with chronic kidney disease. Seminars in Dialysis, 25(4), 428-438.

Zhang, W. B. (2003). Taiwan's modernization: Americanization and modernizing Confucian manifestations. Singapore: World Scientific Printers.

Ziaian,T., Anstiss, H., Antoniou, G., Baghurst, P., &Sawyer, M. (2012).Resilience and Its Association with Depression, Emotional and Behavioural Problems, and Mental Health Service Utilisation among Refugee Adolescents Living in South Australia, International Journal of Population Research, pp. 1-ber 8, pp. 19 – 24.

Zimet, G. D., Dahlem, N. W., Zimet, S. G., & Farley, G. K. (1988). The multidimensional scale of perceived social support. Journal of Personality Assessment, 52(1), 30-41.

Zimet, G.D., Dalhem, N.W., Zimet, S.G., & Farley G.K. (1988).Multidimensional Scale of Perceived Social Support (MSPSS).Retrieved on February 2, 2017 from www.yorku.ca/psyctest/socsupp.pdf.

Zkjadoon, (October 2015). Fundamental Processes of Motivation. Retrieved on February 3,2017 from www.processes-of-motivation.org/author

Zoellner, T., & Maercker, A. (2006). Posttraumatic growth in clinical psychology—A critical review and introduction of a two component model. Clinical psychology review, 26(5)

Notes: